# INTELLECTUAL PROPERTY RIGHTS

Heritage Science and Society under International Treaties

# INTELLECTUAL PROPERTY RIGHTS

## Heritage Science and Society under International Treaties


**A. SUBBIAN**


*Foreword by*

**DR. S. BHASKARAN**

Member-Secretary, Tamilnadu State Council for Higher Education,
Chennai-600 005.

**DEEP & DEEP PUBLICATIONS PVT. LTD.**

F-159, Rajouri Garden, New Delhi-110027

INTELLECTUAL PROPERTY RIGHTS

HERITAGE SCIENCE AND SOCIETY UNDER INTERNATIONAL TREATIES

ISBN 978-81-8450-020-2



Typeset by *S.S. COMPOSERS*,
3190, Mohindra Park, Shakur Basti, Delhi-110034.

Printed in India at *NEW ELEGANT PRINTERS*,
A-49/1, Maya Puri, Phase-I, New Delhi-110064.

Published by *DEEP & DEEP PUBLICATIONS PVT. LTD.*
F-159, Rajouri Garden, New Delhi-110027.
Phones: 25435369, 25440916
E-mail: ddpbooks@yahoo.co.in • deep98@del3.vsnl.net.in
*Showroom:*
2/13, Ansari Road, Daryaganj, New Delhi-110002 • Telefax: 23245122

## DEDICATION

In Honour of the Law enacted by the Government of India, Tamil as classical language—and the contribution by Dravidian Movement and its greatest leader

Periyar E.V.R.
Hon'ble (C.N. Annadurai) Arignar Anna
Hon'ble (M. Karunanithi) Kalaignar

whose life dedicated to Tamil language, literature and especially to Tirukkural, Tamil Scholars, Writers and Poets, over the century.

The earliest Dravidian language developed for literary purposes was Tamil claims "a classic age of its own" and there is a Continuous and Extensive Literature in Tamil.

According to Arignar Anna, "If we analyse the thought and motive force of Rajah Sir Annamalai Chettiar, we will find that he wanted this place (Annamalai University, Chidambaram), to be not only a seat of learning but also a centre of learning and research of Tamil Culture and Tamil Polity. He had the foresight to realise that Tamilians were going to cultivate their special talents and that was exactly why he started and made a success of the Tamil Isai movement. . . Truly great has been our achievement in the field of literature. . . and to present to the world the great Tirukkural which is a Code of Conduct for the entire humanity are something about which we can have pardonable pride and pleasure.

Tamil language has been developed into an instrument of precise and subtle thought and to the beauty and richness of the literature which is contained in it. Dravidian literature, philosophy, art and architecture offer therefore a rich and fruitful field for exploration and critical investigation. . . all that is of real value and beauty in our past heritage, we need this research and investigation."

—Hon'ble (Arignar Anna) C.N. Annadurai
Chief Minister to the Government of Tamilnadu
Annamalai University, Convocation Address,
17th November 1967

# Contents

Phone Off: (044) 2844 6486/2844 5570
Fax: (044) 2844 6486

TAMILNADU STATE COUNCIL FOR HIGHER EDUCATION

**Dr. S. Bhaskaran**
Member - Secretary

Lady Willingdon College Campus,
Kamarajar Salai, Chennai-600 005.

# Foreword

Intellectual Property Rights is one of the important themes in the present context. A galaxy of artists and inventors in India produced a plethora of works, pictures, TV shows, software and other items that are in demand in the global market. This also contributes to the growth of GNP. It is also an important goal in the Indian trade policy to protect Indian Intellectual Property against all kinds of cut-throat competition at the global level.

The work under review is devoted to the international side of Intellectual property. Though it is basically a matter of treaty regimes, one has to look into the Indian legislation for the protection of literary and artistic works and scientific invention. There is parallel to national legislation available on the international level. The author discusses the controlling provisions of all the major treaties in a comprehensive manner.

The author has organized the book is the context of the theories underlying the protection of International Intellectual Property Rights. He illustrates these theories on a selective basis. As a matter of fact, it is concerned with the historic and philosophical foundations of copyright protection. He has also allowed space for scholars who want to extrapolate theories from one topic and apply them to related topics.

There are well-established norms in the norms of Paris Convention, Berne Convention, Universal Copyright Convention, UNESCO Convention, the NAFTA, etc., But the forms also develop through the more subtle legal process of harmonization. The author poses a series of issues which don't seem to have easy solutions. National differences do not disappear as fast as the distance is getting annihilated. An engagement with the issues proposed should follow from scholarly effort in the domain of Intellectual Property Rights. It is reasonable to anticipate that the issues highlighted in this book shall remain a source of contested legal accommodation as nations continue to struggle with the question of what norms, if any, should be established and secured for the protection of Intellectual Property Rights.

This is a rare piece of research work in the virgin field of Intellectual Property Rights. It is rarer still to make significant contribution. As usual, only the Western scholars, especially, the American scholars have been contributing to the study of Intellectual Property Rights, Non-Western scholars face a series of problems in writing good text books. It is in this perspective that one should look at the book under review. The author has taken pains to look into all possible and necessary sources to prepare his magnum opus. Dr. A. Subbian deserves all kudos.

S. BHASKARAN

# *Preface*

In studying the development of Intellectual Property Rights and trying to understand why do we are thinking and it takes particular directions, it has always seemed fruitful to me to look at the interaction, often one-way, between the prevailing situation of the economy and developing tendencies in economic thought.

For my university teaching profession all Professors are (not) being asked to write a sentence or three about why they entered their respective fields. I entered "history" because, as a youth of the language agitation, I wanted intensely to have some understanding of what was going on around me. It was psychologically difficult to grow up during the fluid situation "the uncertainty'. It was easy to become discouraged about getting a "good job" or "any job" and did not giveone, at 22 years, however, the feeling that there were boundless opportunities just waiting for exploitation. I have spent one full year at Chennai from 1969-1970 reading all sorts of literatures especially writings and speeches of Swami Vivekananda and Sri Aruobindo Ghosh, Ralph Waldo Emerson, Gandhi, Romain Rollare, Nehru, Radhakrishnan, Periyar E.V.R., Anna and others. The young people of the 1960's and 1970's (two decades) have had higher positions to worry about, but they have also had feelings of abundant opportunities if advancement in life could be achieved. Some noted teachers both at Alagappa College (Karaikudi), University of Madras and in Annamalai University impressed on me the intellectual ferment of the University, the importance of ideas, and genuine life of the mind that was present at the institutions.

I have always had an interest in the history of economic thought, philosophy ideas, heritage and culture. In the last 16 years I have been giving a course in The Study of History by Arnold J. Toynbee to post-graduate students in Annamalai University. In 2000 we have started giving 5 years integrated programme History and Heritage Management. One question I have been facing in the relative importance of different factors in the development of new ideas.

I was an omnivorous reader, and I added to that a desire to systematize my understanding. As a result, history, my "first love" was not merely a set of dates and colourful stories, I could understand it as a sequence in which one event flowed out of another. This sense of order crystallized during my undergraduate and post-graduate years into a predominant interest in philosophy and intellectual history and ideas in history. It was the study of philosophy of history that turned out to shape my history career in a decisive way. As a result I learned history, philosophy, history of ideas, as I had learned so much by reading. In my case at least, I believe this self-education was much better than any lecturers I could have attended anywhere. Finally, a series of abortive research ideas, each of which seemed to be more of a distraction than a help, culminated in my first major accomplishment, know as the human rights and international and regional organizations.

I would like to discuss two further contributions of mine, which illustrate the relations to current philosophy of human rights, and international organisations and to the world of socio-economic reality.

This is an elaboration of the simple but not easily understood point that in human rights, philosophy ideas and the system everything affects everything else.

I have great taste for museums, heritage and culture and I have visited more than 15 world famous museums both in India and outside India. This also has helped me to have a clear understanding on the Universal Copyright Convention and the UNESCO Convention.

My repeated visit to New Delhi for the last 20 more years have paved the way in one way or other facilitated to visit the leading book stalls and the Sapru House Library,

Delhi Central Library, resulted in collecting a wide range of material which helped for this book.

Already I have been in touch with the leading international intellectual and human rights organisations such as Human Rights, Internet Toranto who were sending periodically on all aspects of my interest. I thank Dr. Suriya, Professor of Library Science for her valuable help.

Atlast it is my bounden duty to thank my Alma Mater Annamalai University and its authorities Respected Founder Pro-Chancellor Dr. M.A.M. Ramaswamy, B.A., D.Litt., D.Sc., MP (Rajya Sabha). Thiru MAMR. Muthaiah, B.E., M.B.A., Member Syndicate, Annamalai University the Vice-Chancellor, and the Registrar. My deep sense of gratitude goes to Prof. Dr. S. Bhaskaran, M.A., M.Litt., M.S., Ph.D., Political Scientist, Member-Secretary, State Council for Higher Education who have spared his valuable time and energy to offer foreward and blessings.

Finally I owe so much for my wife Mrs. S. Mangaiyarkkarasi. son S. Venkatraj, M.E., Lecturer in Electrical Engineering, Annamalai University and daughter Ms. S. Arulmozhinangai, M.E., Lecturer in Computer Science, J.J. College of Engineering all for their moral support. I thank the Vinayaga Computers, Annamalai Nagar. Further this is my third book published by Deep & Deep Publications Private Ltd. New Delhi.

I thank the publisher Sri G.S. Bhatia for the nice printing and publication.

Annamalainagar A. SUBBIAN

CHAPTER

# 1

# Introduction

## Intellectual Property Rights and the Economic Value

*Genius can be spiritual, artistic, or intellectual. It is the intellectual geniuses, working in cooperation with their far more numerous averagely intelligent contemporaries, who have made mankind's material fortune. Intelligence is mankind's only true capital.*

—Arnold J. Toynbee, Experiences

Every country in the world today has its domestic artists Authors, Writers, Scholars, Sculptors, Musicians, Scientists, Mathematicians, Philosophers, Actors, Actresses, Filmmakers, and inventors who stand to increase their income if there is world-wide protection of intellectual property rights. Yet it is quite clear that there is an imbalance among nations regarding the total worth of their exportable intellectual properties. Centuries ago, Thiruvalluvar the greatest among the thinkers in India wrote:

*In sandy soil, when deep you delve, you reach the springs below,*
*The more you learn, the freer streams of wisdom flow.*

—Kural, 396

Centuries afterwards Milton Wrote that

*"A Good Book is the Precious Life's blood of a Master Spirit."*

An exploration of these reasons opens up a window to the present analysis we are concerned, in the study that follow, not only a to provide a description of international intellectual property law, but to look at its underlying dynamic in order to understand why it is where it is today and to predict where it is going.

Many cultural developments—the arrival of the computer age and the appearance of new techniques of literary criticism and legal analysis—have created serious problems for copyright law. Past technological developments have often been met with inadequate legal changes. Government responses to invention as diverse as photography, player pianos, phonorecords, cable and satellite television, and digital recording devices have been criticized with varying degrees of intensity. Contemporary attempts to adapt copyright law to the internet and to digital forms of data storage and transmission have led to another burst of trenchant commentary. Equally sharp critiques have emerged from those familiar with contemporary forms of literary criticism, economic reasoning and legal thinking. The notions that authors always rely on the work of predecessors, that the meaning of copyrighted works changes depending upon the settings in which they are used and the audiences that perceive them, and that authorship is usually by groups or enterprises rather than isolated, creative souls, have placed strains on the continuing use of intellectual property concepts developed a century ago.

## I. DEFINING PROTECTED VALUES

### (a) Appellations of Origin

Appellations of origin (appellations d'origine) are geographical denominations that indicate a product's origin, as well as particularly distinctive and renowned qualities associated with the location.

Within the broad classification of geographical terms, laws in some countries distinguish between indications of source and appellations of origin. An indication of source (indication de provenance) is merely a name designating a product by its source. Unlike an appellation of origin, an indication of source does not represent particularly distinction or renowned qualities associated with the product's origin, although both designations refers to geographic locations.[1]

France has been particularly adamant and outspoken in favour of stricter protection of appellations of origin for a variety of reasons. Foremost among them is that appellations of origin are common particularly in the wine and cheese industries.

In general, French laws are much more protective of domestic and foreign trade names and producers' rights. Further, France's long history of deference to geographic appellations establishes these laws firmly in practice and tradition. In contrast to the French system. United States law is less protective and primarily directed towards consumer protection. International conflicts develop because United States law permits domestic producers to use freely many foreign appellations of origin that would be legally protected in their countries of origin. For example, "champagne" is an appellation of origin in France and Britain, but not in the United States.

**(b) Technology and Wealth**

There is no general agreement on exactly what constitutes technology or how technology should be defined. The United Nations in a document designed to help countries plan their technological development, has adopted a very broad view of technology, referring to it as "a combination of equipment and knowledge." Other commentators, after acknowledging the ambiguity of technology and the fruitlessness of trying to define it with specificity, have settled on a more functional description. For example, some refer to technology as the systematic application of scientific or other organized knowledge into practical tasks. The developed countries appear to have adopted this functional definition. The Organization for Economic Co-operation and

Development ("OECD"), which includes many of the developed nations of the world, proposed that "technology means the systematic knowledge for the manufacture of a product, for the application of a process or for the rendering of a service, including any integrally associated managerial and marketing techniques.[2]

Defining technology functionally adds an element of subjectivity. If "technology is, in fact, the use of scientific knowledge by a given society at a given moment to resolve concrete problems facing its development", then what constitutes technology will vary with the culture and with the level of development.

Authorities have had similar difficulties defining "technology transfer." There has been a general consensus that any workable definition of technology transfer must be functional rather than formal; however the specific definitions have varied. One scholar defined it as "the process by which science and technology are diffused throughout human activity." Another labeled it "the transmission of know-how to suit local conditions." Nevertheless, both authors were careful to point out that the transfer of technology requires a functional component—in order for there to be a true transfer of technology, there must be effective absorption of the transferred technology by the recipient country. Another commentator elaborated, "the important factor in defining technology transfer is that the recipient acquires the capability to manufacture itself a product whose quality is comparable to that manufactured by the technology supplier.

The traditional method of transferring technology has been through investment in wholly owned and controlled subsidiaries. Not surprisingly, this is the form of transfer that transnational corporation favour. They invest in developing markets in order "to protect the existing market, to create new markets, to bypass prohibitive barriers and import restrictions, to take advantage of cheap labour and skills, and to discover or protect raw materials." These interests can best be fulfilled by retaining ownership and control of the technology transferred to a foreign market incident to an investment in that market. Actually transferring the production technology to the foreign country would simply create unnecessary and unwanted competition and diminish profitability.

Joint ventures are long-term relationships involving he pooling of assets, joint management, profit and risk sharing, joint marketing, servicing, and production. In a typical agreement, technology is transferred primarily through technical liaisons, training, and continuing operational support. Perhaps most valuable, the transferring firm generally provides the recipient with on-going technical changes as they are developed during the life of the agreement. Foreign investors have recently become increasingly willing to participate in joint venture and partnerships with firms in developing countries, especially in India since 1990's so long as the majority of the equitable ownership remains in the hands of the transnational corporation.

.Developing countries often lack a strong technological infrastructure, i.e. the "support system" that are necessary for the specific technology to function effectively. These support systems include hardware, technological education, the level of process technologies in the receiving firms, the capability to perform R & D work, and the ability to maintain technology and organizational infrastructure.

One of the consistent problems that third world nations have faced in successfully importing technology is that the technology acquired from developed nations is ill-suited to the third world's needs: "Technology is not usually produced directly for salt." It is therefore not normally developed for use in the third world. The small technology markets in developing countries and the limited profit-making opportunities they offer discourages technology exporters from adapting their technology to meet the particular circumstances of developing countries. Instead, corporations will offer the same technology that they sell in developed countries.

Developing nations are also often unable to discern their technology needs. Recipients normally choose technology needs. Recipients normally choose technology based on imperfect information. The breadth of choices is often so overwhelming that the recipient is unaware of the full range of alternatives. This problem has become known as the "information paradox." The idea is that when someone is looking to acquire technology, he is ignorant of exactly what he is getting, otherwise there would be no need to acquire it. This paradox reveals that in transfer agreements there is always an element of suboptimality of information, which often leads to inappropriate technology being transferred.

By pursuing a "technology at any cost" strategy, developing countries failed to import technology at a rate that would allow them to study the imported information so as to develop internal sources of its production.

The attempt by developing countries to leap stages of development by the important of technology significantly in advance of the technological skills of the recipient economy will mean both that the technology is in expertly, utilized, and that the relevant expertise is not given an opportunity to develop. This failure has contributed to the underlying problem—the technological dependence of many third world nations. The dependence is likely to continue until those nations are able to increase their ability to deal with and develop technology.

The final reason cited for the difficulties that third world nations have had in developing technologically is that most of them lack a coherent, strategic plan for development: "The immediate post-war or post-independence period in the developing countries was marked by a total absence of any policy specially dealing with technology." Although the last decade has seen that developing countries enact laws and regulations dealing with imports of technology, the legislative policies have been largely ad hoc and uncoordinated in nature and have had a short-term perspective. This is very much in an alarming condition in India.

### (c) Economic Consideration

*International Trade*

Intellectual Property and International Trade[3]

From one angle, intellectual property rights derogate from the norms of free competition in order to overcome the "public goods" problem inherent in the commercial exploitation of intangible creations and to elevate routine technical skills to progressively higher levels.

The changing nature of innovation under modern conditions, and the corresponding pressure such changes exert on conventional assumptions about the nature of competition itself, have exacerbated this unsatisfactory state of affairs. Almost without realizing it, let alone questioning it, traditional legal lore has assumed that manufacturers of most unpatented goods sold on the general products market can fend for themselves without governmental intervention to restrain the exercise of their competitors' legal rights to imitate. To this end, the patent system functions negatively by driving all unpatented innovation onto the general products market where free competition prevails.

The mixture of legal norms applicable to intellectual creations, including trade regulation laws, is evolving in two opposing directions. One trend favours the reduction of market-distorting practices that affect both domestic and international trade in the traditional objects of protection; the other tends to increase legal restraints on trade, including barriers to entry, affecting new objects of protection that would otherwise have to endure the rigours of free competition.

By providing exclusive property rights in return for the production of scarce intellectual goods, statutory intellectual property law seeks to overcome the risk of market failure that inheres in public goods generally and to ensure that free-riders do not appropriate the benefits that would otherwise accrue to investors in research and development. The positive role of these disciplines is widely acknowledged despite a lack of empirical support. Nevertheless, policymakers concerned to promote investment in important new technologies often overstate the supposed benefits of specific intellectual property regimes while ignoring the negative economic functions of these regimes in relation to the complementary operations of competition law generally. If it was true that intellectual property laws balanced incentives to create against opportunities to compete in the specialized markets for qualifying intellectual goods, a healthy by product of these laws was that courts and legislators traditionally drove non-qualifying intellectual goods onto the general products market where free competition prevailed. The negative economic functions of a mature patent system, for example, have been summarized in the following terms:

1. Non-patented innovations remain subject to price competition and are free to imitate if disclosed;
2. Undisclosed, unpatentable innovations are free to reverse engineer but not to steal;
3. Patented inventions are not infringed by non-equivalent innovation;
4. Unfair competition law may not repress product imitation in the absence of confusion.

While providing temporary monopolies to stimulate the production of high-risk, intangible creations, intellectual property law supplies statutory periods of artificial lead time to compensate, at least in part, for the loss of natural lead time that occurs when intellectual goods are subject to rapid imitation. When no statutory exclusive rights apply, the availability of natural lead time largely depends on unfair competition norms operating through laws protecting trade secrets and confidential information. What seems insufficiently understood is that these laws determine the pace and direction of competition based on ordinary or routine skills by requiring second corners to reverse engineer undisclosed, unpatented innovation by proper means.

In practice, the mesh between intellectual property law and the laws governing confidentiality and trade secretes was imperfect even during the nineteenth century, when traditional forms of engineering occupied the forefront of attention and clear lines still separated theoretical from applied science as well as industrial from artistic property laws. Of particular concern in this period were commercial designs, both aesthetic and functional in nature, whose creative contribution is usually embodied in products sold on the general products market. Because neither classical intellectual property law nor classical trade secret law guaranteed industrial designers sufficient lead time against slavish duplication, free-riding second comers could appropriate the benefits accruing from investment in innovative design without contributing to the costs of research and development. As a result, both statutory intellectual property laws and the general laws of unfair competition are still struggling to fill this gap in most industrialized countries.

By now it has become evident that today's information technologies, together with other important new technologies, such as integrated circuit designs and biogenetic engineering, slip through the cracks between intellectual property law and trade secret law into that same netherworld of chronically insufficient lead time that previously engulfed industrial art. Stated simply, today's most valuable technologies often fail to meet the non-obvious standard of patent law because they partake of merely incremental advances beyond the prior art, while their functional character remains alien to both the spirit and economic assumptions of copyright law, which implements cultural rather than industrial policies. Yet, such technologies obtain little or no natural lead time in classical trade secret law because they consist essentially of intangible scientific or technical know-how that becomes embodied in products sold on the open market. Any third parties who obtain the tangible products can quickly duplicate the valuable information they contain and thereby appropriate the fruits of the innovator's investment in research and development, with no corresponding investment of their own.

Under modern conditions, in other words, a major problem with the kinds of innovative know-how underlying important new technologies is that they do not lend themselves to secrecy even when they represent the fruit of enormous investment in research and development. Because third parties can rapidly duplicate the embodied information and offer virtually the same products at lower prices than those of the originators, there is no secure interval of lead time in which to recuperate the originator's initial investment or their losses from unsuccessful essays, not to mention the goal of turning a profit.

Responding to the lack of protection for applied scientific know-how as such, governments have tended either to reform the patent and copyright laws in an effort to accommodate subject matter for which the classical regimes are inherently unsuited or to multiply hybrid legal regimes granting exclusive property rights to unpatenable innovation that has nowhere else to go. Both tendencies generate cumulative protentionist effects that offset the long-term competitive gains expected from major harmonization exercises.

Under the rubric of recent developments, one may note a revived interest in the patenting of computer programs (despite a successful campaign to bring software within the Berne Convention on the excuse that patents were unavailable); a legislative proposal to lower the non-obviousness standard for biogenetic progresses affecting recombinant DNA in the United States; and a proposal to protect non-copyrightable databases under *sui generis* regimes in the European Union. The protection of plant varieties internationally has shifted from a modified copyright approach to a modified patent approach without elevating the prerequisites of eligibility, just when most developing countries will find themselves obliged to protect plant varieties under the TRIPS Agreement. This is the real problem India is facing.[4]

To complete the picture, one should recall that the protection of innovative functional designs under patent-like standards in the utility model laws some countries enacted a long time ago has given way to mandatory protection of virtually all integrated circuit designs on modified copyright principles in countries adhering to the GATT. This, in turn, has led the United Kingdom to protect virtually all functional designs in an unregistered design right, operating on modified copyright principles, that requires no appreciable creative contribution to qualify. A variant of the United Kingdom's unregister design right has been endorsed by the Commission of the European Union, and when sale protection of functional designs in the European Union would increase the pressure on the United States to follow suit. Meanwhile, the United States federal courts already protect product configurations for an indenite period of time under a spurious theory of "appearance trade dress"; the Swiss unfair competition law of 1986 permits innovators to interdict slavish imitation of technologically novel products until the costs of research and development have been recuperated; and the Japanese unfair competition law of 1993 prohibits slavish imitation of most product configurations for a period of three years.

These developments compromise the competitive ethos from within. Traditionally, trade secrets laws invest competitors with an absolute right to imitate every unpatented, non-copyrightable product provided they reverse-engineer its innovative features by proper means. Notwithstanding the competitive mandate handed down from the nineteenth century, the overall trend today is to override classical free-market premises and to organize in their stead a system in which virtually every product sold on the products market comes freighted with the exclusive rights of intellectual property laws.

## (d) The Economics of Intellectual Property Rights Protection

### *The Economic Impact of Intangibility*

At the core of all intellectual property theory lies the basic observation that information has economic value—both to individuals who possess it and to society as a whole.[5]

It is hard (perhaps even impossible) to imagine an economic system in which ideas do not play a central role; in this sense, at least, intellectual goods are as fundamental as any other class of commodities. The economic characteristics of ideas, however, set them apart from the material goods that form the focus of most economic thinking. To illustrate this, consider a "pure" intellectual good—an idea that can be both transmitted and stored without cost or degradation. Although a substantial initial investment may go into the development of such a good, once it exists the marginal cost of providing it to consumers is zero: the "supply" of any existing idea is effectively unlimited. In this respect, pure intellectual goods present problems similar to those posed by more conventional "public" goods such as highways, wells and lighthouses. Inventors are unlikely to invest more in the fixed costs of innovation than they can recoup from the sale of new ideas to consumers; but at zero marginal cost, optimal allocation occurs only when producers provide their ideas to the public free of charge.

Two additional, distinctive attributes of intellectual goods—attributes shared with neither private goods nor public goods—aggravate this market failure. The first of these is the possibility of "secondary production": the purchasers of an intellectual good can resell it to third parties with little or no diminution in value, and they can do while leaving their own holdings intact. In this regard, intellectual goods occupy a precarious middle ground between public goods, which usually flow from a single source and cannot be resold, and private goods, which can be resold but, once resold, are no longer available to the original purchaser. As a result, any release of a pure intellectual good on the open market eliminates the inventor's monopoly, producing a competitive environment in which price rapidly falls to zero.

The second distinctive attribute of intellectual goods, discontinuous marginal utility, complicates the situation still further. Unlike both private and public goods, an idea is only valuable to a given consumer the first time she receives it: "When an individual consumes the intellectual good '2 + 2 = 4' for the first time, something new has been learned and personal welfare is enhanced. When the consumer receives the same message a second time, however, its value is reduced to zero." This state of affairs dramatically hinders marketing, since buyers rarely know the value of information until they have sampled it, but once they have done so, their incentive to purchase vanishes.

The upshot of all this is an inherent instability in markets for ideas. Because inventions are costly to develop but inexpensive to imitate, society will systematically underinvest in the creation of knowledge. At the extreme, rational producers will refuse to invest in innovation at all, preferring to wait and appropriate new ideas from the few individuals for whom invention is its own reward. In short, without intervention, a free market in pure intellectual goods is impossible.

## 2. CONFLICTING THEORIES OF ECONOMIC VALUE[6]

The debate on intellectual property rights at the GATT level has thus far been dominated by the following issues: the question of jurisdiction (the WIPO GATT debat), the interpretation of the negotiating mandate of the Punta del Este Declaration, and procedural questions (the precedence of the anti-counterfeiting code negotiation and the pace of negotiations on TRIPS *vis-a-vis* other negotiating groups in the Uruguay Round). Some believe that the debate has focused on form rather than substance, and hence has failed to generate results. If one tries, however, to identify substantive issues that are at the core of the debate, changing the focus would not help bring the negotiating parties any closer to consensus. There are major conflicts in the way different nations approach the issue of intellectual property rights protection lurking behind procedural discussions.[7]

At the legal level, the conflict reflects a century old debate on the territoriality of intellectual property rights laws and its implications for international trade. Another legal dimension of the debate is to what extent infringement of private property rights can be attributed to the state, justifying external reprisals. The Uruguay Round can be interpreted as a new attempt to promote universality in the protection of intellectual property rights. Previous attempts, beginning with the Paris Convention for the Protection of Industrial Property of 1883, have always encountered difficulty in imposing strict international law standards in the area of intellectual property rights. the continuing debate is even more complex because of its ambitious coverage and the widespread perception that in rencent years that India is trying to translate its domestic provisions into international standards.

The debate also carries clear political connotations. After all, a common definition of international leadership is based on the capacity of a country to maintain a relative primacy in the generation and commercialization of new technologies. Some analysis interpret the growing concern of industrialized nations with intellectual property rights as an attempt to control the diffusion of new technologies or "as a weapon in the struggle of 'haves' against 'have nots'." Accordingly, the ultimate goal of the industrialized countries would be to freeze the existing international division of labour by way of the control of technology transfers to the Third World. Another political dimension of the debate from the perspective of Least Developed Countries has to do with the role of foreign capital in these intellectual property rights protection, at least in the short run, would be transnational corporations. In most Third World countries, a reform of intellectual property laws perceived to favour foreign capital would be highly controversial.

There are also significant philosophical differences along the North-South divide with respect to intellectual property rights. In the First World, intellectual property protection is usually presented "as a fundamental right comparable to rights to physical property." The criticism of countries with "defective" intellectual property systems is often designed to stress the high moral ground from which these attacks are made. The thesis that natural law provides a firm basis to the notion of inherent rights in products of the mind, however, is at best debatable. One can make an eloquent case of the importance "to conceive of ideas as property, and of property not solely as material but also as spiritual." Yet, the history of the evolution of national patent systems suggests that "economic expediency" has usually dominated legal and moral considerations. As a consequence, any attempt to present a country's intellectual property system as a model of "enlightened" virtues is bound to face a great deal of skepticism in the Third World. Moreover, in contrast with developed economics, Least Developed Countries tend to assign a higher weight to "social" interests (often loosely defined than to private interests. Intellectual property systems always entail a compromise between private and social interests. Arguments against intellectual property rights protection for pharmaceutical and food products, for example, are often based on social considerations, such as the objective of avoiding price increases in health and nutrition.

At the core of the conflict between industrialized countries and Least Developed Countries, however, are some basic economic issues. A common belief was that lawyers took intellectual property rights protection too seriously while economists took the issue too lightly. Economist's took the towards intellectual property rights, however, have been changing significantly over the last decade. The growing share of knowledge intensive products in international trade, the economic impact of new copying technologies, the possibilities of world-wide integration brought by communication networks, and the increase in international technological rivalry have magnified the economic significance of "piracy." At the same time new technologies (computer software, semiconductor chip design, etc.) are challenging existing patterns of intellectual property rights protection. Consequently, there is growing interest in the economics of intellectual property rights. Nevertheless, the analysis of the costs and benefits of more sound intellectual property systems for Least Developed Countries is still in its infancy.

The conventional reasons for intellectual property rights protection—to promote investments in research and development (R & D) and technological innovation, and to encourage the disclosure of new knowledge - are not enough to make an economic case for the adoption of intellectual property laws. First, one can argue that there are other institutional arrangements which could in theory generate the same results of the concession of legal rights in new knowledge. As Dasgupta and Stoneman point out, the theory of public goods suggests at least two other solutions for the problem of efficient production and allocation of knowledge: (1) the direct production of knowledge by the government which would "allow free use of it, and finance the expenditure by the imposition of lump-sum taxes"; or (2) the encouragement of "private production of knowledge by the imposition of (differential) subsidies for their production and the levying of lump-sum taxes to finance these subsides."

It is, however, important to recognize that the economic rationale for intellectual property rights protection goes beyond the issue of underproduction of knowledge in the absence of government intervention. It requires that the benefits associated with increased production of knowledge be greater than the costs due to its underutilization, a possible by product of monopolization. The literature tends to support the proposition that a net positive welfare effect results from intellectual property rights protection. This conclusion, nonetheless, becomes disputable when the focus of analysis changes from a closed economy (or from a global perspective) to an open economy. Berkowitz and Kotowitz, for example, point out that a national government "is bound to value the welfare of its own citizens or residents more heavily than that of foreigners." In this context, they were able to drive results showing that for a Least Developed Country a shorter period of patent protection (*vis-a-vis* an industrialized country) may be optimal in terms of national welfare. Lyons adopts a more provocative position based on these results, stating that "[t]here appears to be little reasons for small countries to adopt a patent system."

The implications of these results for the North-South debate on intellectual property rights, however, have to be qualified. First, the model is developed for a small country "in which little invention takes place and/or in which invention markets are competitive." Soem of the newly industrialized countries (NICs) of the Third World no longer fit this description. Second, the model assumes away the possibility of retaliation against defective intellectual property systems. As recent United States actions against Korea, Taiwan, and Brazil, as well as European Community measures against Indonesia suggest, the possibility of intellectual property-related trade retaliations has to be taken into account for an adequate evaluation of an intellectual property-system reform. Finally, the model does not capture some of the benefits that sound intellectual property systems may generate.

Despite these considerations it is important to recognize that for a Third World country a reform designed to increase intellectual property rights protection will tend to generate a welfare loss at its initial stages. Because Least Developed Countries are typically net importers of technology, a usual consequence of a more strict regime of intellectual property laws would be an increase in royalty payments of foreigners. A related cost would be the displacement of firms devoted to "piracy." From social perspective, the cost of dislocation of "priates" will only be relevant as long as foreigners benefit from the process (either by an increase in imports or by an increase in license fees paid by domestic firms to the foreign owners of intellectual property rights). As MacLaughlin, Richards, and Kenny point out the "transfer of sales or royalty payments to other nationals would represent merely a transfer of income from one member of society to another." In this context, this income transfer would not generate a social welfare loss.

Other social costs associated with there reform would be the opportunity cost of additional reform would be the opportunity of additional domestic R & D and the eventual loss of consumer surplus brought by higher prices that could result from the "monopolization" process. The issues of the opportunity cost of additional R & D has received little attention in the debate since most analysts seem to profess an unlimited admiration for the benefits of investments in R & D. Without disputing the importance of R & D. Without disputing the importance of R & D for economic development, one should also take into account its related costs. In Least Developed Countries, human-capital tends to be the scarcest factor of production. As a consequence, an increase in domestic R & D will increase the demand for this scarce resource with potential implications for other productive activities and could even have a negative short-term impact in terms of income distribution. Another source of potential costs, which were not considered in the model, are the local subsidiaries of transnational corporations. Local R & D by these companies can be translated into future royalty payments abroad if intellectual property rights "reside with the parent company, regardless of the location of the research." The model also does not take into account the costs of establishing an effecting an effective, intellectual property system (from the organization of a "cadre" of patent examiners to the costs of enforcing intellectual property rights). For a small Least Development Country, these costs can be substantial.

Turing now to the social benefits that a Least Developed Country would achieve by enforcing more strict intellectual property rights, one could list the following impacts. (a) cost savings associated with new technologies developed by additional R & D and by the disclosure of new knowledge; (b) cost savings associated with technological transfers that could only occur under more strict intellectual property rights protection; and (c) additional investment fostered by the new regime of protection. Items (a) and (b) can be interpreted as the main channels through which the benefits of technological change are translated into economic growth. Other potential benefits could accrue in the form of higher quality products becoming available for consumption and through the contribution of better national intellectual property rights protection to world technological growth. The magnitude of this contribution is an open question, but it seems reasonable to assume that the impact of any individual intellectual property reform in the Third World would be marginal at best.

**(a) The Case Against Intellectual Property Rights Protection**

Those who oppose more strict intellectual property rights protection tend to dispute the benefits . . . . partially based on the hypotheses that domestic R & D will not respond significantly to the reform, that the growth impact of any additional R & D will be marginal, or that capital formation and technological transfer are not very sensitive to intellectual property rights protection. Some alternative formulations . . . are; local incompetence; a very inelastic supply of human capital; the argument that intellectual property rights protection is only one of the relevant variables which explain R & D and that it can be ineffective in the absence of additional conditions (such as a larger stock of human capital); the belief that modern technology is carried forward by large enterprises (particularly transnational corporations); and doubts about the net contribution of foreign capital to economic development.[8]

The criticism is also directed to the cost aspects of an intellectual property-system reform. First, it is argued that the weight of additional royalties would be disruptive given the foreign-exchange constraints faced by many Least Developed Countries. Second, a high value is assigned to the perceived benefits of having access to technology in the cheapest possible way. According to this approach, by "taxing" imported products of the mind, Least Developed Countries would be lowering the costs of important inputs in the productive process and they would increase consumption possibilities. The question of dislocation of "piracy", however, does not received much attention from those who oppose more strict intellectual property who oppose more strict intellectual property laws in the Third World for tactical and legal reasons. For some countries, particularly those with problems of enforcement of intellectual property laws, it would not be wise to acknowledge the magnitude of the problem. For many Least Development Countries the problem simply does not exist since from a legal standpoint their intellectual property systems comply with international agreements, such as the Paris Convention (which allows each country to choose its own patent conditions as long as there is no discrimination against non-nationals). As Barbosa notes, entrepreneurs in countries with "defective" intellectual property systems, from a United States perspective, could at best at best be called corsairs with all the legal licenses to operate.[36]

**(b) The Case for Intellectual Property Rights Protection**

The economic arguments for intellectual property rights protection in the Third World are built around the concept of self-interest. Emphasis is usually placed on the right social rate of return from investments in new technology and the tendency for under-investment in this area when intellectual property rights are not well-protected. The effectiveness of local R & D is heralded and the micro benefits of sound intellectual property regimes is suggested by case studies at the firm level. Some analysis, such as Sherwood, recognize that these benefits are difficult to quantify, but they tend to stress that small firms and universities will become much more active in the process of technological innovation under enhanced intellectual property rights protection.[9]

An argument which is becoming quite influential is the thesis that presently "technology drives investment" and to the extent that technology "is reluctant to flow where it is not protected" the lack of an adequate level of protection could stunt technological transfer and foreign investment. The relationship between technology and investment can also be explored at the domestic level based n the proposition that enhanced intellectual property rights protection, particularly trade secret, laws, would be an important stimulus for local capital formation.

Turning to the social costs of a reform, analysts tend to downplay the importance of the displacement of pirates. This attitude reflects strong assumptions about labour mobility in the Third World coupled with the belief that growth in sectors benefited by the reform would rapidly absorb displaced workers. The potential loss of consumer surplus is also downplayed because these benefits would be achieved at the high cost of fostering imitation and copying instead of invention and creativity.

A final comment worth making at this point concerns the role of bureaucracies in the intellectual property systems of the Third World. these bureaucracies are quite influential in the debate and tend to adopt a critical view of First World proposals for enhanced intellectual property rights protection. Their attitude is often influenced by ideological interpretations, such as the concept of technological imperialism. It is important to recognize, however that their attitudes also reflect the predominance of the scientific ethos which has at its basis the norm of complete disclosure. This "culture", as Dasgupta poses it, is hostile to the view of knowledge as a private capital good that is the foundation of the so-called mature intellectual property systems of the industrialized economies. Consequently, the dialogue between technology-oriented interests and government bureaucracies, an important domestic fact of the intellectual property rights debate, tends to be a difficult one.

### (c) The "Economics" of Database Protection: A Case Study

The copyright laws of the United States and the European Union have become key forces in the international competition for market share in one of the most dynamic sectors of the world economy. The United States and the European Union have embarked on divergent regimes for the copy right protection of computer databases. The aim of European Union law is to protect local database developers by granting them ownership of the data collected of their compilations. In contradistinction, the aim of United States law is to maximize market efficiency by protecting only creative selection and arrangement of data and leaving the underlying facts free for the taking.[10]

At the center of the division between the two regimes is a basic provision of United States copyright law; the "thin" protection granted to the facts in a data compilation. The protection is "thin" because the compiler of a database can only gain copyright for the creative way in which he has organized the data he collected; he does not, however, gain any protection for the effect, or "seat of the brow", he has invested in the collection. No matter how many thousands of hours or millions of dollars are spent gathering data, traditional copyright law grants only a "thin" copyright in the creative organization and always leaves the facts collected free to be used by someone else.

The United States copyright approach to data compilations adheres to the creative selection approach. The Copyright Act of 1976 was interpreted definitively in the context of data compilations by a unanimous decision of the U.S. Supreme Court in *Feist Publications, Inc.* v. *Rural Telephone Service Co.* In an opinion by Justice O'Connor, the Court held that alphabetical listings in a telephone book did not contain the minimum level of creativity required for copyright. The *Feist* Court explicitly rejected the "sweat of the brow" proposition that the creator of a data compilation such as a telephone book should be economically rewarded fir his effort regardless of the creativity it exhibits.

In contrast, the European Union has abandoned the fact/ expression distinction for data compilations. In order to spur domestic development of computer databases, the "sweat of the brow" doctrine is at the heart of the Commission of the European Communities' Proposal for a Council Directive on the Legal Protection of Databases (Proposed Directive). Unlike *Feist*, which coves all compilations, the Proposed Directive is specifically targeted to computer databases. The Proposed Directive contains a two-tiered approach to database copyright. The first tier grants a copyright in creative selection and arrangement, which is largely consistent with existing international copyright law as embodied in the Berne Convention, and consequently with United States law as articulated in *Feist*. The second tier, however, is a *sui generis* provision which pro-hibits unfair extraction or copying of the facts in an otherwise unprotected work. While the commission asserts that such an approach does not extend a copyright to facts, in actuality it has the effect of granting to the original compiler a limited "ownership" of the facts.

The drafters of the Proposed Directive appear to be interests in increasing the European share of a market central to the economic development plans of most industrialized nations. Intellectual property from movies to microchips is the engine driving United States foreign trade at the expense of many of her staunchest competitors. In 1990, the United states enjoyed a $ 12.6 billion trade surplus in copyright and patent license transactions; it was the only G-7 nation to run a surplus. In the same year, worldwide revenue in online databases was just over $ 9 billion. Though just a small segment of the larger intellectual property market, the database industry is among the fastest growing, they accounted for only one quarter of the total revenue. This is because non-profit producers (governments) still produce the majority (fifty-four percent) of European databases, whereas American databases are produced largely by the private sector (seventy-two percent).

In a desire to reward the author, and hence encourage production of new works, copyright essentially grants the author a monopoly over the reproduction and dissemination of his creative expression for a limited period of time. Thus, copyright is also a tax to society, because the author may set any price he chooses for the work, though the work faces potential substitutions if the price is too high and buyers opt instead for other, similar works. Competitors are prohibited from copying expressions without the author's consent. To produce new works, competitors must pay to license, or they must start from scratch. Hence the public may be burdened by higher prices or limited access to the copyrighted work. Copyright thus establishes a tax on readers, publishers, and competitors for the purpose of rewarding writers. In order to protect the copyright holder while mitigating the burden of his monopoly on his competitors and customers, the protection is limited to creative expression for a specific period of time. In contrast, if the purpose of copyright were solely to rewards the author, copyright would be absolute in duration and scope. The limit is important because the purpose of copyright is not solely to reward the author, but rather to induce production at the minimum possible cost to society. The law, by liming the ownership of data, thus favours its free movement and therefore contributes to the general progress of society.

In contrast, the policy behind the sui generis protection in the European Union's Proposed Directive is intended to maximize profit in information services for European providers of information services. This policy choice is not rooted solely in economics; European law also recognizes a moral right to intellectual property which is absent in United States law. Fundamentally, however, the Proposed Directive is intended to favour European database publishers at the expense of their customers and non-EU competitors.

The European Community's Proposed Directive for the Legal Protection of Databases embodies the "sweat of the brow" doctrine. It lags behind the United States in database development because the Union took this position. The strength of the Directive's approach is that it grants a property interest to an author for the work he expended. Unlike the convolutions of Feist, the "sweat" doctrine is relatively straight forward as a legal principle.

The Proposed Direction was enacted with the provisions of the Berne Convention for the Protection of Literary and Artistic Works in mind.

Specifically, Article 2(5) of the Berne Convention provides:

> Collections of literary of artistic works such as encyclopedias and anthologies which, by reason of the selection and arrangement of their contents, constitute intellectual creations shall be protected as such, without prejudice to the copyright in each of the works forming part of such collections.

Thus, Article 2(5) grants protection to collections of artistic and literary works where the selection and arrangement is sufficiently creative.

The Berne Convention did not, however, contemplate protection for electronic databases, and no specific protection is outlines. In the first tier of its two-tiered approach, the Proposed Directive seeks to fill this void by making explicit the protection of database compilations exhibiting sufficient creativity in selection and arrangement. Thus, the first tier simply consolidates a standard to which the great majority of member states and the United States already adhere, and explicitly extends this protection to computer databases.

In contrast to the harmonizing effect of the first tier of the directive, the second tier represents something of a departure from the approach of the vast majority of Berne Convention signatories by creating an ownership right allows the database developer to prevent the unauthorized extraction or re-use of the contents of a database for commercial purposes. The developer thus owns the data he has compiled, regardless of the eligibility of the database for protection under the first tier.

In order to mitigate the monopolistic effects of the ownership right, the Proposed Directive also requires that the original compiler issue licenses to secondary compilers. This compulsory license if imposed when the database has been made publicly available and is the only source of a work or material.

### (d) Copyright as an Economic Policy Lever

From cars to computers to guns, we now take it for granted that all manufactured goods are made from interchangeable parts. A single supplier will sell commodity nuts, bolts and brake shoes to automobile manufacturers. A host of personal computer makers build their machines from the same chip. British gunsmiths claimed 150 years ago that it was impossible to make something as precise as a gun from interchangeable parts; highly skilled craftsmen were required to file each component, at an enormous increase in cost. But Samuel Colt's small company ultimately dominated the world market for guns by eliminating the need for custom-developed parts.

The revolution took place in manufacturing because standard interchangeable parts could be produced by a number of companies operating in a competitive market. From the parts could be produced by a number of companies operating in a competitive market. From the parts manufacturer's perspective, costs were reduced because a single part could be sold to any number of finished product producer's perspective, costs came down because competitive bids could be solicited from a range of parts manufacturers.

This environment was a sharp contrast from a market in which the makers of customized parts could charge higher prices based on their protected market position. Their protected positions resulted from the cost and time associated with producing specialized parts for a single potential buyer. Competitors were reluctant to enter a market where they would be forced to start from scratch in order to service a single buyer who already had an entrenched relationship with the original developer of the part.

The same evolution from proprietary (produced by a single producer to fit a single assembly) to interchangeable (produced by multiple producers to fit multiple assemblies) parts that revolutionized the production of goods must continue to work in the production of information. From legal databases to industrial specifications to names and addresses of telephone subscribers to lists of registered trademarks, the market for electronic information will grow most quickly if the underlying data is free to subsequent compilers. This will ensure a competitive market by eliminating the protected market position of original database compilers. Competition flourishes when subsequent compliers are not forced to start their data base by going out and rediscovering the same data. Buyers benefit at the prices of databases lowers through competition. The database market benefits as more databases are sold at a lower price.

The kind of competitive market that will allow this evolution to continue is a market where the average long-term price of a database is as close as possible to the database's marginal cost. The marginal cost of a good is the cost to the manufacturer (or author/publisher) of producing one additional unit. In a perfectly competitive market, all firms are to small in relation to the overall market to affect price. Thus, equilibrium for a profit-maximizing firm occurs where marginal cost equals the price set by the market. In other words, where the cost of producing one additional unit is equal to the revenue earned from selling it. Market price does not rise above marginal cost in a competitive environment because no firm may charge more than another; any attempt by a single firm to raise prices results in a loss of sales as buyers opt for lower priced products. If the market price were to drop below a producer's marginal cost, he would not gain enough revenue from the sale of a unit to cover his expenses in producing it, and would ultimately be forced to drop out of the market.

In contrast to this competitive market scenario, a copyright in underlying data will lead to a market more analogous to a monopoly. A monopoly is a market in which a seller may dictate supply, and hence price, because no alternative seller is available. Buyers in these markets pay more than they would in a competitive market, and thereby inefficiently transfer resources to the monopolist. In the context of databases, this situation is analogous to the market for custom gun parts in that once a compiler owns the data copyright, subsequent compilers will be reluctant to incur the costs of starting from scratch and entering a market already dominated by the original player. This leaves the original compiler in a protected market position in which he can charge monopolistic prices until a subsequent compiler can generate the same data from scratch.

This is not to say that in a competitive market every producer's price must always be equal to marginal cost. On certain occasions, a producer may invent an innovative new product with features that make it unique in the market at a specific point in time. During this "monopoly window" where the producer's product is unique, he may charge a price higher than other competitors who are bound to the marginal cost price. This higher price is not inefficient for two reasons. First, the higher price reflects the greater value of the product; if the product is not worth more, customers may opt to buy from lower priced competitors. Second, the "monopoly" price charged will only last fro the limited period of time it takes for competitors to match the innovation and for prices to return to a marginal cost level in expectation of the next innovation. The pioneer's position is not protected by the copyright system; it is protected by his own ingenuity and the speed with which he brings a new product to market.

Given the efficiencies of a competitive market where long-term average price approaches marginal cost, the question for copyright policy makers is what form of protection should be granted to ensure investment in innovation of information products while allowing the commodity raw material, data, to move quickly and at low cost among suppliers of databases and between suppliers and customers. Assuming that the evolution of the database industry is analogous to the evolution of manufacturing industries, the lower costs of innovative production will increase competition and eliminate some competitors, the market will grow exponentially as less expensive, better products continue to attract new populations of customers. In order to evaluate the copyright options in light of these economic assumptions, it is illustrative to trace a database through its competitive life cycle, and to compare the effects of United States and European law on the likely investment by the complier and the resultant cost to the consumer at each juncture of the product life cycle. The resulting analysis demonstrates that while United States and European law would have similar effects on database protection, in most respects the two approaches differ in one critical area: the United States approach ensures that database developers are free to rely on an inexpensive and plentiful supply of data, while the European approach adds cost and promotes inefficiency.

**(e) Identification of New Markets**

In a competitive environment, development of a copyrightable database usually begins with the identification of a market niche and potential customers.

United States and European Union law are identical in their protection at this early stage. Producers who successfully identify original categories of information that are useful to users in a new market would enjoy two protected positions. First, developers would enjoy a time-based monopoly for the period of time that their product was the only one on the market containing the new category. For example, a database developer offering information to retailers on food buying trends of Latino customers in San Antonio could charge a premium price for the information as long as that developer was the only source. The amount of the premium would depend only on how well they had identified a market for the product. Second, both United States law after Feist and European Union law under the first tier of the Proposed Directive would recognize a copy-right in that information product because it is based on the creative selection of data and creates an original category. Copyright in creative selection and arrangement spurs investment in new products, as producers enjoy limited protection for their innovative category selection and organization.

Investment in market identification and category selection, not the ownership of data, is the proper source of advantage for a database in a competitive market. In a competitive market, developers of a novel format would gain copyright protection for that format, and set prices according to demand for their ingenuity. They would be released temporarily from the pressures of marginal cost pricing; as long as their product is either the first one available in the market or more ingenious than other available products, they can charge a premium price. This typically brief monopoly window is not, however, detrimental to the market because competitors may take the data and compete based on another novel format. The welfare of the market increases as consumers get better products through competition and developers get more customers because of the better products they are forced to develop to stay in business. Resources are not simply being transferred from customers to monopolists who are not driven to innovate. Consumers are paying higher prices because they perceive greater value in the innovative product they are purchasing.

**(f) Assessments of Multiple Data Sources**

After a market for the data has been identified and

useful categories of data developed, database developers must find sources of data to deliver to their customers. Occasionally, the required data may come from a single source. However, more often than not the data will come from multiple sources whose contents must be sampled and selected for usefulness in the particular database. For example, a demographic database may draw upon public sources, such as census data, property tax records, and voter registration files, as well as a wide variety of proprietary sources that contain data on the target group, such as purchasing patterns, or subscriptions to catalogs and periodicals. Often, the effort of collecting the right data involves extracting a needle of fact from a haystack of irrelevant information.

The cost-benefit analysis applied to the selection of data will differ depending on the legal regime. Under United States law, the cost-benefit analysis is relatively simple. Regardless of the originality in the selection and arrangement of the sources, the underlying data in the work is free to anyone provided they do not take the format. Thus, an American compiler of a new database would simply take the best quality data and target it to his market, provided he was not infringing upon the original compiler's creative selection and arrangement. Thus, the absence of copyright protection for data under the United States regime maximizes the power of market forces on databases that are already developed. Data is free because its marginal cost is zero. Absent transmission costs, it simply does not cost any more to deliver a completely developed database to the tenth subscriber than it cost to deliver it to the ninth. Profit is properly stripped from the ownership of underlying dat.

Of course, while the data is free from copyright protection, many other mechanisms are available to protect it from competitors. Access to electronic information is, to a great extent, governed by contract. Software algorithms can make it difficult to access information without agreeing on how the information will be disseminated and reused. However, new distribution methods, such as on-line information gateways (the much ballyhooed Internet is a prime example) and easily portable compact disks containing vast compilations of material, are expanding access to parties who may not be in contractual privity with the database proprietors. These trends weaken contractual control but should not shake the basic logic behind copyright protection limited to creative selection and arrangement.

In contrast to the United States approach, the Proposed Directive's "neighbouring rights" scheme grants certain protection to the basic as well as providing for traditional copyright for the creativity of the compilation. The original compiler thus owns the facts he has compiled for a limited statutory period. This arrangement skews pricing because the artificial monopoly allows the original compiler to charge a price above what he would charge in a competitive scenario until another compiler develops the data from scratch.

The Proposed Directive purports to limit the inefficiencies of this artificial monopoly by compelling the original compiler to license his data to any developers of derivative compilations if his work was the only source of the data in question. Compulsory licensing exhibits many of the same "bad tax" characteristics as those exhibited in an absolute copyright monopoly. In addition, the potential for abuse of a compulsory licensing system by large compilers, such as telephone monopolies, is enormous. Because original compilers who enjoy protected status would be unlikely to easily grant licenses to secondary compilers, compelling such licensing would often be settled through long and costly civil litigation.

Finally, the second tier of protection under the Proposed Directive is anticompetitive because it is not reciprocal. Non-EU database developers (principally American) will not be allowed to use the data developed by European developers protected by the directive. Moreover, American developers will face competition from European competitors operating in the United States under the provisions of Feist, which provides that data is free to all subsequent compilers. It remains an open question whether a European developer would be allowed to take the data of a non-EU developer and then gain an ownership interest in the copied data. Such a development could be highly injurious to both the marketplace and worldwide database suppliers because regardless of where databases are developed, many will be competing for the same global customers. Unfortunately, these unequal conditions will endure until bilateral agreements are worked out between the United States and the EU member states.

**(g) Preparing the Database for Market**

Once data has been secured, either through original collection, licensing or the simple taking of unprotected data, depending on the legal scheme, the contents must be edited and refined for use in the new database and then blended into a presentation format. The goal is to organize and deliver the information in a way that enables the intended user to access needed information efficiently. Furthermore, most commercially significant databases are to some degree dynamic, requiring updating and revision either consistently or periodically.

Here, the economic effects of the two regimes will be most apparent to end users. Under the United States system, the cost of the database, and its resulting competitive advantage will be concentrated in producing an innovative product. Because the only legally sustainable competitive advantage available under the United States system will be its creative selection and arrangement, this stage of the product cycle will be fertile ground for investment. Users will benefit as producers are forced to compete by creating more user-friendly systems, for matting databases more cogently, any by creating hardware and software tools that enhance the ability of users to gather and synthesize unrelated data.

The cost of a database under the European scheme, on the other hand, will be reflected in the cost of gaining access to proprietary data. Because the original compiler owns the underlying data, the price charged for it will be a premium based on the lack of alternative sellers. For the potentially long period of time it will take competitors to either negotiate a licensing agreement or develop the data from scratch, the original compiler will have limited incentive to invest in more effective and easier-to-use products.

Clearly, the collection and assembly of information as well as the selection, coordination or arrangement of data are often extremely time consuming and expensive. The successful development and distribution of a database often depends on the solution of complex marketing problems. The process also calls for sophisticated knowledge of information science, the study of information seeking behaviour, and of the details of storage and retrieval system and computer programs. if the resulting compilation seems simple to the user, it is precisely because of the complex web of authorial activity that went into its design and execution.

In short, United States law recognizes that these complex factors are at the root of the competitive advantage of a compilation. The United States system rewards these important investments through the copyright protection of creativity. The European Union's Proposed Directive, on the other hand, will draw investment away from these strategic competitive features as EU developers struggle to compete at the less demanding stage of the original compilation of data.

The best argument for the United States copyright regime is that it most closely approximates a free market for data compilations with commodity data as the central feature. The price of a database will be set by its development cost and how well it has been designed through the various stages of the product development lifecycle. In contrast, the European scheme allows and sustains monopolies based on the original compilation of data. This scheme will allow original compilers to set monopoly prices limited only by inefficient compulsory licensing schemes.

The European Union's effort to protect domestic competitors now will be harmful to the market for databases in the short-term and to the Europeans themselves in the long-term. In the short-term, because data will be purchased or developed from scratch each time, the large number of works produced by EU developers will be expensive. In the long-term, the Europeans will ultimately suffer as non-EU competitors accustomed to competing for global customers based on the quality of their product will become more and more difficult to beat in the market place. These competitors, hardened by the market and forced to innovate, will beat the Europeans on every price performance front. It would be far better for the Europeans to rely on their ingenuity and face the reality of the market now.

Ultimately, the division between the two regimes represents the dam over which information will not easily flow. More than perhaps any other commodity, data must be allowed to move without barriers in order to allow the world economy to grow in the most efficient manner possible. Consequently, rationalization of the two approaches to the copyright protection of computer databases should be an indispensable part of negotiations between the United States and the European Union, both in the multilateral GATT environment and in more focused bilateral talks.

## 3. THE COMMON HERITAGE OF MANKIND

Intellectual property has always played a unique role in the economic evolution of industrialized nations. The history of patent and trade secret protection is filled with technological advances which have driven the industrialization engine of development. From the early days of the printing press to the onset of CD-ROM production and distribution in China in the 1990's, developing countries have similarly utilized the ability to produce and market copyright protected works of foreign authors as the backbone for their economic advancement. Developing countries do not generally possess a large body of intellectual property created by their own authors and inventors which can be marketed internationally. In the absence of sufficient nationally—created works, such developing countries have often used the intellectual property of other nations to enhance their industrial capabilities. Even the United States, in its early days as a newly emerging industrial nation, used its copyright laws to protect its nascent publishing industry. These laws did not grant other nations' authors the right to protect their works from the voracious requirements of the US domestic publishing industry.[11]

The need for access by developing countries to intellectual property protected works has arguably grown more severe in the present technologically driven global economy. Much technology includes intellectual property elements. Thus, attempts to restrict a country's internal access and use of such technology through the enactment of international protection norms or procedures are seen by some developing countries as a direct challenge to their ability to play a significant role in the world economy.

Many scientific developments in the areas of medicine and agriculture also contain intellectual property elements. This unique role as an instrument of public health and safety further supports the desirability of providing unrestricted access to intellectual property.

Given intellectual property's undeniably historic role in the industrialization of a developed country and in improving the health of its citizens, many developing countries asset that intellectual property should be considered the "common heritage of mankind."

**(a) Ayurvedic Heritage: Yoga**

Acording to Justice Dr. V.R. Krishna Iyer: "Indian intellectual property, in the ancient field of Ayurveda, may come under the skullduggery of MNCs using the dubious device of piracy and patenting of Ayurvedic pharmaceuticals. Our pliable Central Government may repeatedly amend the 1970 Act and Indian Ayurveda may well become an exotic MNC pharmacopoeia.

The accessibility and affordability and authenticity of Ayurvedic medicines will be adversely affected if the patent laws are so changed by the cunning and clout of MNCs to bring them in line with their interests. In this context, we must remember our constitutionally mandated fundamental duty under Art. 51A(f) to "value and preserve the rich heritage of our composite culture." Our medicinal legacy, a few thousand years old, is Ayurveda, derived from the Maharishis and supplemented by tribal medical and other plural systems native to the soil. It will be betrayal of the fundamental right to life (Art. 21) and duty if we allow insidious invasion by macrocorporates committing piracy of our ancient formulations and drug wonders, with a view to practice 'golden deer' packagery, and thereby alienate Indian producers of Ayurvedic pharmaceuticals from their own country.

This is not a theoretical apprehension but an operative misappropriation against which the sovereign India, as the defender of its people's health, must take preemptive steps. Swaraj jurisprudence, with sensitive nationalism and concern for the health of the people, must use parliamentary legislation and WTO litigation, to defend our unique system of medicine from conquest by patent—a peril to ignore which is to jettison our priceless pharmacopoeia asset well known globally for its curative glory. In this context, the nation must conscientise itself so that patents can not be granted for any Ayurvedic or tribal medicine since it involves no invention but belongs to India's widely known indigenous materia medica. Insidious foreign invasion and stealthy transmission of our drug wonders can never be novelty, invention or creative innovation, a *sine qua non* of patent claim. We may note at this point that neither TRIPS nor other international agreements will bind the Indian people unless legislation is made in implementation.

The implementation of the TRIPS does not adequately reflect concern for the right to health of the people. Parliament has a solemn obligation to protect the fundamental right to life under Article 21, of every Indian. Western medicine, now that product patents are included by amendment in the patent law, will rise in price sky high. In this view it is just, fair and reasonable and consistent with international human rights law to legislatively defend the native systems of medicine against piracy and patentisation.

Already, Germany and other countries are committing covert robbery of our herbal therapy and biodiversity. They are taking patents in their country on the new that patents in their country, because of TRIPS provisions, will bind our country. India must, with all emphatic opposition, resist the application in our country or elsewhere the validity of patents of Ayurvedic drugs. Even under the existing patents law, no patent can be granted unless there is clear case of invention claimed by the patentee. It is outrageous that any German can claim any invention of an Ayurvedic drug. So also of herbal medicines popular all over India. What we have to do is to drive home the point that Ayurveda, Siddha, Unani and trial medicines are not secret therapies, never German serendipities, but public property available to anyone who reads the relevant texts and meets any medical practitioner of the system. A data base, comprehensive in scope, plenary in planned presentation, collected with painstaking investigation and made available with appropriate sources and references to anyone interested, will defeat the pretension of any foreigner who urges a phoney plea of discovery.

Apart from drugs and medical herbs, there are a wealth of medical treatments by way of oil massage, eye exercises and Yoga practices which are fantastic in their curative benefits. Kerala has a glorious tradition in these therapeutic procedures. Tamil Nadu has an excellent native orthopedic system and special oils and ointments. So too Kerala. These cannot be smuggled and patented.[12]

The science of ayurveda (ayur means life and veda means knowledge) has walked in from hideaway rural and urban pharmacies into urban India's medicine cabinet and the world's consciousness. The impact is significant. The stressed in India and the world increasingly search out ayurveda massages and cures for a hundred ailments ranging from migraine to paralysis. And global drug companies are tumbling over one another in their rush to research biocures and patent processes. It is easy to see why. Modern research has confirmed at least 60 uses of the humble neem tree. It's nice to see that a form of healing that began about 5,000 years ago is till yielding its mysteries to leading-edge research."

**(b) Great Heritage**

The main theme of all these discussion is the great heritage of our country. It is about a great country, a culture, a civilization that has withstood the onslaughts from other cultures over many millennia and proved itself to be stable, viable, and self rejuvenating.

**(c) Regain Self Confidence**

Unfortunately, in our country, during 300 years of British rule, the Britishers succeeded in destroying our spirit, self-confidence and self-pride, dinning into generations that we are incapable of anything, that Indians have no culture, no background and only things from the West are the best. Unfortunately, generation after generation imbibed this and now it is difficult for us to believe that we are a great nation, that we have been the torch holders of ethics and dharma for almost 7000 years and that our art, music, culture, science and medicine were shining during the centuries when the western countries did not even exist as nations.

**(d) Inner Strength and the Marvel of the Human Brain**

Reverting to the topic of inner strength: the idea that all of us can reinforce or efforts with our inner strength gains proof when we study this marvelous creation, our own brains.

This science of tapping the potential of our nervous forces has been offered to the World by our forefathers, the great Vedic Seers, who by intrusion and practice discovered that everyone of us has the potential not only to live a full and happy lie, but all had inherent powers to control nature and to go beyond time and space. This is the great Science of Yoga, 'Yoga is a precise science, a practical science and a provable science.

For ordinary human beings like us, Yoga and Meditation offer an easy way of improving our efficiency and equanimity. We need not worry at our stage about the various supernormal powers that are claimed for the intense practice of yoga. Through modern science we know that such extraordinary achievements are possible through the development of our brain powers. But these are not our goal. Our goal is to be efficient and successful, to be clam and happy and to be kind and generous to all human begins. Apart from the future goal of preserving human generations, the immediate fruit of yoga and meditation is a vast improvement in our daily life. What other treasure do we need to be happy and successful?

Luckily for mankind, our ancients in India have evolved an excellent way of improving and modifying brain function through the technique of yoga and mankind will be fortunate if it realizes this on time.[13]

It should be freely available to all. Such free availability includes the right of transfer to developing countries without payment of compensation so that these countries can utilize this important heritage as instruments of public policy.

The efficacy of this 5,000-year-old holistic science, first noticed in an Indus Valley seal of a yogi and later codified by Patanjali in the 2nd century B.C. is accepted without question as a superb mind, body and soul exercise. Yoga schools have proliferated in thousands all over the world, and yoga teachers are the rage in urban India and among karma tourists.

As a common heritage of mankind, instead of being protected by more stringent protection standards, they reason, such standards should be reduced, if not completely eliminated.

### (e) Traditional Perspective of the Developing World

Formation of an international standard of protection for intellectual property sounds like a simple task. Problems arise, however, when one actually attempts to claim a property right to information in the global arena. The difficulty stems from divergent concepts of property and ownership, as well as the elusive character of the term "information." Different legal principles exist from country to country, stemming from the particular social, political and ideological experiences of each. Unsettled definitions of ownership and property with regard to information are most evident when one compares the developed and developing worlds.[14]

Changing patterns of trade and technology revealed the schism between the developing and developed worlds in terms of intellectual property protection. The cost of creating intellectual property soared as research and development began requiring large-scale production, open international markets and protection against free-riding imitators. At the same time, the cost of pirating intellectual property plummeted as new technologies, such as photocopy machines, video cassette recorders and computer systems, lowered reproduction expenses. While these changes in trade and technology occurred, the developing world and the developed world adopted divergent attitudes toward the protection of intellectual property.

Because they are not major producers of intellectual property, developing countries have little incentive to vigorously protect it. Weak protection is justified on the grounds that the developing world needs maximum access to Western intellectual goods for its development and that stringent standards of protection are debilitating. Some developing countries maintain that knowledge and information are "the common heritage of mankind" and therefore should be made available at low cost. Most views are grounded in the premise that efficient use of knowledge is a fundamental requirement for economic growth. Therefore, the argument runs, technological information should be provided with minimal restriction because Third World development is in the interest of all nations.

Inadequate protection of intellectual property in developing countries occurs at both the substantive law and enforcement levels. On a substantive level, many developing countries fail even to recognize the three traditional areas of intellectual property protection: trademark, patent and copyright.

There are several reasons for non-recognition. First, lax protection offers economic benefits to developing nations. Because pirates of intellectual property incur minimal production costs and no royalty payments, they are in a better position than legitimate producers to satisfy demands in developing countries. Moreover, by copying only successful products, pirates avoid the risk of market failure and, in the short run, enrich themselves and the country in which they operate.

Second, developing counties tend to have scarce government resources. As a result, they resist spending on the enforcement of foreign intellectual property rights. As with the importation of capital, developing countries often view the importation of intellectual property as a means of dominating and exploiting the economic potential of the importing country. Paying for imports or royalties is thus seen as an economic burden fostering a negative balance of trade.

At the enforcement level, many developing countries provide weak or non-existent protection of the intellectual property laws they have enacted. And unlike Western countries, developing countries have few strong lobbies of inventors, authors or companies that would benefit from strict intellectual property laws or the enforcement thereof.

From the developed world's perspective, information is a valuable commodity upon which its livelihood depends. Indeed, for some developed nations, the transfer of technology represents the major component of their income. These countries demand strict protection of their ownership rights, for organized piracy undermines the very incentive structure that trademark, patent and copyright laws were designed to promote.

Moreover, inadequate protection also undermines the goal of free trade. Absent sufficient protection, creators cannot recover the cost of their research and development. The result is lower production, fewer trading opportunities and higher costs to the consumer. In other words, piracy cuts directly into the developed country's profits and undermines its competitive edge.

**(f) The Economic Liberalization View**

Recent efforts towards economic liberalization in developing countries have made them more willing to strengthen intellectual property protection in order to attract foreign investment for local development. Empirical data suggest that pharmaceutical research and development is conducted most commonly in countries that protect intellectual property, and that areas where protection is increasing have been receiving increasing shares of research and development expenditures from US pharmaceutical firms. In addition, the availability of intellectual property protection in a developing country may encourage foreign firms to invest in product development specific to the country's needs. Stronger intellectual property protection may also facilitate technology transfer, since patent holders are more willing to sell technology to countries that guarantee ownership rights. Stronger protection also encourages local inventors to keep their technology in the country. Inventors from developing countries with weaker protection currently patent more heavily in the United States than do inventors from other developing countries.[15]

The parameters of the developing-country intellectual

property debate have been determined thus far by the need to protect high technology, and not by intellectual property issues unique to the developing world. Recently, however, increased interest in the economic potential of developing countries' rain forests has expanded the context of the debate, suggesting that developing countries have economic needs which are left unmet by the intellectual property system as it now exists. The motivations behind developing countries' and their inhabitants' growing insistence on increased property rights to biological material used in technological enterprise both correspond with and diverge from their historical reasons for adopting traditional intellectual property law systems. Much of this tension is evident in the intellectual property implications of medicinal plant and crop variety research.

The developed world's pharmaceutical industry has been a prominent source of the heightened interest in the rain forest, as pharmaceutical companies have begun to explore the forest more intensively for medicinal plants and information on their possible uses.

The developed world's renewed search for new plant material has been accompanied by a growing interest in the traditional knowledge of indigenous peoples. Native healers and other members of indigenous groups can draw members of indigenous groups can draw attention to specific plants, while explaining their physiological effects and describing the processes through which they convert raw plant material into purer compounds. Such information can provide valuable clues to the identity of active molecules, greatly expediting their isolation in the laboratory. In fact, traditional knowledge has long been an integral part of drug development. Approximately three quarters of the plant-derived compounds currently used as pharmaceuticals have been discovered through research based on plant use by indigenous peoples.

Like the pharmaceutical industry, the international seed industry depends on plant genetic materials derived from crop varieties selected and improved by farmers in developing countries.

Along with the rain forests in which many of them developed, the traditional cultures of indigenous peoples are disappearing rapidly, making it likely that their typically orally-preserved knowledge of medicinal plants and agricultural varieties will be permanently lost. Like the rain forest, cultural knowledge has been assigned little economic worth, although it too is valuable for biotechnological innovation. Proposals for intellectual property reform with respect to cultural knowledge consequently mirror those regarding ownership off valuable plants: in both cases, the compensation for and recognition of such ownership, as a legitimate form of intellectual property deserving protection, is advocated as a means of providing economic incentives currently absent from the system.

Extending protection to the knowledge of indigenous peoples challenges the conventional distinction created by the practice of protecting unique knowledge but not unique raw materials. Increasing the scope of intellectual property protection in this way also raises questions about the patent ability of knowledge that belongs to a group rather than an individual. Although the findings of a research group affiliated with a university or corporation are patentable, the cultural knowledge of an indigenous group and even the secrets of healers within a group are not, since they are considered to be public, common knowledge.

The desire for increased foreign investment as a means of achieving internal economic development has been a major impetus for developing countries' recent efforts toward providing enhanced intellectual property protection. Although the intellectual property policy debate has focused in the past on protection for high-technology products, new concerns specific to the developing world pose a challenge to the traditional debate. Specifically, the rain forest's economic promise for both developing and developed countries has revealed economic needs of developing countries which are left unaddressed by the existing intellectual property system.

The three types of response to these concerns—political action, multilateral co-operation, and private business transactions—reveal the developing countries' new attitude towards intellectual property while demonstrating their willingness to take control of property rights relating to their unique natural resources. While the success of each solution will depend in part upon cooperation by private and public institutions in the developed world, the direction of change will be determined largely by the innovations through which developing countries respond to the complex tensions among state and individual property rights and ecological concerns regarding the rain forest.

### (g) Perspective of the Developed World

Developed countries uniformly view intellectual property as embodying pure property rights, entitled to comprehensive international protection in order to assure a full economic return to creators and owners. Reducing the potential for uncompensated, infringing uses by enacting and enforcing international protection norms is perceived as beneficial for both developed and developing countries. By assuring a higher economic return to the authors of copyrighted works and inventor of patented inventions and trade secrets, such norms encourage such authors and inventors to expend the necessary research and development funds to develop such works. Thus, intellectual property, contrary to being a "common heritage of mankind" is, in fact, an individually developed property right whose use should be compensated as fully as any other property.

Developed countries further assert that viewing intellectual property as a common heritage of mankind is harmful to developing countries since it denies these countries the ability to develop their own intellectual property. By denying protection to intellectual property, developing countries, they reason, lose the economic incentive to their own authors and inventors to create native-developed technology which could then be exported to other countries.[16]

## 3. CASE STUDIES IN CONFLICT

### (a) The Caribbean Basin and Copyright Protection

Increasingly dependent upon the sale of information, the United States deems the international protection of intellectual property a vital trade issue involving its competitive advantage in the world market.

The United States argues that inadequate protection of

copyrights has definable detrimental economic effects. At a time when it can hardly be afforded, the problem has resulted in the large-scale loss of jobs in the United States. Further more, the production of intellectual products has become extremely costly, requiring research, development, and large-scale production expenses. Increasingly, the United States needs an expansive international market to recover its investment costs. Unrecoverable costs, resulting from inadequate copyright laws and enforcement, discourage production of copyrightable material due to a loss of incentives and unavailability of funds.[17]

The United States stresses that inadequate copyright protection causes other identifiable "trade distortions." For example, pirated products imported into the United States displace sales of legitimate items on the domestic market. In addition, if products are pirated in non-US markets, they decrease United States exports to those markets. Furthermore, pirated parts exported from those non-US markets to third countries again displace United States exports. In contrast with the view of Caribbean countries, the United Sates argues that lack of enforcement is equivalent to a trade barrier because inadequate enforcement deters international trade.

Recent approaches to solve the problem have been trade-based, with the United States holding trade pacts hostage to its demands for better copyright protection.

By contrast, Caribbean countries have an unenthusiastic attitude toward their own laws as well as toward international copy-right laws. Their attitude is due in part to their perception that copyright law limits free access to intellectual property, thus hindering economic development.

Despite their ambivalence regarding copyright law, a significant number of Caribbean countries are signatories to international copyright conventions. Therefore, the inadequate protection of intellectual property in the Caribbean is more closely attributable to nonexistent or ineffectual enforcement of the law than to a total lack of substantive copyright laws.

A major enforcement effort would be necessary to adequately protect Asian copyrighted material in the Atlantic Achieving sufficient enforcement of copyright laws demands complex and very costly administrative and judicial systems.

The infrastructure required to support such systems is severely lacking in Caribbean Basin countries. Basic services, as well as skilled workers, technicians, and administrative personnel, are either scarce or completely lacking. Further infrastructure problems include substandard communications facilities, airports, roads, and other means of transportation. The problem is compounded by the notoriously slow bureaucracies of many Caribbean countries.

The public, of course, would bear the cost of developing the judicial and administrative infrastructures necessary for copyright law enforcement. Developing countries in general are reluctant to allocate scant government capital to the enforcement of intellectual property laws. In the Caribbean, a severe shortage of foreign currency, coupled with the belief that available resources are better spent elsewhere, renders the enforcement of foreign copyright laws a secondary concern. Many view piracy as having the benefit of producing desperately needed intellectual property at little cost to he public and with less sacrifice of the funds demanded for the development of infrastructure.

The inability or mere unwillingness of government and judicial officials to enforce copyright laws may also stem from political instability and widespread corruption. Enforcement efforts are thwarted when enforcement officers can be bribed to allow incidents of infringement to escape the sanctions provided for by the law.

In addition, many Asian countries simply have no tradition of protecting intellectual property. The lack of tradition contrasts with the United States, where copyright law is so ingrained in US jurisprudence as to be included in the Constitution. Unlike the United States, Asian countries have limited number of authors, inventors, or companies that would lobby for, or benefit from, sound intellectual property laws. Therefore, US outrage as to "mere" copyright violations are sometimes met if not with bafflement, then at least without complete understanding.

**(b) Thailand and Pharmaceutical Patents**

A patent represents a government grant of a "monopoly" of limited duration on the use of an invention or discovery. Although patent laws vary from country to country, if an invention is novel, useful, and not obvious, and if the invention fits within the statutory categories of protectable inventions, it is generally patentable. Much of the controversy in international patent law surrounds variations, from country to country, in patentable categories. Because the owner of a patent can charge a royalty for the use of the patented invention, if a country refuses to recognize a patentable category, such a refusal will necessarily affect the cost of using a given technology in that country.

Western countries generally believe that a patent system provides the best overall incentive to encourage invention. although this assertion is difficult to prove, it forms Western industrialized countries, including the United States. This implicitly assumes that all economics necessarily benefit from an increased number of inventions. When an invention is granted patent protection, investors are more willing to invest because profits are higher if competition is reduced. Western Industrialized Countries also believe that patents encourage the development or transfer of the technology necessary to utilize the patent. Thus, according to the Western view, a system of patent laws can lead to economic development despite the cost of the royalties.[18]

While the US Government and businesses subscribe to the views of the majority of other Western Industrialized Countries and contend that all countries would benefit from granting and enforcing patents on pharmaceuticals, many countries, including most Third World nations, do not grant patents for inventions is agriculture and medicine. These countries may fear drastic price increases that would result from paying royalties on patented pharmaceutical and agricultural technology as well as a loss of control over technology that is vital to national development. The Thai Patent Act, before its recent revisions, served as a typical example of the limitations developing countries place on their patent laws.

The Thai Patent Act ("Act"), originally passed in 1979, is the primary source of patent protection in Thailand. On February 27, 1992, the Thai Legislative Assembly passed a revision of the Act. The revision was intended to satisfy US objections to the 1979 Act.

The United States objected to several provisions of the Act as originally ratified. The strongest compliant of US patent owners was that the 1979 Act excluded pharmaceutical, agricultural, and biological products from patent protection, thereby causing a significant loss of revenue. US owners also complained the fifteen years was an insufficient term for patent protection. Finally, the 1979 Act provided that a patent must be worked in Thailand; otherwise, the patent would be subject to either a compulsory license or revocation.

**(c) US Pressure on Thailand**

In 1991, Thailand became one of three countries identified as a priority country under Special 301 for its failure to enforce copyrights and for deficient patent protection for pharmaceuticals.

The Thai government reaction was reserved. Then Primary Minister Chatichai Choonhavan was unconcerned about US threats, taking the view that what the United States did not buy, Japan would. Current Prime Minister Anand Panyaachun's more circumspect stance has been to recognize that the United States is now Thailand's largest export market and a world economic power, while at the same time indicating that the national interest must come first.[19]

In 1987, the Thai government responded to US pressure to provide for stronger copyright enforcement and penalties by putting amendments to the Copyright Act before the legislature. However, significant opposition arose to the proposed legislation with a political intensity that resulted in an election, a new coalition government, and a reexamination of the entire copyright issue. the strongest opposition came from those arguing that change to Thailand's intellectual property laws amounted to capitulation to US bullying. Two years later Primary Minister Chatichai's defiance of the United States on the GSP issue was widely supported in Thailand. Thailand accept cuts in GSP benefits from the United States rather than altering its intellectual property laws.

The prevailing view in Thailand is that the government should not yield to US pressure on intellectual property right.

For examples, the government minister responsible for negotiating with the United States during 1991 was referred to as a "traitor" for allegedly yielding to US demands.

In the pharmaceutical area, those opposed to change in the Patent Act, such as the Thai Patent Act, such as the Thai Pharmaceutical Manufacturers Association, argue that foreign drug monopolies will take over the Thai market and this will lead to higher prices and a reduction in the availability of drugs to the poor. Other arguments against the Patent Act amendments can be raised, such as questioning the necessity of increasing intellectual property protection for US nationals when they already hold more patents, trademarks, and copyrights in Thailand than Thais, and bemoaning the increased outflow of royalties to be expected with enhanced intellectual property protection, but these are not significant positions taken by opponents to change in Thailand.

It is tempting to evaluate the Section 301[20] experience by determining whether its use has led to changes that benefit the Untied States. However, it is more appropriate to evaluate the Section 301 experience by looking from both the Thai and US point of view. Four specific criteria can be used: short-term economics; long-term economics; impact on the international regime (GATT); and short-term political impact.

From the US point of view, the operation of Section 301 and its threat of embargoes has had an immediate positive economic effect. Thailand's intellectual property laws and practices are being altered to comply with the US demands. US companies can anticipate an immediate economic return. The immediate economic effect in Thailand of changes forced upon it by US use of Section 301 is one of expected increased cost for certain pharmaceutical drugs and increased government expenditures on enforcement of intellectual property law. There will also be an increase in royalty payments made to the United Sates because of increased intellectual property protection. The Thais will derive little short-term economic benefit from the changes made in response to Section 301 action.[21]

Moreover, there exists resentment about the one-sided nature of the US Section 301 policy. The United States uses economic coercion to force change on Thailand, yet Thailand can expect no reciprocity from the United States when internal US policies are in question, such as subsidized rice exports that unfairly disadvantage Thai rice producers.

In the long-term, Thailand may be able to see some positive economic impacts from adopting the US recommendations. As an economic matter, some conclude that the protection of intellectual property rights, including patent protection for pharmaceuticals, should lead to substantial long-term benefits in the form of increased investment and developing technology. Moreover, it can be argued that if Thailand is to emerge as one of the newly industrialized countries, its intellectual property laws and practice must be brought into line with those of industrialized countries. The problem is that it is unclear whether industrialization precedes, or follows, intellectual property protection leads to increased investment and economic development. However, it is difficult to reconcile this approach with the experiences of Japan, Taiwan, and Hong Kong. For example, Japan did not recognize certain types of patents until 1975, although today it is one of the strongest supporters of US efforts. As one author has commented:

Though apparently it cost them international respect at the time, the Japanese policy of tolerating the copying of imports appears to have benefitted their economy in the early period of development without producing longterm negative effects. Looking at the Japanese experience, a country presently in the early stages of development might choose a similar course.

It is worth noting that one study determined that the degree of intellectual property rights protection afforded by Thailand matches its current stage of economic development.

Where the international trading system is weak, as it allegedly is in intellectual property protection and trade dispute resolution, it can be argued that Us unilateralism will lead the way in developing new and necessary responses to these issues. Section 301 results in pressure to agree in areas where a lack of international discipline is, in the long-term, capable of undermining the entire international trading system.

While increased use of the GATT dispute settlement process is not inherently bad, the deadlines on GATT adjudication and compliance imposed under the US law are unrealistic.

More importantly, the United States itself does not comply with the standards, nor does it easily accept adverse GATT ruling. Regarding intellectual property, it is argued that a new approach is necessary to increase standards or protection.

US pressure on Thailand regarding intellectual property protection may have created significant short-term political costs in Thailand. As previously noted, there is significant opposition to Thailand's perceived capitulation to US pressure. The current unelected Thai government is in a position of not having to respond directly to such pressure. With elections coming a politician's stance on standing up to US pressure could be important. Moreover, former military leader General Suchinda Kraprayoon expressed irritation with the US government's perceived meddling in Thai internal matters and has been quoted as saying that the United states was not the "world's big boss", and that "if I were the Thai Government, I would not allow the US to treat me this way." It has been speculated that the United States has softened its stand on Thai intellectual property issues because of the fear that resentment of any US action could lead to greater political instability.

From the US perspective, Section 301 has been successfully utilized to further its short and long-term economic and international interests. However, it is clear that utilization of Section 301 against Thailand has not been without its costs. Resentment of US pressure tactics has created an anti-US political constituency in Thailand where none had existed and has created significant problems for the civilian government as Thailand seeks to regain democratic processes. The resentment is increased because of the one-sided nature of the US action—demanding changes from Thailand without rectifying US inadequacies and GATT inconsistencies that are detrimental to Thai interests. The unilateral nature of the US action does not create confidence in international rules upon which Thailand is dependent.

The perception in Thailand, regardless of how the dispute is portrayed by the United States, is of a stronger, more powerful friend publicly bullying its smaller, more vulnerable partner into complying with unwanted laws and practices. It is a perception that will not be really forgotten in The Land of Smiles.[22]

## 4. TRANSPLANTATION

### (a) Transplanting Intellectual Property Values

Much of the early scholarship in the area of comparative law focused on the importation, reception and/ or transplantation of one system's jurisprudence to another. For example, Roman legal concepts were "received" into much of Europe through their rediscovery in the Middle Ages and the "adoption" of these concepts into the emerging laws of countries such as France and Germany. Early differences between common law countries, such as England and the United States, and civil law countries, such as France and Germany, often arose as a result of the differing degrees to which Roman law concepts were adopted into each country's legal system. Efforts at developing international standards of protection for intellectual property rights, whether through accession and compliance with substantive norms contained in bilateral or multinational treaties, or through the revision of present national laws as part of a country's effects to "harmonize" its laws with other nations' treatment, necessarily require consideration of many of the same factors which affected earlier instances at reception and transplantation.[23]

Regardless of the status of a country as a developed (industrialized) or developing (less industrialized or newly industrialized) country, its efforts to create or revise existing intellectual property law norms must being with consideration of the effect the adoption of another country's norms will have—not merely on those laws affecting intellectual property—but on the country's historical and cultural treatment of such underlying issues as the ownership and use of intangible property, the protection of information and public access to ideas, information and expressions.

**(b) Legal Transplants**

A "legal transplant" may be defined as any legal notion or rule which, after being developed in a "source" body of law, is then introduced into another, "host" body of law. A classic example is found in the Corpus Juris Civilis, the compendium of Roman Law which the Emperor Justinian commissioned almost fifteen centuries ago. Law encapsulated in the Corpus Juris has found a host in Continental European law over the last thousand years. This process has been called the "reception" of Roman law into modern European law.

Copyright law governs how literary and artistic works may be exploited. The rise of copyright might have begun when paper and printing were first invented in China. Copyright statutes were in fact first instituted during the eighteenth century in Europe. With ever-accelerating technological advances, media exploitation has crossed national borders with increasing frequency and speed. As a result, there has been increasing pressure to extend and harmonize copyright law internationally. Legal transplants have served as a common device for achieving this end.[24]

For example, in the middle of the nineteenth century, France threatened not to renew its commercial treaty with Belgium. At a condition of renewal, France required Belgium to adopt a copyright law, this at a time when French law provided a model for copyright on much of the European continent. The British Copyright Act of 1911 is another example: it was transplanted throughout the British Empire in the twentieth century, until such time as British colonies and dominions became independent and enacted their own copyright laws, more or less on the British model. Not all of these jurisdictions, however, fall squarely within Anglo-American legal culture: Quebec, India, and Israel, most notably, also draw upon different, pre-existing traditions.

How do transplants work? This question may take empirical and normative forms. Empirically, we may ask about the fate of transplanted law in passing from a source to a host body of law. This inquiry becomes problematic to the extent that linguistic, cultural, or historical perspectives change when moving from the source to the host body of law. Does the transplant nonetheless work much as it did in the source law, is it modified in form or substance in the different host law, or is it simply rejected by it? Normatively, to the extent the transplant takes place without significant change, we have to ask: is such slavish reception justified? And, if so, by reference to whose values?

### (c) Realist Arguments for Transplants

A legal "realist" would treat the law, to quote Oliver Wendel Holmes, as a "body of systematized prediction" concerning the likely behaviour of lawmakers and agents, from legislators through judges to the police. One could then make decisions in the light of such predictions or, where necessary, attempt to change the institutions o the law resulting in predicted, but unfavourable behaviour.

If, for example, a lawyer warned a business client, that the law of another country was not adequate to protect creations in which the business had invested, the business could then seek to have copyright law thought to be effective at home transplanted into that country. The rationale seems simple enough: a country protects its nationals' property on its own soil with its laws, and comity generally leads other countries to protect foreigners' property on their soil, except for intellectual property which has not benefitted from this approach. One response to foreign failure to protect copyright would be proceedings, such as those in the United States, in which the business may petition its own government to use threats of trade retaliations against countries abroad serving a pirate havens.[25]

### (d) Normativist Arguments About Transplants

What might be called "normativist" positions pick up where realist arguments leave off. In this century, Hans Kelsen re-articulated the basic argument of such positions, namely that statements about facts, about what "is", cannot serve as adequate bases for statements about how the law "ought" to work. While realists might dwell on how a notion or rule "is" transplanted from one body of law into another, normativists would ask why the transplant "ought" to have effect as law. Normativism can be elaborated into different approaches to transplants.

The most ambitious of these approaches is "universalist" normativism. In a seminal analysis, Kant attempted to derive one over riding norm universally valid for any system of law. In copyright, arguments have been made for legal transplants on the basis of supposedly universal, "permanent cultural values." The title of the first copyright statute, the British Statute of Anne of 1710, already anticipates this sense of some common, higher aim of copyright law by setting out "the Encouragement of Learning" as the purpose of the statute. During the eighteenth century, in Enlightenment Europe, such notions as "learning" or "science" were broadly understood in include all products of mind, including literature, music, and the fine arts, that might advance human consciousness of the world.[26]

Another approach might be called "systemic" normativism. Kelsen elaborated such a position, defining a system of law as including literature, music, and the fine arts, that might advance human consciousness of the world.

Another approach might be called "systemic" normativism. Kelsen elaborated such a position, defining a system of law as including only such rules as may be generated consistently with its own underlying norms. This position may serve as the basis for arguing that transplants may not be understood as foreign notions or rules that a system of law passively takes on. If one system received law from another, as European civil law incorporated Roman notions, its own constitutive norms would at least have to validate them. From this point of view, universalist aims for copyright, such as "learning", "human consciousness", or "permanent cultural values", are at best window dressing, not justifications. Indeed, for systemic normativism, values as such, whether universal or local, cannot form the basis for adopting legal rules, since values themselves must derive from underlying norms for legal purposes. As a result, to understand the normative basis, for example, for the reception into China of the Berne model of copyright, some norm of Chinese law would have to be invoked. One could invoke the Chinese provision that, in the event of any difference "between the Civil Law of the People's Republic of China and its international treaties, the latter shall prevail."

However, this principle itself seems to be borrowed from continental European approaches to international treaties, raising the question of what underlying Chinese norm in turn validates it as a basis for further transplants.

**(e) Relativist Challenges to Transplant Analysis**

"Relativism" involves the suspicion that our own linguistic, cultural, or historical perspectives distort our knowledge of other such perspectives. Benjamin Lee Whorf encapsulated this position in speaking of language as "a vast pattern-system' made up of "culturally ordained . . form and categories" that channel our "consciousness." This point of view does not lead to arguments against transplants as much as it makes them seem difficult, if not impossible, to analyze from our own, necessarily biased perspective.

The Italian maxim *traduttore, traditore*—translator, traitor—succinctly conveys the lesson of relativism. In the common and civil laws, whose languages share European roots, basic notions like "right" or "law" do not take on meaning consistently.[27]

Starting at the linguistic dimension of relativism, we thus quickly encounter its cultural and historical dimensions. It is well and good to say the copyright law is to enhance "permanent cultural values" or to protect "the most sacred of properties." Nonetheless, such notions of "law" and "culture', not to mention "Property" and "the sacred", if taken together, seem to refer to manifold processes not easily disentangled. As a result, we run the risk of encountering radically different types of entanglements of law and culture; indeed, the very concept of "law", not to mention "culture", may vary from place to place and period to period. Further, it cannot be assumed that the effect of law on culture will be as simple to see as that of a tool applied to raw materials, say, the mark of a chisel used on a piece of marble. Generally, and certainly in copyright, we have to take account of intricate and subtle feed-back mechanisms between legal and other cultural processes, notably by way of the media.

Relativism, if carried far enough, leads to a kind of solipsism. It highlights epistemological obstacles that would make it difficult, if not impossible, to know just how transplants from a source law might operate in an exotic host law. The fact that languages are translated, however, gives us reason to believe that these obstacles are not insurmountable, even though "[t]ime, distance, disparities of outlook or assumed reference make this act [of translation] more or less difficult].

In transplants, we face the problem of translating terms from one language into another. Where transplants include open ended notions, such translation becomes problematic.

In one of its dominant forms, linguistic relativism has focused on the tendency of differently structured languages to lead to different descriptions of reality. For example, the Hopi Indians, in the southwestern United States, have been observed to employ a verb system that enables them to make finer discriminations of the phases and unfolding of natural processes than one could easily do in any European language. It is nonetheless possible to learn to speak an exotic language with some competence, albeit imperfectly: if, hypothetically, we were dropped into the midst of a tribe with an unknown language, we could with increasing success translate as "rabbit" a word we heard the tribe repeatedly use while hunting, pointing to, or eating what appears to us to be rabbits. There would still remain the hard cases of all-too-frequent, open-ended notions: for example, the French word bois accurately translates into the English "wood" or "woods" often enough, but it is not clear whether *le Bois de Boulogne* is best translated as "Boulogne park" or the "Boulogne Woods."

If we shift our attention to legal language, the problem of translation becomes much more complex. Legal discourse fulfills a large range of "performative" functions in implementing norms rather than merely making "true or false" statements about facts. However, some commentators still look to factual reference, not merely to test translations from different languages, but even interpretation within the same legal language. For example, realists suggest that, unless the law indicates the behaviour it is to control by its very "words", it represents nothing but vague "paper rules'. The fact of the matter is that legal discourse remains endemically riddled with value-landen, open-ended notions that resist factual clarification. Such discourse nonetheless allows legal practitioners to communicate, at least within relatively homogeneous legal cultures. Furthermore, conceptions of "fact" and "law", and of how facts relate to the law, vary from culture to culture. It often becomes necessary to understand these conceptions to disentangle meanings in other laws.

Of course, different legal notions differ in the extent that they are open-ended. For example, in the Berne Convention, the notion of "publication" is more precisely.

## 5. HISTORICAL PROBLEMS

### (a) Printing Privileges and Copyright Monopolies

Since the late Renaissance the French Crown regulated that publishing industry; Convention, do not benefit from Berne minimum rights. Anglo-Australian incomprehension before Aboriginal art and Berne purism concerning unlisted works tend to have comparable effects with regard to transplanting relevant law. Either way, the "common core" meaning of the Berne notion of "work", historically the European meaning, is made the standard for non-European works.

In moving from language to culture, we have to widen our framework of analysis. Legislators or treaty drafters might blithely use a notion like "work" without contemplating the entire range of cases in which it might not always have clear meaning. It is in applying the notion in trouble some cases that difficulties might arise in interpreting the rules that it helps to articulate. These cases are likely to be entangled in complex cultural settings, in which a variety of factors come to bear on interpreting possibly applicable rules.[28]

Such cultural inquiry might be broken down into the following questions: First, who, in the community of legal practitioners, has power to interpret a rule? Some systems tend to decentralize such powers in judges with discretion to refashion law case by case, while others tend to centralize them in legislators. Second, what values and theory direct the interpretation of rules? Some values are relevant to all law, such as equity and reliability, while others become relevant only in specific fields such as copyright. As well as encapsulating such values, legal theory may also entail premises about law itself that, depending on their tenor, differently guide the interpretation of legal language defined than the notion of a "work." Berne "publication" is defined by rather objective criteria, notably the requirement of making hard copies available to the public. The very fact that the case law has developed converging interpretations of Berne "publication" indicates that this notion is only marginally open-ended. By contrast, Article 2 of the Berne Convention only illustrates the notion of a protected "work" with an open-ended list of examples, and there is still debate on how to interpret this notion. Commentators offer conflicting answers to the questions: does the Berne Convention or national law determine the defining criteria of works, such as "originality" and "creativity"? and what legal effects, if any, follow from placing a work in the Berne list? Of course, if the language of the Berne Convention authoritatively defined "work", it would control how this notion was transplanted into the national laws of Berne countries; otherwise, domestic lawmakers would have discretion in defining it. The courts tend to ignore all these issues for the simple reason that there is a rough and ready consensus worldwide on the sense of "works." There are nonetheless, frequently enough, hard cases in which courts disagree on how to apply this notion. Cases of factual compilations, industrial designs, and computer programs are among the most notable.

## Notes and References

1. Lrie E. Simon, "Appellations of Origin: The Continuing Controversy", 5 *Journal Intl. Law Bus.* 132. Copyright 1983 North Western School of Law, Excerpt Reprinted with permission.
2. David M. Hang, "The International Transfer of Technology: Lessons that East Europe can Learn from the Failed Third World Experience", 5 *Harvard Journal of Law,* Science and Technology 209. Copyright 1992.
3. J.H. Reichman, "Beyond the Historical Lines of Demarcation: Competition Law, Intellectual Property Rights, and International Trade After The GATT's Uruguay Round", 20 *Brooklyn Journal International Law.* 75 Copyright 1993 by the Brooklyn Law School.

4. Biswajit Dhar, C. Niranjan Rao, "Third Amendment to Patent Act: Reflections on a TRIPS—Complaint Law" *Economic and Political Weekly,* April 9, 2005, OECD, Genetic Inventions, Intellectual Property Rights and Licensing Practices: Evidence and Policies, 2005, 15.
5. Mark C. Suchman, "Invention and Ritual: Notes on the Interrelation of Magic and Intellectual Property in Preliterate Societies, 89 Columbia Law Review 1264. Copyright 1989 Directors of the *Columbia Law Review* Association, Inc.
6. Carlos Alberto Primo Braga, "The Economics Intellectual Property Rights and The GATT: View from the South", 22 *Vanderbilt Journal of Transnational Law* 243, Copyright 1989 *Vanderbilt Journal of Transnational Law.*
7. Pradip Thomas, GATS and Trade in Audio-Visuals Culture, Politics and Empire", *Economic and Political Weekly,* August 16, 2003; 3485-3493. K.M. Gopakumar and Tahir Amin, "Patents (Amendment) Bill 2005: A Critique", *Economic and Political Weekly,* April 9, 2005. 1503-1505. The Patent (Amendment) Bill passed by Indian Parliament, March 22, 2005, "Two Cheers for Patents" (The Leader) *The Hindu,* March 24, 2005.
8. Carlos Alberto Primo Braga, "The Economics of Intellectual Property Rights and The GATT: View from the South", 22 *Vanderbilt Journal of Transnational Law* 243. Copyright 1989 *Vanderbilt Journal of Transnational Law.*
9. Carlos Alberto Primo Braga, "The Economics of Intellectual Property Rights and The GATT View from the South", 22 *Vanderbilt Journal of Transnational Law* 243. Copyright 1989 *Vanderbilt Journal of Transnational Law.*
10. Charles Von Simson, "Feist or Famine American Database Copyright as an Economic Model for the European Union" 20 *Brooklyn Journal of International Law* 729. (1995) Brooklyn Law School.
11. Doris Estelle Long. "The Role of Intellectual Property in Developing Nations." (1995)
12. V.R. Krishna Iyer, "Piracy of Ayurvedic Heritage", *The New Indian Express,* 13th October 2003.
13. B. Ramamurthi, "Sixty-fourth Convocation Address", Annamalai University, 6th March 1997.
14. Tarakkalagher Giunta, Lily H. Shang, "Ownership of Information in a Global Economy", 27 *George Washington Journal of International Law and Economics* 327. (1994) George Washington University.
15. Kirsten Peterson, "Recent Intellectual Property Trends in Developing Countries", 33 *Harvard International Law Journal,* 277 (1992) President and Fellows of Harvard College.
16. Doris Estelle Long. *The Role of Intellectual Property in Developing Nations.* (1995)
17. Valerie L. Hummel, "The Search for A Solution to The US—Caribbean Copyright Enforcement Controversy" 16 *Fordham International Law Journal.* 721 (1993) Fordham University School of Law.

18. Stefan Kirchanski, "Protection of US Patent Rights in Developing Countries: US Efforts to Enforce Pharmaceutical Patents in Thailand", 16 *Loyola of Los Angeles International and Comparative Law Journal*, 569. (1993).
19. Ted L. McDorman, "U.S. Thailand Trade Disputes: Applying Section 301 to Cigarettes and Intellectual Property", 14 *Michigan Journal of International Law* 90. (1992).
20. Robert A. Cingue, "Making Cyberspace Safe for Copyright: The Protection of Electronic Works in a Protocol to the Berne Convention", *19 Fordham International Law Journal* 1258, (1995) Fordham University School of Law.
    (a) Ted L. McDorman, "U.S. Thailand Trade Disputes: Applying Section 301 to Cigarettes and Intellectual Property", 14 *Michigan Journal of International Law* (1992) Ted. L. McDorman.
    (b) Theordore H. Davis, "Combating Piracy of Intellectual Property in International Markets: A Proposed Modification of the Special 300 Action", 24 *Vanderbilt Journal Transnational Law*, 505 (1991) Vanderbilt University School of Law.
21. *Supra* Note 20.
22. Editor's Note: For a detailed discussion of Special 301, See Chapter.
23. *Supra* Note 11.
24. Paul Edward Gellen, "Legal Transplants in International Copyright: Some Problems of Method", 13 *University of California Los Angels Pacific Basin Law Journal*, 199, (1994) Regents of the University of California.
25. Paul Edward Gellen, *Ibid.*
26. Paul Edward Gellen, *Ibid.*
27. Paul Edward Gellen, *Ibid.*
28. Jane C. Ginsburg, "A Tale of Two Copyrights: Literary Property in Revolutionary France and America" 64 *Tulane Law Review*, 991, (1990) Tulane Law Review Association.

CHAPTER

# 2

# *The Purpose of Copyright Law*

*The art of writing is the highest of those permitted to man as drawing directly from the soul, and the means or material it uses are also of the soul. It brings man into alliance with what is great and eternal. It discloses to him the variety and splendor of his resources. And there is much in literature that draws us with a sublime charm—the superincumbent necessity by which each writer, an infirm, capricious, fragmentary soul, is made to utter his part in the chorus of humanity is enriched by thoughts which flow from all past minds, shares the hopes of all existing minds, so that, whilst the world is made of youthful, helpless children of a day, literature resounds with the music of united vast ideas of affirmation and of moral truth.*

—Ralph Waldo Emerson

The purpose of Copyright Law is to encourage authorship. When we embody that encouragement in property rights for authors, we can lose sight of a crucial distinction: Nurturing authorship is not necessarily the same thing as nurturing authors. When individuals, authors claim that they are entitled to incentives that would impoverish the milieu in which other authors must also work, we must guard against protecting authors at the expense of the enterprise of authorship.

## I. COPYRIGHT AND PROPERTY

Copyright law is a legal scheme, prescribed in the constitutions and put in place by national legislatures like Indian Parliament Rajya Sabha Lok Sabha and US Congress, to encourage and protect the enterprise of authorship.[1] In the 280 years since the enactment of the first copyright statute, the technicalities surrounding copyright have assumed diverse forms, but the essential mechanism has remained constant. The system creates legal rights akin to property rights.

According to a currently popular mode of analysis, property rights in intellectual works are necessary because intellectual creations pose a public goods problem: The cost of creating the works is often high, the cost of reproducing them is low, and once created, the works is often high, the cost of reproducing them is low, and once created, the works may be reproduced rapaciously without depleting the original. In a world in which such reproduction is not restrained, an author will be unable to recover the costs of creating a work and will therefore forgo the creative endeavour in favour of something more remunerative. To provide the author with a market in which he or she can seek compensation for his or her creation, we establish property rights in her work and allow her to sell or lease these rights to others. Thus, the copyright system encourages authors to create and encourages distributors to purchase rights in authors' creations so that the distributors may sell those creations to the rest of us.

The model for these property rights is real property. We cast the author's rights in the mould of exclusive rights of control. Invasion of these rights is actionable on a strict liability basis, akin to the traditional formulation of trespass to land. We describe the exceptions to the exclusive control attending ownership as privileges. Copyrights are fully alienable, subject to a copyright statute of frauds. They may be inherited, bequeathed, mortgaged and distributed equitably upon divorce.

## 2. ORIGINALITY AND AUTHORSHIP

Treating intellectual property as if it were real property, of course, can be problematic. The aspects of intellectual property that create the public goods problems that the property regime is intended to repair also make it difficult to fit intellectual property within the real property rubric. One difficulty, discussed at length in a recent research by Professor Wendy Gordon, is that intellectual property lacks the tangible qualities associated with real property.[2] In the face of intellectual property's lack of "thingness", the law must supply alternative concepts to take the place of physical boundaries.[3]

What is copyright's analogue to (boundaries)? Surprisingly, the system demands no comparable analysis or evaluation until actual litigation occurs, and there is remarkably little analysis even during litigation. There is nothing that you need to prove in order to ensure that your copyright endures until fifty years after one's death. To provide the illusion of boundaries confining one's property rights, we invoke a copyright postulate.

This concept of originality is a keystone of copyright law. A work is ineligible for copyright protection except to the extent that it reflects original authorship. "Authorship" is a term used to describe the requirement of a non-trivial amount of creative expression; originality requires that the expression "owe its origin" to the authors[4] rather than be copied from another source. Where a work of authorship is based on preexisting sources, copyright will protect only the portions of it that are original. Thus, originality determines the boundaries of the copyright. Its mirror images defines the scope of copyright infringement since the statute protects the author only from another's copying, or use, of the original portion of her/his work and does not prohibit the independent (and thus original) creation of other similar works.

The principle of limiting copyright protection to only those aspects of a work that are original with its authors, while remarkably easy to state, proves to be impossible to apply. We lack the capacity to ascertain the sources of individuals' inspirations. Thus, the boundaries of copyright are inevitably indeterminate. To mitigate the mischief this could cause, we rely on the public domain.

The concept of the common heritage or public domain is another import from the realm of real property. In the intellectual property context, the term describes a true commons comprising elements of intellectual property that are ineligible for private ownership. The contents of the public domain may be mined by any member of the public the Buddha's *Dhammapada* the *Bhagavad Gita, Mahabharata, Ramayana* of Tulsi Das, *Ramayana of Valmiki.* From the Emperor Harsha (7th Century) we have three plays which have stood the test of time in the theatre, as well as two Buddhist hyms. The *Nagananda,* a *Bodhisattava* play, Bana's *Harshacaritra,* are depicting the intellectual genius of the time. Harsha's contemporary, the pallava king Mahendravarma I's comedy is marvellous.

The lay understanding of the public domain in the copyright context is that it contains works free from copyright. Works created before the enactment of copyright statutes, such as the immortal *Manimegalai* and *Silappadigaram* Thiruvalluvar's *Thirukkural* Tholkappiyar's *Tholkappiyam* the Tamil Grammer Panini Grammar; Patanjali's *Yogasastra, Yogasutra,* Alberuni the great scholar wrote his *Book of the Hind,* Bharathiyar's poems, Sekkizhar's *Periyapuranam, Thevaram* and *Thiruvasagam* the four thousand *Prabandhas* composed by twelve Alvars (as Tamil vedas); the work of Nanak *Granth Sahib* of the Noble Book; Kambar's *Ramayanam* Kalidasa's works most quoted work is the lyric poem *Meghasandesa* 'Cloud Message", the short empic *Kumarasambhava,* 'Origin of Kumara', the longer epic *Raghuvamsa* illustrating the four ends virtue, wealth, pleasure, and release, Kalhana's *Rajatarangini* a detailed history of Kashmir, Narasimha's drama out of the novel *Kadambari* were the greatest contributions of that age and Kautilya's *Arthasastra.* The immortal Tamil literatures *Pattuppattu* (The Ten Songs). *Ettutogai* (Eight Anthologies); *Padinenkelkanakku* (The Eighteen Minor works) are available from fourth grade classes to Universties across the nation to use without permission from any publisher or payment of any royalties.

Another class of old works in the public domain are works once subject to copyright, but created so long ago that the copyright has since expired, such as Annie Besant's *India*. An even larger class of uncopyrighted works in this country entered the public domain because they were ineligible for Indian copyright or failed to comply with a formal prerequisite for securing it. India's first copyright statute expressly thrust all published works by authors or writers, poets into the public domain. That policy continued for the next century, until it was grudgingly replaced with an extension of copyright to foreign works conditioned upon compliance with Indian procedures. Both domestic and foreign works fell into the public domain through inadequate compliance with statutory formalities. Although his/her second class of works became less significant when Indian Parliament eliminated most formal prerequisites and international distinctions in 1988, and in 2005 it represents a massive body of public domain works.

But the class of works not subject to copyright is, in some senses, the least significant portion of the public domain. The most important part of the public domain is a part we usually speak of only obliquely: the realm comprising aspects of copyrighted works that copyright does not protect. The concept that portions of works protected by copyright are owned by no one and are available for any member of the public to use is such a fundamental one that it receives attention only when something seems to have gone away. Although the public domain is implicit in all commentary on intellectual property, it rarely takes center stage. Most of the writing on the public domain focuses on other issues: Should the duration of copyright be extended? Should we recognize new species of intellectual property rights? Should Indian intellectual property law cut a broad preemptive swathe or a narrow one? Copyright commentary emphasizes that which is protected more than it discusses that which is not. But vigorous common Heritage public domain is a crucial buttress to the copyright system: without the public domain, it might be impossible to tolerate copyright at all.

## 3. THEORETICAL JUSTIFICATIONS

Copyright protection, once limited to maps, charts, and books, now extends to an extraordinary variety of products that saturate our society. Copyright cases no longer can be classified within subject-matter lines, and courts and commentators have sought to articulate general principles dividing what copyright protects or should protect from what it does not or should not.

Meanwhile, the term "public domain" has fallen out of fashion as a description of unpredictable aspects of copyrighted works. Courts and commentators speak instead of "uncopyrightable" or "nonprotectible" material. The distinction is a minor one, but the new vocabulary obscures the positive rationale for denying copyright protection and, instead, draws attention to the negative rationales. As Indian Parliament has enacted statutes expanding the range of subject matter entitled to copyright, the categories of material that copyright does not protect have struck many as increasingly anomalous. The Indian copyright patent law has been ammended in 1994 and in 2005. Protectors of the "common heritage" or public domain have found themselves on the defensive. When they have explained why it is that copyright should not protect ideas, facts, stock scenes, titles, or characters, they have attempted to explain what aspects of copyrightable works of authorship it is that ideas, facts, stock scenes, titles, or characters lack. These arguments have in turn been vulnerable to attack.[6]

The debate over copyright in factual works furnishes one example of this phenomenon. Copyright does not protect facts, theories about facts, or the research that yields them, it is said, because facts are not original. The eminent Professor Melville Nimmer described it this way:

> The "discoverer" of a scientific fact as to the nature of the physical world, an historic fact, a contemporary news event, or any other "fact", may not claim to be the "author" of that fact. If anyone may claim authorship of facts, it must be the Supreme Author of us all. The discoverer

> merely finds and records. He may not claim that facts are "original" to him, although there may be originality and hence authorship in the manner or reporting, i.e. the "expression" of the facts. Since copyright may only be conferred upon "authors", it follows that quite apart from their status as "ideas", discoveries as facts per se may not be the subject of copyright.[7]

Thus articulated, the argument invites its own rebuke. As Professor Jane Ginsburg has aptly demonstrated, such an analysis rests on what Ginsburg has dubbed the "Platonic fact precept."[8] The fallacy of the Platonic fact precept is its tenet that facts are already there, suspended in the ether for the hapless researcher to stumble upon. Facts, however, do not exist independently of the lenses through which they are viewed. Those lenses may be theoretical, methodological, or perceptual; they may be coloured by experience or bias or may be shaped by the scope of the researcher's inquiry. Researchers seeking to unearth facts must sift through available evidence, design new avenues of inquiry, choose among myriad conflicting indicia, and supply interpretive paradigms to structure incoherent collections of minutia. Researchers can thus be said to be composing their facts as they go along. In this sense facts are no more "out there" than are plots, words, or sculptural forms. If one discards the Platonic fact precept, it is hard to maintain the position that facts and theories about facts are still less original than other works of authorship that copyright protects. Denial of protection must be predicated on some alternate ground.

A proponent of the economic analysis of law might argue that because copyright's purpose is to provide incentives for the creation of works that are valued by society at large, copyright should protect the portions of such works that society most values. Because the most valuable contribution of many factual works is the facts themselves, she might continue, copyright ought to protect those facts. Its failure to do so arguably deters the appropriate level of investment in fact findings, which results in under-production of valuable fact-based works. A rival economist might retort that non-copyright incentives already encourage a plethora of fact-based works; a third might suggest that protecting facts would impose inefficient transaction costs on later authors who wish to incorporate the same facts in their works.

Among these economists some hypothetical economists illustrates a problem endemic to their approach. Their models are most helpful when empirical data is available to test their conclusions. In the absence of empirical data, the result of economic analysis is dictated by the model's placement of the burden of proof. Economists who begin with the assumption that the copyright incentive should be no greater than necessary to encourage authorship will conclude that the case for increased protection is, at best, "not proven." Economists who start with the assertion that any diminution of or condition on the copyright incentive should be eschewed until its proponents demonstrate that it will not, at the margin, deter authorship, will similarly leave the argument unpersuaded. Most arguments over the appropriate scope of copyright protection, unfortunately, occur in a realm in which empirical data is not only unavailable, but is also literally uncollectible.

The weary proponent of a vigorous public domain in general, and of a public domain in facts in particular, turns to precedent as a justifications. We should not protect facts, she argues, because a long line of copyright cases forbids it. This argument dissolves when the directory cases are raised. Indeed, even if the directory cases are dismissed as *sui generis* and fundamentally misconceived, there is ample precedent deciding almost every copyright issue in almost every conceivable direction. The myriad variations among decisions make it possible to assemble long lines of cases to support—or refute—any position. The copyrightability of works of fact is no exception.

This weakness in the common justifications offered in support of the public domain takes different forms with respect to different categories of unprotected material. When explaining courts' failure to protect *scenes a faire,* some commentators have explained that *scenes a faire* and indispensable to the expression of common theme.[9] This explanation, if accurate, would pose a particular case of the idea/expression merger problem, denying protection to expression to avoid giving a monopoly in unprotected ideas. Only when one examines the cases to ascertain what sorts of *scenes a faire* have been denied protection does the explanation dissolve. Nor is it plausible that the use of sand dollars for currency or seahorses for transportation would strike a trial court as essential to express the idea of an underwater civilization. The lack of protection given to *scenes a faire* seems to lie more in their triteness than their necessity. But why that should be so is rarely explained.

Indeed, the justifications for the public domain become least satisfactory at the most fundamental level. Why is it that copyright does not protect ideas? Some writers have echoed the justification for failing to protect facts by suggesting that ideas have their origin in the public domain. Others have implied that "mere ideas" may not be worthy of the status of private property. Some authors have suggested that ideas are not protected because of the strictures imposed on copyright by the first amendment in the U.S. constitution The task of distinguishing ideas from expression in order to explain why private ownership is inappropriate for one but desirable for the other however, remains elusive.

## 4. ON ORIGINALITY

To return to first principles, let us go back to the concept of copyright as property. The realm protected by copyright is privately owned; the unprotected realm is the public domain. What we rely on in place of physical borders, to divide the privately owned from the commons and to draw lines among the various parcels in private ownership, is copyright law's concept of originality. Copyright's threshold requirement of originality is quite modest. It requires neither newness nor creativity, but merely creation without any copying.

By now it should be obvious that the law purports to draw lines on the basis of "facts" that cannot be ascertained. While our two fictitious authors may call for opposite legal conclusions in the world of black-letter law, we have no way of telling them apart in he real world. The problem is not merely that we must determine the credibility of an author's account of his intentions; rather, the problem is that the author's intentions are irrelevant to the determination of originality versus copying. Copyright infringement requires neither bad motive nor guilty mind.

The determination of originality, however, is our benchmark for ascertaining the scope of an author's private property in the contents of her/his works. The determination of copying is our gauge for ascertaining whether she has trespassed on another author's rights. And only when we can be sure that she has never encountered the similar work of a prior author can we confidently detect that difference between the two. Courts have avoided confronting this paradox through the use of procedural devices and presumptions that allocate the burden of proof. But where an ultimate fact is unknowable, the allocation of the burden of proof is determinative.

Thus, is an infringement action, a plaintiff may prove that the defendant copied her/his work by introducing evidence that the defendant had access to her work and produced a work that is substantially similar. According to most authorities, the plaintiff's evidence of access and substantial similarity shifts the burden of persuasion to the defendant to disprove copying. The defendant is permitted to rebut the inference by introducing evidence that the accused work was independently created, that is, not even subconsciously copied from the plaintiff's.

If the defendant cannot disprove exposure to the plaintiff's work, however, it is difficult—to say the least—for her to demonstrate that the similarities between the works reflect neither conscious nor unconscious copying. Lacking such evidence, the defendant might try another strategy, realizing that no plaintiff's work could surmount the test of copying to which defendants' works are subjected. If the plaintiff's work is not itself original, then the plaintiff is not entitled to a copyright. Defendant, therefore, tries to introduce evidence impeaching the originality of the plaintiff's work by producing similar works to which plaintiff had access and probably subconsciously copied. Plaintiff, however, waves her certificate of copyright registration (a prerequisite to suit), which is prima facie evidence of the validity of her copyright, including the originality of her/his work. Since defendant cannot produce direct evidence that plaintiff copied the prior similar works and does not receive the benefit of an access-plus-substantial-similarity inference, the attack on the plaintiff's copyright comes to naught. And defendant's own certificate of registration has no probative value as a defensive measure.

There are two conclusions the author wishes to draw from the foregoing discussion. The first is that the concept of originality is a poor substitute for tangible boundaries among parcels of intellectual property because it is inherently unascertainable. The second conclusion is more controversial: The concept of authorship (within the meaning of the copyright law) and the concept of infringement (also within the meaning of the copyright law) are, for practical purposes, synonymous.

Originality, it is said, is the means that copyright uses to bound the property that an author may claim under copyright. Prominent commentators discuss originality as if it were an actual legal condition that a court could ascertain. Judicial decisions similarly invoke the concept of originality. They do not, however, essay the task of determining whether and to what extend a plaintiff's work is original. The procedural devices mentioned earlier permit them to avoid that particularly slippery task. The corollary that copyright tolerates a plurality of similar works so long as none of them is the product of unauthorized copying is also a bedrock concept of the law and is equally chimerical.

This is not to suggest that every copyright claim succeeds, or even that most succeed. It is merely to suggest that despite the esteem which the concept of originality commands in copyright law, the concept is irrelevant to the resolution of actual cases. Instead, courts have evolved flexible principles that allow the finders of fact to decide infringement cases in accord with their gut impressions.

The first of these principles is the rule that the similarity between a plaintiff's and a defendant's works must be "substantial" to support an inference of copying. Substantiality has both qualitative and quantitative elements.

The determination of substantial similarity is largely subjective, thus permitting the finder of fact to give effect to its intuitive judgment of the perceived equities in a case.

The second principle allowing resolution of actual cases on subjective grounds is the privilege of fair use. Fair use is the darling of the commentators, who routinely nominate it to assuage any danger of overprotection; it has received much more limited application by contemporary courts. It can operate as a safety valve to rescue worthy defendants from the perceived injustice of an infringement judgment should the substantiality wicket fail to operate.

In practice, these two principles are often conflated, but they allow the system to achieve rough justice in actual disputes. The fact that the borders supposedly supplied by the concept of originality are entirely illusory has not much hampered courts in deciding the cases before them. If the concept of originality in copyright cases, however, is indeed as chimerical as the author has described, then its status as the *sine qua non* of copyright raises intriguing questions.

What is it about the concept of originality that so inspires our confidence that we ignore the fact that it fails to perform the tasks we assign to it? In other property contexts, we might find that more disturbing. Imagine, for example, that the land on which my house sits is adjacent to my neighbor's, and that somewhere between our houses is neem tree. Both of us avail ourselves of its neem fruits, leaves for medicine but we do not know to which of us it belongs. Should the issue arise, we believe that somewhere in the bowels of the sub-registrar of registration is a recorded document that supplies the answer. Believing that to be the case, neither I nor my neighbor bothers about actually visiting the Office of Registrar to determine who owns the tree. If the Office Registrar is in fact a mere myth, a sign on the door of an untenanted office, neither of us will discover the fact, and neither will worry that the boundaries of our properties cannot be proved.

One day, however, some folks across the street go to court in a dispute over which of them owns a neem tree. Both confidently expect the evidence from the Office Registrar to resolve the litigation; instead, however, the court decides the case by awarding the tree to the party who makes the best neem fruits. One would expect such a ruling to cause concern; at the least, one would expect real estate lawyers, realtors, and banks to being to advise their customers to take up baking with a vengeance. After a series of similar rulings, scholars would write articles bemoaning the failure of courts to consult the Office of Registrar courts would comment that the system seems unjust. Landowners inept at baking and the banks that hold their mortgages would soon insist on some alternative method for settling title to trees. Newspapers would publish editorials exhorting the city either to put a real Office of Registrars in the room with that sign on the door or to replace it with something equal concrete.

In the alternate universe of copyright law, of course, no analogous commotion has occurred. The continued esteem for the concept of originality as the rule for settling title to copyright cannot stem from its pragmatic advantages in drawing actual boundaries, so it must be attributable to its other characteristics. Two such characteristics come to mind. The first is that the concept of originality must have enough symbolic power to subdue its vaporous reality. This symbolic power is rooted in its apparent reflection of what we would like to believe about authors and the authorship process. The second characteristics is that it must have a companion, some other force in its universe that dissipates the pressure to draw reliable boundaries. That companion, of course, is the public domain. The two characteristics are not unrelated.

## 5. ABOUT AUTHORSHIP

Let us return to the conclusion that is labeled controversial earlier: Copyright law defines authorship and infringement so that they are indistinguishable in a concrete world. An author transforms her/his memories, experiences, inspirations, and influences into a new work. That work inevitably echoes expressive elements of prior works. Whether it infringes the copyright in the prior works depends upon the conscious and subconscious processes within the author's mind. We cannot verify them; neither can she/he. If this author's work lands in a copyright suit, the legal conclusions that will be drawn will depend in the first instance on facts (such as whether she is suing or being sued and whether she is holding a certificate or registration) that have nothing to do with the nature of the authorship process.

Why does this not seem more disturbing? Perhaps because the story seems so hypothetical. It might describe a quandary faced by the author of *Ancient History of India* (1975) who confesses to a glancing acquaintance with the earlier.

But it is not going to happen to real authors like A.L. Basham's *The wonder that was India*. The idea that subconscious copying occurs rarely and only at the margin springs from a fancy that I term the "romantic model of authorship'. According to the romantic model, creative processes are magical and are, therefore, likely to produce unique expression. The expression is unique because the real author is using words, musical notes, shape, or colors to clothe impulses that come from within her/his singular inner being. This mysterious inner being may be the repository of impressions, experiences, and the work of other authors, but the author's individual sensibility recasts that raw material into something distinct and unrecognizable.

Indeed, some would deny that "recast" is an appropriate verb to use in describing the creative process. An author's artistic sensibility may be affected or shaped by what she experiences, they would argue, but the images of those experiences enter her subconscious on a one-way journey. What the subconscious disgorges is no mere recasting of preexisting material, but something wholly new. Anything less would be theft.

This romantic model of authorship is implicit in much commentary about copyright, and it underlies our tolerance for the presumptions and procedural devices that seem to make the concept of originality do the work that the law assigns to it. Because this model establishes the distinction between creation and copying as central to our conception of authorship, copyrightability is identified with originality: A work is copyrightable if and to the extent that it is original, or so we are comfortable with a presumption that the works they register for copyright are original. We believe in the idea that expression is created from thin air and the correlative notion that the universe of creative expression is infinite, so we are ready to conclude that similarity of expression is created from thin air and the correlative notion that the universe of creative expression is infinite, so we are ready to conclude that similarity of expression must reflect plagiarism. And we worry not a bit that our conclusions are unverifiable because they reflect our intuitive beliefs about reality.

Let us offer, however, a competing metaphor for the authorship process, drawn from the case of any leading publishers. In discussing the copyrightability of mezzotint engravings that reproduced public domain paintings, Judge, Jerome Frank observed: "A copyist's bad eyesight or defective musculature, or a shock caused by a clap of thunder, may yield sufficiently distinguishable variations. Having hit upon such a variation unintentionally, the 'author' may adopt it as his and copyright it." This formulation depicts authorship as a more modest achievement. Of course, was addressing the specific situation of the author who imperfectly reproduces a pre-existing work, but this image of the individual whose apparent creativity is the product of imperfect eyesight, flawed execution, or unrelated circumstances can serve as a metaphor for authorship in general. The metaphor suggests that transformation is the essence of the authorship process. Some of this transformation is purposeful; some of it is inadvertent; much of it is the product of an author's peculiar astigmatic vision.

An author, be she writer, composer, or sculptor, seeks to communicate her own expression of the world. Her views of the world are shaped by her experiences, by the other works of authorship she has absorbed (which are also her experiences), and by the interaction between the two. Her/his brain has not organized all of this into neat, separable piles entitled "things that happened to me", "things I read once", and "things I though up in a vacuum" to enable her/his to draw the elements of her/his works of authorship from the correct pile. She/he did not, after all, experience them so discretely. A snatch of a tune he/she heard was infected by the shape of the place where she was sitting when she was sitting when she heard it; her/his sense of a pattern she/he saw was colored by that day's saw was colored by that day's weather; a conversation she overheard was tainted by the book that she/he was reading at the time. Her/his memories of the song, the pattern, the conversation, filtered through her/his experience, may in fact seem quite unlike the objects she believes they represent. The counterpoint between a sound from one memory and a smell from another may express something quite different from what either seems to say alone. But when the author mines the raw material for her/his next work, significant portions of it will be the stuff of the outside world mediated by her/his experience. It is unsurprising, then, that parts of her work will echo the works of others.

To the author engaged in finding concrete form for immaterial impulses, each phrase, tone, or configuration of expression may seem new at the moment it takes shape. The author will often not recognize the antecedents that she/he has absorbed in the past and recasts and recombines as she works. Such amnesia about the sources of one's diction is a blessing that enables the work to proceed without the paralysis that would follow from examining each accretion for echoes of prior works.

Any serious minded authors characterization of authorship as a combination of absorption, astigmatism, and amnesia is not intended to diminish its merit. Indeed, my position is that this mixture is precisely the process that yields the works of authorship we wish to encourage through the copyright law. The strong form of this argument is that all authorship is the product of astigmatic repackaging of other's expression, but this strong form is unnecessary for our purposes. We can relay instead on a milder and hardly controversial variation: All works of authorship, even the most creative, include some elements adapted from raw material that the author first encouragement in someone else's works. If this description is accurate, it implies that the romantic model of authorship, taken seriously, would do grave disservice to the authors it seeks to describe.

Were we to take the legal concept of originality seriously, we would need to ensure that authors' copyrights encompassed only those aspects of their works that were actually original. We could not draw the boundaries of an author's property in the contents of her work until we had dissected her/his authorship process to the preexisting elements from her astigmatic recasting of them. As argued earlier that such a dissection would be impossible in practical terms. If it were possible, the author confident that authors would not welcome it.

Absent such dissection, however, we risk granting broad and overlapping property rights in the subject matter of copyright. If each author's claim to own everything embodied in her work were enforceable in court, almost every work could be enjoined by the owner of the copyright in another. That prospect is at least as repellent as the specter of merciless dissection raised above.

To avoid choosing between the two, we rely on the public domain. Because we have a public domain, we can permit authors to avoid the harsh light of a genuine search for provenance, and thus maintain the illusion that their works are indeed their own creations. We can tolerate the grant of overbroad and overlapping deeds through the expedient assumption that each author took her raw material from the commons, rather than from the property named in prior deeds.

The essence of my argument is this: Originality is a conceit, but we like it. To the extent that we are tempted to forget that originality is a conceit, it can be a dangerous principle on which to base a system of property. Most authors would agree in the abstract that the raw material that authors use in their work must be left free for all authors to use. Individual authors can nonetheless dispute the applicability of this abstract principle to a situation in which they see something that they think of as their own in a later author's work. We could force each copyright owner to demonstrate her right to claim such aspects of her work by requiring her to prove their originality, but we would have to accept that she would often be unable to do so in any meaningful way. We could instead tolerate a world in which all authors must seek permission from each of their predecessors, but few but works of authorship would be likely to appear in such a system. Instead, we rely on a commons, and we draw the boundaries of that commons by recalling the fact that the concept of originality we purport to reply on is a mere apparition that we cannot afford to test.

## 6. RESCUING THE SYSTEM

There is, (however, another) set of interests threatened by the phantasm of originality: the copyright system's interests in preserving its own integrity. The problem of overlapping claims, alluded to above, invites gridlock in the courts as parties request judicial resolution of insoluble disputes. This set of interests, the author think, best explains the recent impulses of some courts to expand the borders of the commons. To illustrate this problem the author offer a final parable.

Imagine the familiar plot of a novel for children. You remember this book: Our heroine (hero) is an unpopular, bookish sort, small for her/his age and, typically, a book she/he has never seen before: worn, plump, and red. (For some reason, the book always seems to be red). It is magic book. Indeed, it seems to be written especially for our heroine (hero). She/he reads the book, certain at first that it is some sort of joke, but then discovers that the magic in the book really works. It takes her/his to strange alternate universes, where she meets alien creatures and ultimately performs brave deeds that save at least a small part of the world. The class bullies no longer trouble her.

Imagine as well a contemporary author of books for children who has just finished a manuscript along these lines. Her/his lawyer remarks in passing that she/he recalls reading something of this ilk to her/his son. (The son was entranced). Indeed, now that she/he thinks of it, she/he has a vague recollection of enjoying a similar books borrowed from the library some thirty years ago. Our author becomes concerned.

At this point, our author and her lawyer would like to file an action to determine with whose conditions she/he must comply. Imagine now that they file an interpleaded suit, depositing the plot of the novel with the court and joining the dozen prior authors as defendants. Each of the dozen files a counterclaims to quiet title in the plot; five other authors of similar stories seek to intervene.

The court before which this suit is brought faces a quandary. There is no rule of decision that can resolve the issues in dispute. Theoretically, each of the authors before the court may be entitled to claim ownership of the plot on the ground that she originated it; it is, after all, the sort of plot that any bookish child with a taste for fantasy might have thought up on her/his own. On the other hand, any or all of the authors may have consciously or subconsciously copied the plot from some prior some prior source. The question cannot be determined directly, and the presumptions and procedural devices that usually make this determination unnecessary are of no assistance here, because the court has no basis on which to apportion the benefits and burdens of the procedural devices among the parties before it.

When we are confronted with an insoluble problem in overlapping deeds, pragmatic concerns may out weigh doctrinal ones. It ceases to matter why this plot is claimed by so many authors; the important thing is that it is. The court could dismiss the case on procedural grounds—the plot of a novel is after all an unfamiliar res. This rescues the court from the spectre of having to make any decision, but it leaves the children's book industry in disarray. Next week, some composers are sure to show up with a dispute over chord progressions. The court could instead award exclusive rights in the plot to one progressions. The court could instead award exclusive rights in the plot to one particular author—perhaps the one who bakes the best cherry pie. This solution would seriously inconvenience the other authors, who would presumably incur liability for their use of the plot unless they could disprove access to that author's book. The court could avoid that particular difficulty by awarding the plot to all of the authors could avoid that particular difficulty by awarding the plot to all of the authors before it. This answer would, of course, hinder the authors of the future, but perhaps the world has enough literature about magic books already. Finally, the court could decide that without some principle on which to base a decision, the plot must belong to the commons. This decision relieves the parties of having to produce inconclusive evidence of originality, relieves the court of having to reach a decision with no basis for doing so, and relieves the law of having a predicament posed by overlapping deeds.

Our parable is about plots, of course, but it is also a metaphor for scenes a faire. Scenes a faire are common; hey are the property shared among the overlapping deeds. Some scenes a faire are common because they are trite; some become trite because they are common; for others it is hard to figure out whey they appear so frequently. There is no particular reason why a magic book should be red; if the book is always red or even often red, however, that is a scene a fair. When we grant deeds without doing title searches, we risk significant overlap. We can often fashion rules to permit us to decide between two or three competing claimants, if not necessarily on strictly doctrinal grounds. At some point, however, the frequency of overlapping claims to something in particular will itself become the problem. Assigning that something to the commons is the copyright law's most practical defense.

This leads the author to an observation about some recent cases. Some courts have been increasing their resort to the scenes a faire doctrine during the last decade. These courts have been responding to a real and troubling trend. If access to a prior work is the basis for presuming that similarities represent actionable copying, then one would expect a marked increase in everybody's access to everything to carry with it increasing inferences of infringement. The copyright law has defined access as "reasonable opportunity to view" since before the development of modern methods of mass dissemination. Disproving access is, in most cases, no longer possible. It is not surprising, then, that the pressure of overlapping claims to common material has increased and that the courts have felt it necessary to rely on the public domain in ever more sorts of cases. We may be approaching an era in which familiar solutions to the chimera of originality become insufficient; there may soon come a day when we have to give the notion up.

## Notes and References

1. Gordon, "Fair Use as Market Failure: A Structural and Economic Analysis of the Betamax Case and Its Predecessors", 82 *Columbia Law Review*, 1600 (1982); Gorman "Fact of Fancy? The Implication for Copyright", 29 Bull Copyright Society, U.S.A. 560, 560-561 (1982).
2. Gordon, "An Inquiry into the Merits of Copyright: The Challenges of Consistency Consent and Encouragement Theory", 41 *Stanford Law Review* 1378-79 (1989).
3. *Ibid.*, 1378-84.
4. Burreow-Giles Lithographi Co. 1.
5. Mira T. Sundara Rajan, "Bharati and His Copyright", *The Hindu*, 22.12.2004.
6. Rajeev Dhavan, "The Patent Controversy", *The Hindu*, 10.12.2004, See for further details, The Leader "Delayed Action on Trademark Law", *The Hindu*, 25.09.2003.
7. Nimmer, "The Subject Matter of Copyright Under the Act of 1976" 24, *University of California Annual Law Review* 978, 1015-1016 (1977).
8. Ginsburg, "Sakotaging and Reconstructing History: A Comment on the Scope of Copyright Protection in Works of History after Hoehling V. Universal City Studios, 29 Bull. Copyright Society U.S.A. 647, 658 (1982).
9. Brinson, "Copyrighted Software: Separating the Protected Expression from Unprotected Ideas, A Starting Point" 29 B.C.L. Review 803, 814 (1988).

CHAPTER

# 3

# The Harmonizing Role of Historical Accuracy

*Every great achievement is a vision in the soul before it becomes a fact of history.*
*If is true that facts dominate life, it is equally true that facts themselves obey the force of mind.*
*Ideals control the world. They will triumph over the blind forces.*

—Dr. S. Radhakrishnan
Punjab University Convocation
Address December 23, 1930.

The French and US copyright systems are well known as opposites. The product of the French Revolution, French copyright law is said to enshrine the author: exclusive rights flow from one's (preferred) status as a creator. For example, a leading French copyright scholar states that one of the "fundamental ideas" of the revolutionary copyright laws is the principle that "an exclusive right is conferred on authors because their property is the most justified since it flows from their intellectual creation." By contrast, the US Constitution's copyright clause, echoing the English Statute of Anne, makes the public's interest equal, if not superior, to the author's. This clause authorizes the establishment of exclusive rights of authors as a means to maximize production of and access to intellectual creations.

Pursuing this comparison, one might observe that post-revolutionary French laws and theorists portray the existence of an intimate and almost sacred bond between authors and their works as the source of a strong literary and artistic property right. Thus, France's leadings modern exponent of copyright theory, the late Henri Desbois, right as springing from the creative act. If copyright is born with the work, then no further state action should be necessary to confer the right; the sole relevant act is the work's creation.[1]

Despite these paradigms, the differences between the US and French copyright systems are neither as extensive nor as venerable as typically described. In particular, despite the conventional portrayal, the French revolutionary laws did not articulate or implement a conception of copyright substantially different from that of the regimes across the Channel and across the Atlantic. The French revolutionary sources themselves cast doubt upon the assumed authorcentrism of the initial French copyright legislation. The speeches in the revolutionary assemblies, the texts of the laws, and the court decisions construing the laws, and the court decisions construing the laws, all indicate at least a strong instrumentalist under current to the French decrees of 1791 and 1793. Similarly, while the law of US letters predominantly reflects and implements utilitarian policies, US law was not impervious to authors' claims of personal right. Indeed, some of the earliest US state copyright laws set forth author-oriented rationales of which any modern Frenchman would be proud—and from which some revolutionary legislators might have drawn considerable inspiration.

Historical accuracy may promote future legislative harmonization; now that increasing US participation in international copyright agreements and policy-making bodies calls key features of the US copyright system into discussion, one can properly argue that US copyright has not always been different from that of its Continental partners. The comparison of systems shows that their distinctions are neither original nor immutable. A copyright regime's initial instrumentalist formulation does not preclude later reception of more personalist notions of protection. By the same token, a modern author oriented copyright system's reference to its utilitarian past may assist its absorption of newer productions perhaps remote from the core of the *beaux arts*.

## I. CULTURAL PROBLEMS

The artistic resource of a nation or a region has always been part of the fabric or glue of its culture. The significance of works or art as rallying points for a nation or a cause are well known. Picasso's "Guernica" is a good example of the symbolism and the power that an image by an artist can create, related to a political cause. This now world famous work was a protest to the bombing of the city of Guernica, Spain, during the Spanish Civil War. The piece itself has become a symbol of the Spanish nation as it now exists. The painting, which resided in the United States for a number of years, was recently returned to Spain, and now has a prominent place in a new museum, the Reina Sofia Museum of Contemporary Art in Madrid. "Guernica" is now owned by the Spanish people. It is but one example of the intrinsic, cultural, political importance of artifacts and art works to the national interest of a country.[2]

Harry H. Chartrand defined the importance of intellectual property rights for the arts industry:

> Intellectual property rights provide the legal foundation for the industrial organization of the arts and sciences. But legal systems are products of specific cultures and different cultures recognize differing creative rights. In this regard, and in addition to problems about agriculture, GATT negotiations are floundering due to these differences. This trade dispute has implications not only for the global knowledge industry but for cultural sovereignty of the post-modern nation state.

The arts today pose a different problem than they did at the time of the creation of the United Nations Charter.

They are now commodity-oriented rather than people oriented and thus are more accessible to a world audience. The potential for the art market of the next century is enormous if the communication giants of today create the proposed networks, bringing images, sound, and text into every home in the globe. The individuals who are able to create and orchestrate the images, write the texts, and create the sound or music are going to be extremely valuable human commodities in the future and will control the knowledge base. This will be an extremely valuable commodity in a sound/image society. Consequently, this is a factor in world trade that will be increasingly important to all nations in the next century, and the foundation for dissemination and ownership must be created in this century. The issue is critical of future development of arts in the world community as their role in the world economy continues to grow during the next decade.

For the first time in our history as a world a nations, the world community has the capability and the opportunity to communicate with the population in a multi-media format, i.e., sound, imagery, language, and real time moving imagery. The capability exists to transmit and convey information, almost instantaneously, so that world cultures, world art forms, and world artists can interact in ways which transcend geographic barriers. The communication system provides a mechanism for every country to explain its own culture and its significant contributions to the arts. This capability has commercial and educational implications. It should assist us in arts appreciation and provide a balanced view of the arts and cultures of the world.

However, the arts have become an economic battleground in which the issues go beyond the economic concerns into the cultural domain. The French have been very adamant in current. GATT talks about the necessity to preserve the French culture at any costs. A free media market in the European Union Nations would open up more markets and audiences for media products from the United States. This would threaten the guidelines set-up in France and other European Union Nations which stipulate that 50 percent of the programming on television must originate in that country.

This increases the necessity for communication and information exchange, but calls for a structure and process in which all can share the wealth without one part of the world exploiting the other.

## 2. HARMONIZATION

Intellectual property rights have been viewed classically as territorial in nature. As such, the recognition of any particular form of intellectual property, the scope of rights granted the owner of such property, if its existence was recognized, and the degree of protection afforded such rights were traditionally creatures of domestic laws. Since a nation's laws reflect the historical, cultural, economic and philosophic views of the country in question, standards for intellectual property protection necessarily diverge.

So, long as markets remained relatively isolated, the lack of uniform standards for the protection of intellectual property had little global impact. With the coming of the industrial age, and the increasing internationalization of the marketplace for intellectual property, the need for a uniform standard of protection became increasingly the subject of debate between nations. By the late 1880's two international treaty regimes had been established specifically to address the problem of international intellectual property law protection. Both the Berne Convention for the Protection of Literary and Artistics Works[3] and the Paris Convention for the Protection of Industrial Works[4] recognized the supremacy of domestic law in the area of intellectual property protection by basing their primary emphasis on the provision of national treatment. Yet each sought to develop some degree of uniformity among the laws of the member countries by establishing minimum standards which signatory nations agreed to incorporate in their domestic laws.

Treaty regimes such as the Berne and Paris Conventions serve a useful role in the development of a single international standard for intellectual property protection. Given the increasing complexity of multinational negotiations, however, the negotiation of such regimes can be a time consuming, and not wholly successful, process.

Multilateral negotiations during the Uruguay Round for the General Agreement on Trade and Tariff that ultimately resulted in the Agreement on Trade Related Aspects of Intellectual Property Rights ("TRIPS") lasted nearly ten years and resulted in an agreement that largely adopted the minimum standards established by the Berne and Paris Conventions.

As a supplement to multinational treaty negotiations, many nations have sought to resolve the problem of conflicting domestic laws by seeking to harmonize their laws with those of like situated countries. Such efforts at harmonization are based upon the theory that, even if identity of domestic laws cannot be achieved, at least the most harmful differences can be minimized to afford a more uniform standard of protection. Transplantation of ideas and laws from other countries is a well established occurrence. Present day harmonization efforts are based upon the implicit view that common history, common philosophy, common economic goals, even common legal systems can be used as a basis for the successful transplantation of rules and norms from other countries.

## 3. THE CULTURAL IMPACT OF INTELLECTUAL PROPERTY FORMS

Just as the decision to protect intellectual property is governed by the cultural, historical and philosophical background of a country, so too the forms of protection that are selected reflect the cultural imperatives of a country like India. This phase of arguments reviews the role that culture plays in the selection of which of the different forms of intellectual property to adopt. It begins with an examination of the role of copyright in the protection of a country's cultural heritage. The phase then explores the use of patent laws in protecting biodiversity and the problem of trademark protection. It ends with a brief examination of the conflict between culture, trade secret protection and the encouragement of foreign investment opportunities.

## 4. COPYRIGHT

### (a) The Protection of Art and Literature

Few would dispute that at least one segment of a country's cultural heritage is represented by its native-authored art and literature. Copyright has often been viewed as a source of encouragement for the development of home grown literary and artistic works since it promises economic recompense for the public use of such works. The early founders of the Indian republic in the preamble of the Constitution in the Directive Principles of State Policy recognized the critical role that copyright protection could play in the development of the arts by expressly providing for the enactment of appropriate copyright legislation "to promote the progress of . . . the useful Arts." The founders of the Indian republic has recognized the protection of historical mounments Arts, Architecture, literature and culture.

Since most domestic copyright laws are designed to protect artistic and literary expression, they have limited usefulness in protecting works of pre-literate societies, such as rituals, customs, folklore and other works which are not fixed in a tangible medium of expression. Such "unfixed" works, however, may be as important to a country's cultural heritage, and therefore, perceived to be as worthy of protection, as other classical forms of artistic or literary heritage. Thus, traditional, Asian-centric of Indian centered views of intellectual property protection, limited as they are to fixed literary and artistic works, do not include within their purview all artistic works which a country may desire to protect.

Traditional, views of intellectual property protection pose an added problem in providing an acceptable form of protection for all culturally desirable works of a particular culture of society. All creative endeavors to a certain extend build on what has come before. There is an old adage that there is no such thing as a truly new novel or genuinely original art. There are only advancements on what has come before. Copyright protection necessarily restricts subsequent authors' and artists' ability to use freely prior works so long as such works remain subject to protection. The necessary tension between protection and access motivates most decisions regarding the scope of protection afforded under a country's domestic copyright laws, including the existence and scope of any fair use or compulsory licensing exceptions. Consequently, even if a country chooses to enact domestic copyright laws, it may shorten the period of protection or narrow the category of protected works in order to protect culturally worthy works. Conversely, countries may protect aspects of works which have fallen into the public domain in order to protect the cultural integrity of such works. Thus, the form and scope of protection selected by an individual country will reflect the cultural imperatives sought to be served by that country's laws.

**(b) The Protection of Indian Folklore as Culture**

Folklore is usually transmitted orally, by imitation or by other means. Its forms include language, literature, music, dance, games, mythology, rituals, customs, handicrafts and other arts. Folklore's basic traits are: (i) it is passed from generation to generation by unfixed forms; (ii) it is a community-oriented creation in that its expression is dictated by local standards and traditions; (iii) its creations generally are not attributable to individual authors; and (iv) it is being continually utilized and developed utilized and developed by the society in which it lives. Indian folklore perpetually identifies a nation's cultural history and is considered a fundamental element of a nation's cultural patrimony.[6]

Because of its evolutionary and unfixed form, external sources subject folklore to substantial threats. Indian folklore, especially within developing countries, is being consumed by mass communication and importation of foreign cultural works. The risk of total dissolution of folkloric culture is prevalent if preservation actions are not taken. Economic exploitation of folkloric works has also been usurped by outside forces to the point that, even within a nation's own territory, nationals pay foreign publishers for reproductions of their own cultural works. Indian folkloric works also are victims of integrity violations in that they suffer mutilation, distortion, and misappropriation, particularly when recreated outside their national habitat or without authorization. For example, an Indian or Americans production company could capture any tribal rituals or Indian traditional cultural festivals on film or tape and, upon return to Bollywood or Hollywood incorporate the recording into a television documentary, movie, radio program, or advertisement without any obligation to remunerate the African or Indian performers for exploiting the ritual and without any obligation to accurately attribute the ritual to its creating tribe or to the constitutions.

In general, the legal structure of copyright is ill-suited for adequately protecting folklore. Copyright laws recognize solely an individual author's creative expression as the authorship in a work and normally require fixation of the work in a tangible medium before limited duration rights will vest. Copyright entitlement does not retroactively extend to those works in existence prior to the enactment of copyright laws. Since folklore violates these generally established conditions, it is condemned to wallow in the unprotected marshes of the public domain unless special provisions are created to excuse its unqualifying nature.

A handful of states has extended legislative protection to works within the public domain. Public domain legislation is designed to "prevent or sanction use of public domain works in such a way as to prejudice their authenticity or identity."[7] Protection covers either works whose copyright protection has expired or works that would have been under copyright if such a system had existed at the time of their creation or had extended protection to their creation or had extended protection to their class of works. In some instances, protection extends beyond works of national origin to include foreign works.

To avoid stifling any creativity or distribution, public domain legislation strikes a balances between freedom of use and preservation of integrity. Sanctions are imposed only on those uses that violate the work's essence, cultural value, or reputation. Thus, modern adaptations, translations, or republications are allowed as long as the work's character is maintained.

Authority to control public domain usage is vested in either the state or an agency designated by the state. In some instances, prior authorization is required before a national can exploit a public domain work. Other states preserve free use if the work's integrity is preserved.

One primary motive behind public domain statutes is the desire to retain safeguards on the author's personality through the moral rights of paternity and integrity. The state can act as the primary assertor of these moral rights if moral rights expire with economic rights or death, or as the secondary protector of moral rights if moral rights are perpetual had extend to the author's heirs.

A second motive for public domain legislation is the preservation of a state's cultural heritage. States adopt protective laws that will safeguard the cultural interests of the public, which implies that no confusion should exist between the original works and works resulting from any use made of it, and prevent abusive or prejudicial forms of the work from entering the public market. Noted public domain theorist Carlos Mouchet justifies this protections by sating:

> Once a work has fallen into the public domain, it is in the public interest that its artistic integrity should be maintained, that the name of its creator should not be omitted , that the title by which it can be identified should not be removed or modified, that the work should not be reproduced in any imperfect or rough form, etc.

**(c) Mouchet goes on to say**

> When the State introduced administrative or penal measures with a view to the protection, safeguard and defence of a piece of cultural property, it is . . . acting . . . as the representative of the interests of the community.[8]

Thus, public domain legislative acts as a cultural consumer protection device by forestalling any intangible cultural product that misrepresents a pres-existing work. The state's interest in the author's contribution to its cultural heritage is preserved, and society is not misled by cultural impostors.

Additional requirements on the use of public domain works have been enforced by some states under the legal rubric of domain public payant. Domaine public payant is a legislative scheme that imposes a fee for the use or economic exploitation of works in the public domain. Funds received are funnelled into societies that provide for the welfare of creative workers and their families or into state administrative agencies for the promotion of cultural activities and exchange.

Domaine public payant is characterized as a protector of cultural heritage because it can provide the financial means for nations to protect and preserve their cultural creations, particularly folklore. In practice, however, domaine public payant mainly functions as a promoter of intangible property by assisting authors to generate intellectual works, which benefit both the immediate society and its cultural heritage. In some ways, the system of domaine public payant effectuates a transfer of the author's economic rights at expiration of copyright to the state or to a delegated artists' association.

Public domain legislation is the most prevalent method states choose to protect and expolit their folkloric creations. States can readily classify folklore as a segment of their public domain and thus can control folklore's usage.

The main drawback to relaying on the public domain and domaine public payant is the lack of an international structure to enforce these protective measures extraterritorially. Because the bulk of abuse arises outside the borders of the country of origin, effective protection of a state's folkloric heritage is sometimes unachievable.

In countries that both extend moral rights in perpetuity and designate and authority to enforce those rights for folkloric works, folklore can secure relief from paternity and integrity violations. In most states, however, moral rights are condified within copyright law and satisfaction of copyright prerequisites precedes any grant of moral rights.

The public has a legitimat interest in ensuring that its cultural works are preserved as their creators intended so that their inherent cultural value will not be lost or distorted. Some states recognize this interest by directly creating a public cause of action for integrity violations. This public interest justification also cohesively links moral rights with a state's rationalization for copyright. If the goal of copyright is the creation of works for society, it is counter productive for works to be inaccurately disseminated, particularly if cultural works tell members of a society who they are.

One major criticism of state control over a public domain work's integrity is the potential for censorship by the state, i.e. the state can control current creations by controlling access to their public domain inspiration. To avoid censorship possibilities, a state would need to implement guidelines as to what preserving the integrity of a work entails. A forum should be provided for consultation of public domain use issues. Experts suggest that designation of a publicly accessible, national depository, like the National Libraries New Delhi, Kolkata, Mumbai, Chennai and National Archives Indian Historical Records Commission, and State Arichives Raja Rammohan Roy Library Foundation Kolkata Oriental Manuscripts Library Chennai, Saraswathi Mahal National Library Thanjavur. The Asiatic Society of India and Libraries in various parts of India can act as a references for satisfying the use guidelines and as a resource for accuracy in dissemination and conserving the Indian Heritage and culture. One should note that these laws must balance preservation interests and public usage interests so that cultural development will continue to progress.

Intangible cultural property merits convention protection for several reasons. First, intellectual creations comprise a significant portion of a state's cultural patrimony and the actual reflections of culture. Second, intangible property facilitates societal development because each intellectual work expresses the dimensions of a society and each work tells the members of its creating society who and what they are. Third, intangible cultural property evokes the same response of cultural nationalism from a nation's people as tangible property. For examples: The Great Caitya-hall, Karli, Mumbai Central, 1st century B.C., Buddhist Temple, Bodha Gaya, Bihar, 5th-6th century A.D., Kailasanatha Rock-Temple, Ellora, 8th century A.D., Shore Temples, Mamallapuram end of 7th century A.D., Apsaras of Khajraho,

10th-11th century A.D., Wheel of the Sun's Chariat, Temple of Surya, Konarak, Orissa, 13th century A.D., Sculpturas on the Madurai Meenakshi Temple 17th century A.D. instills the more sense of pride in Indians as any other International Monuments, yet only the Monument is eligible for international convention protection. Thus it became common to refer to "Indian Architecture" and "Indian Art", "Indian Music" and "Indian Culture", "Indian Mathematics", Indian Science and Technology", when, in fact, one was referring to an astonishing variety of architecture, art, music and culture within a political entity called India and Intellectual Property Rights Legislation.[9] Lastly, Intangible cultural property constitutes part of the "common heritage of mankind" and, as such, merits protection from destruction.

Intangible cultural property faces the same threats of destruction and inaccurate preservation that haunted tangible property prior to the Hague Convention. Mass media and piracy undermine intangible property, rather than armed conflict. Lastly, the "decontextualization" dilemma that plagued tangible property (i.e. if a work is taken out of context, a loss in value and information occurs) directly threatens forms of folklore and mirrors the loss suffered if works are not reproduced fully or accurately.

Multiple goals motivate the tangible property protection offered by conventions. Although preservation of physical works is the obvious objective, such action serves to achieve other goals, such as maintaining the work's integrity, facilitating distribution or access, ensuring truth and certainty, preserving the cultural identity of a particular people as well as the expression "embodied in the work", retrieving information, and preserving a cultural creation for the benefit of the "common heritage of mankind."

### (d) The Role of Cultural Exclusions

Although culture exists in forms that may not readily lend themselves to intellectual property protection (such as the Art and Architecture of South Indian Temples the Great Wall of China or the Mayan Ruins at Chichen—Itza), those forms which lend themselves most readily to mass marketed commodification usually fit well within the confines of traditional copyright protection.

The increasing commodification of culture, in the form of mass marketed novels, sound recordings, motion pictures and television programs, has led to a growing demand to protect the culture of the importing nation from the deleterious effect that exposure to non-domestic culture may have on the development of native-grown, and more particularly, native-inspired works. One of the significant trends in international trade law in recent years has been the development of free trading zones between nations, such as the Treaty of Rome (establishing the European Community), the Canadian Free Trade Agreement and the North American Free Trade Agreement. Despite this focus on reducing trade barriers, thereby insuring a freer flow of intellectual property protected works, recently exclusions have been made to such free flow of goods based on the cultural content of such works. The EC, with its recent. "Televisions Without Frontiers",[10] Directive establishing quotas for the amount of non-domestic television programming broadcast through-out the EC, the Canadian Free Trade Agreement and the North American Free Trade Agreement with their express exclusion of certain goods from the free-trading provisions of these treaty regimes based on the cultural content of such goods,[11] all represent recent efforts to narrow free trade objectives on the basis of cultural imperatives. Since the goods affected by such exclusions are most often subject to copyright protection, it appears that the use of copyright to protect culturally significant works has come full circle.

## 5. PATENT

### (a) Biodiversity

The trade dispute over intellectual property protection descended on the 1992 World Conference on Environment and Development in Brazil at an awkward time; like an unwanted house guest, no amount of ignoring it could make it go away. Persistent and intractable, the controversy confounded negotiations on the 1992 Convention on Biological Diversity to such an extent that it left the treaty little more than an impotent desideratum. The treaty attempts to promote diversity of species by encouraging development countries to preserve their diminishing rain forests, wilderness areas, and wetlands. Yet it also calls for the "equitable sharing" of the economic benefits from patented processes using rare plant and animal species found in developing countries. These two goals are not necessarily irreconcilable, but the way diplomats attempted to combine them in the treaty set the bloc of less-developed countries at loggerheads with the United States, which refused to sign the agreement on the grounds that it did not go far enough in guaranteeing patent rights affected by the treaty.[12]

Diplomats came to Rio de Janeiro in 1992 to negotiate environmental agreements, not trade issues, and the Biodiversity Convention was to be one of the crowing accomplishments of the Earth Summit. But patent protection is normally a trade issue—and a very conventional one. Thus it is not altogether surprising that the negotiators were able to address the issue of intellectual property rights in only a superficial way. The difficulty that arose underscores both the intrinsic links between environmental and trade issues, and how little the relationship is understood by advocates on either side. The longer this intellectual estrangement continues, the longer it will take to realize the goal of sustainable development, which was the theme of the Earth Summit.

Sustainable development means that current generations must leave future generations an environment and a stock of natural resources that is as good and as plentiful as those it received from past generations. The philosophy also says that technology and social organization affect the capacity of the biosphere to meet the economic demands placed on it. International trade is one of the most important forms of social organization by which natural resources are transformed into economic prosperity, but there has been little progress in clarifying the environment related aspects of trade or the trade-related aspects of environmental protection. Intellectual property rights, already a contentious trade issue even without taking environmental arguments into account, is one piece of the sustainable development puzzle that needs deliberate and careful attention. Instead, the biodiversity convention deals with the issue in the worst possible manner: by equivocation in hopes that the controversy will simply go away.

What is needed to repair the Biodiversity Convention is a determined international effort to agree on core principles around which some consensus may be built. This discussion introduces one possible approach: the development of a new category of intellectual property right that would be distinct from normal commercial patents and more relevant to the special circumstances and goals the Biodiversity Convention seeks to address.

The Biodiversity Convention raises two types of economic issues: the effect on the economy of a developing country of monopoly rent created by a patent, and the need to pay for environmental costs that are external to normal market forces.

Strictly speaking, rent is "payment for the use of a resource."[13] The rent for labour is wages; for capital, it is interest. For ideas and innovations, rent takes the form of royalties on patents or copyrights. When patents are protected, the royalties create monopoly rent that will last until the expiration of the patent or until the development of slightly modified imitations and alternatives.

The rationale for creating monopoly rent is that the firm may have necessary expenses that are in addition to the typical opportunity costs of capital and labour it had to pay to produce a certain level of output. Research and development, for example, of ten involve spending money on many research failures prior to the discovery of a marketable new product. The resources spent on the failures do not increase the firm's output nor do they add to productivity, yet they are an unavoidable part of the risk involved in research and development. The idea is that the monopoly rent created by a patent will compensate the firm for these non-productive expenses.

On the other hand, monopoly rent also creates a net welfare loss to consumers. In deciding its intellectual property regime, the state has to decide whether the benefit of creating rents from royalties adequately offsets the loss to consumers.

The magnitude of the social loss may affect the diligence with which a country protects intellectual property through domestic policies. A government will have an incentive to encourage piracy of productive foreign technology if its people are too poor to pay the "legitimate" price and if it has no indigenous expertise to develop similar competing technologies of its own.

On the other side of the debate, patent holders often incur significant costs in bringing their new products to market. The United States pharmaceutical industry says it spent 16 percent of its total sales in 1991 on research and development—nearly $10 billion out of $60 billion in sales. Money for research and development comes from the higher prices made possible by product and process patents; this rent makes up a large part of the industry's total sales. The industry estimate that about 60 percent of the drugs on the market now never would have been developed had firms not been able to recoup their expenses through patent rent.

The incentive for pharmaceutical technopiracy in a developing country is great because the patent accounts for a large portion of the price, and because including the patent rent in the price would prevent a large number of people from acquiring medications for which a demand exists. International trade adds another significant reason: little if any of the monopoly rent from the patent would be transferred to the economy of the pirating country if patents were protected. It would all be repatriated to the country of manufacture, depleting foreign exchange reserves and possibly adding to the country's debt burden.

In addition to the controversy over patents, the Biodiversity Convention also raises the issue of who pays for environmental protection.

Article 16 of the Biodiversity Convention says that,

> The Contracting Parties, recognizing that patents and other intellectual property rights may have an influence on the implementation of this Convention, shall cooperate in this regard subject to national legislation and international law in order to ensure that such rights are supportive of and do not run counter to its objectives.[14]

The reference to "national legislation and international law" in regard to intellectual property rights raises a nettlesome question: which set of international laws? Currently a system of international principles is administered by the World Intellectual Property Organization (WIPO), a United Nations affiliated body charged with facilitating compliance with a system of bilateral treaties and multilateral conventions on intellectual property rights. The principles that have been incorporated within the WIPO regime are generally consistent with he national patent laws of developing countries.

The WIPO treaties, which include the Paris Convention on patents, the Berne Convention on copyrights, and a number of other specialized instruments, gives member states significant latitude in excluding products and processes from patentability. Pharmaceutical products and processes, plant and animal varieties as well as biological processes for producing them, medical treatments for humans or animals, food products, chemical products, computer programs, fertilizers, agricultural machines, cosmetics, and nuclear inventions are among the items that various countries are entitled to exclude from patentability under the Paris Convention. The excluded items can thus be easily copied and widely distributed without regard to royalty payments to the inventor. The WIPO regime also recognizes the right of a country to impose compulsory licensing to ensure that patented products and processes are made available to the public. Developing countries often rely on patent exclusions and compulsory licensing to ensure the dissemination of new technologies in their domestic economies.

Another problem with the above provision in Article 16 is contained in the phrase that calls for the parties to ensure that principles of intellectual property rights (whichever system one may use to define them) "are supportive of and do not run counter to (the Bio-diversity Convention's) objectives. In other words, if there is any conflict between protection of intellectual property rights and the objectives of the treaty, then intellectual property rights must give way. One may argue persuasively that the ecological objective of biological diversity should indeed take precedence over intellectual property rights. But the treaty also aims to achieve an economic goal: the "fair and equitable sharing of the benefits arising out of the utilization of genetic resources. Even though the ecological and the economic goals both may be worthy, the two are different in nature and provide different contexts for weighing the social need to protect intellectual property rights.

The public trust doctrine provides a rationale and legal precedent for placing ecological protection above private property rights. But customary law does not support a similar canonical ordering between the redistribution of wealth and private property rights. If one is to infer such a link, it must be done on the basis of economic theory and not on the basis of customary law. And if one looks to neoclassical economics for a heuristic to determine how to achieve the "fair and equitable sharing" of benefits, the answer provided by theory is straight forward: let the concerned parties negotiate on the basis of their willingness to pay, and the market will reach an outcome that will be fair and equitable. No legislative, administrative, or policy measures by a government would be necessary other than to minimize transaction costs.

Many economists outside the neoclassical school, however, have advanced equally cogent theories that explain how equity between trading nations can in fact diminish over time if market forces are left to themselves. Economists of the dependency school, a group largely identified with developing countries, argue that the path of successive market equilibria creates structural imbalances that leave developing countries at an unfair disadvantage in the international trading system. The structural disadvantage would necessarily increase over time if market forces were to continue unchecked by positive trade policies by both industrial and developing countries.

Biological diversity, the fair sharing of economic benefits, the fair protection of intellectual property rights, and free trade are not irreconcilable despite the complexity of the issues. The real tragedy in this story, however, is not the harm to intellectual property rights but rather the missed opportunity to further the ecological goal of biological diversity. The economic forces that make intellectual property so controversial a trade issue can be used as a potent tool to promote the diversity of specifies, but the treaty as it stands fails to do that. Had it followed the precedent of the ozone protection treaties, the Convention on Biological Diversity would have identified intellectual property rights as an issue to be researched by a special working group that would recommend a specific protocol at the next meeting of the parties. Such a protocol is still feasible; the next section sketches what it might look like.

### (b) Protocol for Products made with Biota from Pristine Ecosystems

The international community needs to develop and accept a special new category of intellectual property principles for products made with biota from pristine ecosystems. Such patents should be treated differently from normal patents on commercial products and processes, and should take account of the special situation and needs of developing countries.[15]

Although other issues could be addressed, the four main points of the proposed protocol would be as follows.

1. All contracting parties—rich and poor—must agree to protect the patents of technologies for pharmaceuticals and other products made from the biota of pristine eco-systems in developing countries. The provisions of this article would apply only to those particular products that arise from national efforts to preserve biological diversity. Patents that use genetically engineered species or common species not protected by a conservation program would be excluded from this provision; protection of those patents would be left to WIPO and the GATT. The patents covered in this protocol would be protected according to the standards of national treatment and most favoured—nation treatment. In other words, all parties would be required to protect this class of product equally, regardless of whether the biota were taken from their own protected areas or those of another party.

2. A Share of the revenues from the sale of pharmaceuticals and other products made from the biota of pristine ecosystems in developing countries must be returned to the countries from which the biota are taken. If developing

countries are to be required to guarantee the monopoly rent included in the price of product made from their biota, then equity requires that they receive a share of that rent. Such a transfer would substantially support the objective of "fair and equitable sharing of the benefits arising out of the utilization of genetic resources."

3. The contracting parties must establish a multilateral fund to help developing counties acquire and distribute life-saving pharmaceuticals made from the biota of pristine ecosystems. An annex would list the kinds of drugs to be covered by the fund: heart medications, malaria medications, and inoculations against HIV, to name a few possibilities.

For the fund to work, the contributions of industrially advanced parties cannot be voluntary as in the case now.

4. The obligation of contracting parties to protect patent rights for technologies to make products from the biota of pristine ecosystems must be without prejudice to any kind of intellectual property not covered by the biodiversity technology protocol.

If these four points are incorporated in a biodiversity technology protocol, both developing and industrially advanced countries would stand to gain. Industrially advanced countries would get assurances that patents related to the Biodiversity Convention will be respected by all parties. In exchange, developing countries would be guaranteed a share of the rent created by the patents, compensating them for their efforts to maintain biological diversity in territories within their national jurisdiction. The special multilateral fund would ensure that higher prices would not put related life-saving pharmaceuticals out of the reach of people in developing countries who may need them. In short, a protocol base don these elements would strike a workable balance between the individual rights sought by industrially advanced countries and the social welfare sought by developing countries. Moreover, it would achieve this philosophical balance in a way that would not place the burden entirely on either side.

**(c) Trade marks India**

Tamil and Hindi movies play through-out the world;

and Tamil and Hindi songs are heard on radios in the far corners of the globe; South Indian Hotels and Bengali Sweet stalls have opened fast food hamburger stands in countries as diverse as U.S.A. and Malaysia, Singapore *Idly* and *Dosa* and *Vada* are sold in almost every country. The Asianisation of culture through the mass marketing of Indian films, songs, and to many Indian families the day starts with M.S. Subbulakshmi's music, at home, and in temples from Kedarnath to Kanyakumari and computer programs has its corollary in what has been referred to as the Indianisation of consumer goods.

In addition to serving as source designators, trademarks increasingly serve as signifiers of cachet in pop culture. Jeans may be roughly equivalent in style or equality, but it is the trademark on the pocket that often informs consumers choices, even when that trademark means that the identical product will cost more than its untrademarked domestically manufactured equivalent. Fears of a new wave of colonization, in the form of brand loyalty to foreign owned marks, is premised in large part on the emerging global market place for trademark bearing consumer goods.

In the Eighteenth and Nineteenth centuries, European nations viewed their colonial counterparts as sources for raw materials and markets for finished products. In the Twentieth Century many former colonial dependents saw themselves placed in the identical situation except the finished products now were trademarked goods. Brand loyalty was encouraged through extensive advertising which made the imported goods more desirable in consumers' mind, even when such goods were roughly equivalent to goods bearing domestic trademarks. In the view of some nations, the protection of foreign marks represents the protection of cultural imperialism at its worst.

Trademark protection, however, is not limited to the protection of foreign source designators. Local brand loyalty is a well recognized fact of most regional markets. Moreover, ethnocentrism and cultural and national pride may all contribute to the development of strong domestic marks. Thus, the protection of trademarks may also serve to develop cultural and national pride.

## (d) Trade Secrets

The protection of secret, commercially valuable information is not so well established as other forms of intellectual property protection. While most nations offer some limited form of patent protection, few protect its sister from—trade secrets. In many instances this refusal to grant trade secret protection is based on historical and philosophical reluctance to limit the access and use of ideas and information absent some cultural reason for doing so. Trade secrets, by their nature, do not usually rise to the level of novelty or non-obviousness required for protection as a patent or utility model. They also rarely, if ever, qualify for the level of originality required for copyright protection. Yet trade secrets drive much of the industrialization of the developed countries.

Methods of manufacture, chemical formulas and plant construction techniques all yield readily to trade secret protection. They also often provide the commercial advantage that gives their owners the edge in the market place.

In order to develop the suprastructure and industrial base to permit continued industrialization, many newly emerging market economies and newly industrialized nations seek foreign investment. Such investment opportunities are often severely limited where countries deny trade secret protection. Multinational chemical, pharmaceutical and industrial companies who consider their trade secrets of vital significance to their economic success have little incentive to invest in manufacturing or research and development facilities when such would necessarily eliminate critical commercial assets. Thus, culture, which may preclude the protection of information qua information, collides directly with economic interest.

## (e) Neighboring Rights

Throughout history, the emergence of new technologies including the printing press, photography, radio and motion pictures, has strained the ability of intellectual property laws to protect the creative and economic interests of those who create or use these new technologies to embody or disseminate their works. With the globalization of the marketplace, the continual introduction of new and faster methods of reproducing, disseminating and communicating works has increased exponentially the need for international standards of protection. These new technologies have stretched the ability of traditional intellectual property forms to cover the needs posed by such new technologies. Instead of expanding copyright to cover these new technologies, many countries rely upon rights that are neighbouring to copyright. This Chapter explores the phenomenon of neighboring rights and the impact of such rights on intellectual property protection issues.

## 6. RIGHTS NEIGHBORING TO COPYRIGHT

### (a) Scope

The term "neighboring rights" is an abbreviation of "rights neighboring to copyright."[16] It was first used in 1948 at the Brussels Diplomatic Conference for the Revision of the Berne Convention. The expression appeared in a resolution with regard to a new subject, not to be dealt with in the old copyright convention itself: the protection of performing artists. The Brussels conference adopted two other resolutions, with regard to the protection of producers of broadcasts, respectively, without, however, using the term "neighboring right." The resolutions expressed the wish that the governments of the Berne Union countries consider the best means of assuring the protection of these three different interests, without prejudice to the rights of authors. This finally led to the International Convention for the Protection of Performers, Producers of Phonograms and Broadcasting Organizations, the Rome Convention of 1961. Here the three interests are bundled together, and although the Convention itself does not use the term neighboring rights, it has been widely used since then in national legislation and in literature to designate the three rights conferred by the Rome Convention.

This should not obscure the fact, though, that several national copyright statutes also cover other "neighboring" or "related" rights. In Germany, for instance, we encounter rights not only of the three Rome beneficiaries but also of organizers of performances, a neighboring right of film producers, a right of photographers (where the photography is not a work), a right in editions of works or texts which are no longer protected, and a right concerning the publication of posthumous works.[17] The United Kingdom also confers a so-called "copyright" on cinematographic films, cable-transmissions and the typographical format of published editions.[18] Sweden has the so-called "catalogue rule", protecting a large number of informational items in "catalogues, tables and similar compilations." In the Netherlands there has long been protection for "non-personal writings" like telephone directories or broadcast listings, which are protected by what could be called a neighboring right, or pseudocopyright.[19]

Rights neighboring to copyright, are, by definition, rights which are not genuine copyrights. They provide a strengthened protection against certain acts of unfair competition which can very loosely be associated with copyright. Only performers rights constitute a special case.

**(b) Historical Development**

In this article, when talking about neighboring rights, the author restricts to the three 'classical' neighboring rights of performers, producers of phonograms and broadcasting organizations.

As defined in discussion 3 of the Rome Convention, performers are actors, singers, musicians, dancers and other persons who act sing, deliver, declaim, play in or otherwise perform literary of artistic works. Their relation to authors and copyright protection has a truly curious history. Of course, before and during most of the nineteenth century, performers did not feel any need for protection along the lines of copyright; their performances could not be fixed on any recording or be reproduced, nor could they be broadcast or otherwise electronically transmitted to a wider public.[20]

The picture changed radically with the inventions of professional sound recording, films, radio, television, cable-retransmission and all sorts of equipment for private recording. This technological revolution made performers as vulnerable as traditional authors to unauthorized exploitation by third partiers Performers had to compete with records and films, and much live music in public places, for instance, was replaced by the increased use of records. The result was an unemployment problem for the whole musical profession. The individual performers needed protection against the unauthorized broadcasting or other communication to the public.

Judge Learned Hand wrote:

> In the vast number of renditions, the performer has a wide choice, depending upon his gifts, and this makes his rendition pro tanto quite as original 'composition' as an 'arrangement' or 'adaption' of the score itself, which Section 1 (b) (of the 1909 copyright Act) makes copyrightable. Now that it has become possible to capture these contributions of the individual performer upon a physical object that can be made to reproduce them, there should be no doubt that this is within the copyright clause of the Constitution.[21]

Also, in Europe, a number of scholars were and are of the opinion that performers should really enjoy full copyright protection and not just a nebulous and weaker neighboring right. Nevertheless, the copyright protection of performers has not carried rough on the international level of the Rome Convention.

Where the status of performers had been pushed down to that of beneficiaries of a right neighboring to copyright, the protection of the organizational and technical achievements and financial investments of producers and broadcasters was now elevated to that same intermediate level of rights neighboring to copyright. They both received full exclusive rights. The producers received the right to authorize or prohibit the reproduction of their phonograms and an optional right to remuneration in the case of broadcasting a record. The broadcasting organizations obtained rights with respect to rebroadcasting, fixation of broadcasts and certain reproductions.

In the literature there was and has been much

opposition to this combination of totally different interests, but pragmatism and contentment combined with a certain degree of agreement between the three interdependent interest groups prevailed. Succinct criticism, however, pervades even the official WIPO Guide to the Rome Convention, and to the Phonograms Convention, where it is said:

> True, the purist may complain that, notwithstanding the skill and talent of a recording engineer or a broadcast producer, the making of a record or of a broadcast is, after all, an essentially industrial act, whereas the performances of artists are of their nature acts of spiritual creation and to mix them up together in one convention creates a hotch-potch. Nevertheless, the Rome Convention has done so, always with the guide-line of stopping the unfair appropriation of the labour of others.[22]

In many national statutes, however, the differences between the unfair competition protection of producers and broadcasters, on the one hand, and the protection of the artistic achievement of the performer, on the other hand, are generally recognized. One of the first symptoms is that moral rights are conferred on performers and not on the other two neighboring right owners. Also, the explanatory memorandum to, for instance, the German Copyright Act of 1965 stresses explicitly the difference between the respective artistic and technical-financial achievements involved. In a very recent Report on copyright, the German government proposed to extend the uniform 25 year-term of protection of neighboring rights to 50 years only for performers, stressing anew the basic difference from the other beneficiaries of neighboring rights.[23] With an amending act of 1990 this has now indeed been realized. Perhaps this consequence goes a little for, but the message is clear. In England, Cornish speaks of "entrepreneurial copyright" in sound recordings and broadcasts.[24] Also in other international literature the fundamental differences are time and again stressed.

There was the fear that some countries might protect neighboring rights but not copyright proper. This objection was indeed addressed. According to Article 24 of the Rome Convention, it is only open for accession by States which are a signatory to either the Berne Convention or the Universal Copyright Convention.

In addition, Article 1 of the Rome Convention prescribes devoutly: "Protection granted under this convention shall leave intact and shall in no way affect the protection of copyright in literary and artistic works."

The Rome convention and the copyright conventions are completely equal and no pre-eminence of copyright has been established.

### (c) Relationship to Copyright

In recent years an international ideological war has been raging over the relationship between copyright and neighboring rights. This war has been unleashed by the International Federation of Phonogram and Videogram Producers (IFPI), one of the most important international pillars of the development and practical implementation of copyright. One the topic of neighboring rights, IFPI now lashes out. Under the leadership of IFPI spokeswoman Gillian Dravies, the thesis that neighboring rights are really copyrights is constantly advanced. It started with the following paragraph in the 1986 report of the WIPO/UNESCO Committee of Governmental Experts on audio-visual works and phonograms:[25]

> Several participants expressed concern that the document (i.e., the preparatory documents of WIPO/UNESCO) did not sufficiently emphasize the creative nature of phonogram producers on the basis of which the intellectual property laws of several countries provided copyright protection rather than neighboring rights protection, if any, to such producers. These participants requested that this point should be taken into account in any future work on the commentary.[26]

In 1961 Producers had succeeded in elevating their purely entrepreneurial status to one of beneficiaries of rights neighboring to copyright, by assimilation with the simultaneously degraded performers. Now, in 1986, they wanted further promotion to full copyright ownership.

It is true that common law countries already use the term copyright in relation to what on the European continent is still called "neighboring rights."

What then is the creative nature of phonogram producers on the basis of which copyright protection should be granted according to those participants in the WIPO/ UNESCO committee quoted above? Nimmer devotes a whole paragraph of his four-volume treatise on American copyright to this question. He quotes the House Report which indicates that "authorship" may be claimed by "the record producer responsible for setting up the recording session." Nimmer then says:

> If the act of setting-up the recording session were the record producers only basis for claiming original contribution to the recording, and hence of authorship, it would be ill based, indeed. This is no more an act of authorship than is the act of one who makes available to a writer a room, a stenographer, a typewriter, and paper. The latter may be setting-up a writing session, but he is hardly the author of that which emerges from such a session. Nor may Congress simply create a legal fiction that a record producer is an 'author' if in fact he is not.[27]

Nimmer then goes on to find another basis in the House Report. It also refers to the acts of "capturing and electronically processing the sounds, and compiling and editing them to make the final sound recording." These are analogous to the acts of a photographer in capturing and photographically processing light images. But, "Nimmer continues," If the author of such originality iphotography is the photographer, the author of such originality in sound recording is the sound engineer who actually performs the task of capturing and electronically processing the sounds. It is true that the record producer may acquire the engineers copyright by virtue of an employment for hire relationship, or possibly by direct assignment, but not merely by virtue of the fact that he 'set-up' the recording sessions. There seems to be no basis for a record producers independent copyright. He can only have a derivative copyright, derived through employment of a sound engineer or through assignment.

Aristotle once wrote: "It is not the deeds that move people, but the words about those deeds." Indeed the question of "copyright" or neighboring rights for producers seems a game of words and a confused game at that. There is, however, an idea in the background. Not only the idea of protecting producers of records and other carriers of information at the same level as authors, but of replacing authors by industry. The first symptoms of this are found in the new English Copyright Act and in the Green paper on copyright of the Commission of the European communities.[28]

On the new English Act and its amalgamation of author's rights and entrepreneurial rights Dworkin writes:

> Whether that portends a development which will permit entrepreneurial rights to overshadow authors' rights, the perennial fear of authors, remain to be seen. In that regard, the introduction of a rental right in favour of producers of sound recordings and films to the exclusion of authors with underlying copyright interests therein is unfortunate.[29]

In the European Communities Green paper on Copyright, it is, for instance, suddenly stated in the context of films and video-recordings that film composers should stop collecting independently their musical performing right royalties on the basis of cinema box office receipts. For economic expediency their rights should pass into the hands of the film producers. Another example from the Green Paper: "The Commission is proud it has concluded a bilateral agreement with Indonesia, which protects sound recordings for the record producers, without any simultaneous copyright protection for the composers of the recorded music."

This realization of a right neighboring to a copyright without a copyright proper is exactly the offending situation which the Rome Convention meant to prevent.

**(d) Relationship to the Paris Convention**

Neighboring rights typically provide the legal mechanism through which countries adhering to the authors right's tradition protect sound recordings, performances and broadcasts without diluting the author's right regime. For example, the United States adopted a neighboring rights strategy when it enacted the Semiconductor Chip protection Act of 1984 (codified at 17 U.S.C. 901-914 (1988).

The Paris Convention covers industrial property, such as "patents, utility models, industrial designs, trademarks, service marks, trade names, and indications of source or appellations of origin, and the repression of unfair competition."[30] It also imposes a general requirement of national treatment on all forms of industrial property as broadly defined in the treaty. The broad coverage of the Paris Convention arguably poses a serious obstacle to experimentation with a neighboring rights approach to new technologies, at least when the moving state seeks to condition its protection of foreigners on material reciprocity, as the United States did in the Semiconductor Chip Act. Although other countries have followed a similar strategy under pressure from the United States, this tactic has been criticized as a regrettable deviation from the national treatment clause of the Paris Convention that invites emulation by the developing countries. Efforts to stipulate an international convention covering semiconductor chip designs have broken down, owing mainly to the opposition of developing countries.

**(e) Relationship to TRIPS**

Neighboring rights under TRIPS receive fairly extensive protection. Performers have the right to prohibit the unauthorized fixation and broadcast "by wireless means" and the communication to the public of their live performance."[31] They also have the right to prevent the reproduction of bootleg recordings of such performances. These rights last "at least until the end of a period of fifty years computed from the end of the calender year in which the unauthorized fixation was made or the performance took place." Producers of phonograms are expressly given the right to control the "direct or indirect reproduction of their phonograms."[32] This right similarly lasts for 50 years, computed from the end of the calendar year in which the performance took place or the fixation occurred. In addition, broadcasting organizations have the right to prohibit the unauthorized fixation, reproduction, and/or rebroadcast by wireless means of their broadcasts.[33] They also have the right to prohibit the unauthorized "communication to the public of such television broadcasts." These rights last for 20 years from, the end of the calendar year in which the broadcast took place.

Any rights granted by member nations to performers, producers and broadcasting entities under TRIPS may provide for "conditions, limitations and reservations"[34] to the extent permitted by the Rome Convention. Such "conditions, limitations, exceptions and reservations" arguably include the right to deny a public performance right to producers and performers of sound recordings, to impose reciprocity as opposed to national treatment for foreign phonogram producers, and to permit, without compensation to the right holder, private use and use for teaching or scientific research.

## 7. THE PROTECTION OF PERFORMANCE RIGHT

The Rome Convention is the only international treaty governing performers rights Like the major copyright conventions, the Rome Convention applies the principle of national treatment to qualified foreigners. This is, nations that are signatories must grant certain foreign performers (and broad-cast organizations and producers) the protections afforded by the Convention minima. Foreign performers, though, are guaranteed national treatment only up to this minimum level because the Convention provides that "national treatment shall be subject to the protection specifically guaranteed, and the limitations specifically provided for, in this convention."[35]

Article 7 of the Rome Convention grants performers

"the possibility of preventing" the unauthorized "broadcasting and the communication to the public" of their unfixed or live work. Rather conveying a property right, the drafters employed the possibility of preventing" language to satisfy broadcasters and authors' groups and to fit into national systems that address performers' rights through systems of law other than property, such as criminal law.

The Rome Convention requires a very low level of protection against the unauthorized broadcasting, use or reproduction of a fixed work. Article 7 specifies that performers shall have "the possibility of preventing. . . ; the reproduction, without their consent; of a fixation of their performance: (i) if the original fixation was made without their consent; (ii) if the reproduction is made for purposes different from those for which the performers gave their consent . . . ; or (iii) if the original fixation was made under the Conventions equivalent of a fair use exception and the subsequent use does not conform with that exception." The many qualifications in this provision satisfy the public's need for widespread dissemination of entertainment, but deny performers full control over their works.

## 8. THE PROTECTION OF BROADCAST RIGHT

In 1961, when the Rome Convention was adopted,

- F.M. radio hardly existed;
- transistor radios were still unknown;
- stereo transmissions belonged to the distant future;
- audio recording equipment was in its beginnings, and cassette recorders were still to be introduced;[36]
- digital audio broadcasting (DAB) was hardly imaginable; and
- wide-spread commercial use of color television was still years away.

In economic terms, the importance of (the rebroadcasting) right lies today in private recording of radio and TV broadcasts. Article 15(1)(a) (of the Rome Convention) nonetheless permits contracting states to make an exception with regard to "private use."[37] As long as this is not supplemented by a levy on recording equipment and/or blank tape, to the benefit of broadcasting organizations, the right of fixation (combined with the generally admitted exception for private use) is rather useless. Theoretically, of course, this right could be helpful in combating deferred rebroadcasts. However, since the Rome Convention does not grant the right of distribution (to a rebroadcaster), a clever pirate will always pretend that he received the recording from a third party, rather than having carried out a fixation himself. As long as (the right of rebroadcast) is not accompanied by a right of distribution, its practical value is extremely limited.[38]

Places where the public go to watch T.V. programmes against payment of an entrance fee have long ceased to exist. On the other hand, the public communication of radio and TV broadcasts on business premises restaurants, hotels, department stores, hairdressers, and so on, is a widespread phenomenon. It serves the business interests in question. However, broadcasting organizations (unlike authors) have no rights in this regard.[39]

In view of the technological development in the field of broadcasting since 1961 and the legislative purpose of, and justification for, the broadcasting organization's neighboring right, a modern version of a neighboring rights article for the protection of broadcasting organizations should include the following detailed rights;

(1) The right to authorize or prohibit (a) the rebroadcasting of their broadcasts ('rebroadcasting' should include both simultaneous and deferred broadcasting, and 'broad-cast' should be clearly understood to include saatellite broadcasting);
   (b) the cable distribution to the public of their broadcasts, both simultaneous and deferred;
   (c) the communication to the public of their broadcasts, whether or not the communication is to a paying audience or is made in places accessible to the public against payment of an entrance fee;

(d) any fixation of their broadcasts via sound or video recorder for other than private purposes, and any reproduction or distribution of such a fixation;

(e) any reproduction of distribution of legally made fixations, other than for private purposes;

(f) any still photograph of a television broadcast other than for private purposes, and any reproduction of distribution of such a photograph;

(g) distribution to the public, by any broadcaster, cable distributor or other distributor, of their programme-carrying signals transported by communications satellite when such distributor is not authorized by the broadcaster to do so.

(2) The right to receive equitable remuneration in respect of private recording of their broadcasts (levy on recording equipment and/or blank tape).

(3) Protection against importation and distribution of fixations or the reproduction of such fixations made without authorization in a country which grants no protection to broadcasting organizations.

An article drafted on the basis of the foregoing provisions could be introduced into any national Copyright Act, regardless of a future revision (if any) of the Rome Convention along the same or similar lines. By virtue of the principle of national treatment, broadcasting organizations from other contracting states would automatically enjoy the same protection.

## 9. THE PROTECTION OF SOUND RECORDINGS

### (a) The Rome Convention

Two major international conventions affect the worldwide protection of sound recordings. The older convention, known as the Berne Convention for the Protection of Literary and Artistic Works, was joined by the United States in 1988. Although the Berne Convention does not mandate the protection of sound recordings, it does cover the international protection of musical compositions. The Berne convention limits its subject matter to "literary and artistic works", and sound recordings are not included. Sound recordings are relegated to the lesser status of a "neighboring right" as covered by the Rome Convention on Neighboring Rights. The United States is not currently signatory to the Rome Convention.[40]

The Rome Convention is the only international convention that affects the decision to enact a performance right in sound recordings in the United States. The Rome Convention is significant because it ensures a right of remuneration to creators of works, such as sound recordings, that are unprotected by the Berne convention. These protections are the so called "neighboring rights." Specifically, Article 12 of the Rome convention provides:

> If a phonogram, published for commercial purposes, or a reproduction of such phonogram, is used directly for broadcasting or for any communication to the public, a single equitable remuneration shall be paid by the user to the performers, or to the producers of the phonograms, or to both. Domestic law may, in the absence of agreement by parties, lay down the conditions as to the sharing of this remuneration.[41]

The remuneration provision of the Rome Convention is based on reciprocity, meaning that a signatory can only withdraw the funds if the withdrawing country has a performance right in sound recordings for foreign nationals. Performers in countries that export royalty-producing creations in greater quantities than they import them are remunerated, thus providing incentive for their government to join the Rome Convention.

**(b) Protection for Rural Performances**

Article 12 of the Rome Convention governs the subsequent use of "phonograms." Phonograms are defined as "any exclusively aural fixation of sounds of a performance or of other sounds." Article 12 provides that "a single equitable remuneration shall be paid by the user to the performers, or to the producers of the phonograms, or to both.[42] Domestic law may, in the absence of agreement between these parties, lay down the conditions as to the sharing of this remuneration."

The Convention, however, specifically allows countries to ratify the treaty with reservations regarding their adherence to Article 12. Reservations may take one of four special forms.[43] The impact of the different reservation varies, but all serve to significantly dilute the effectiveness of the Rome convention by reducing the amount of royalties paid transnationally.

The Rome Convention does not prohibit the imitation of a performance and does address the problem of commercial sound-alikes. Although performers have the possibility of preventing some forms of unauthorized reproduction, "reproduction" is defined by the Convention as "the making of a copy or copies of a affixation." As one commentator states, the term "reproduction cannot be stretched to cover so-called 'sound-alikes.'"[44] The only concession to protecting moral rights in the Rome Convention is found in Article 11, which requires the use of the performers names along with notice symbols.

### (c) The Problem of US Adherence

Although the United States is the world leader in the export of sound recordings, it has not yet joined the Rome Convention, primarily because it does not grant performance rights in sound recordings. Therefore, the United States does not receive reciprocal performance royalties from other countries. In order to join the Rome convention, the united States would have to either enact a performance right in sound recordings so that reciprocity would be a possibility under Article 12, or the United States would have to opt-out of Article 12.[45]

There is little reason for the United States to join the Rome Convention while opting out of Article 12 because it would not gain the funds already set aside by other countries for the public performance of United States produced sound recordings.

## Notes and References


1. Jane C. Ginsburg, "A Tale of Two Copyrights: Literary Property in Revolutionary France and America", 64 *Tulane Law Review* 991, (1990) Tulane Law Review Association.
2. Stanley S. Madeja, "The Arts as a Cultural and Economic Factor in World Trade", 14 *Northern Illinois University Law Review*, 439 (1994) Northern Illinois University.
3. Berne Convention for the Protection of Literary and Artistic Works (As Revised at Paris on July 24, 1971), Article 2.
4. Paris Convention for the Protection of Industrial Property (As Revised at Stockholm on July 145, 1967) Article 1 and Article 5.
5. Doris Estella Long, *China, Russia an the United States: A Comparison of Cultural Choices.* (1996) Doris E. Long.
6. Cathryn A. Berryman, "Towards More Universal Protection of Intangible Cultural Property", 1 *Journal of Intellectual Property Law.* 293 Copyright 1994 Journal of Intellectual Property Law Association.
7. Working Group on Works in the Public Domain, *Copyright Bulletin,* Vol. 13, No. 4 at 33, 34 (1979).
8. Carlos Mouchet, Problems of the "Domaine Public Report", 8 *Columbia VLA Journal of Law and Arts* 137, 146 (1983).
9. A.G. Krishna Menon, "Rethinking Architecture", *The Hindu,* Folio, August, 1999.
10. For a more detailed Discussion of the "Television without Frontiars" Directive, See Chapter Two.
11. For a detailed Discussion of these and other forms of cultural exclusions, see chapter six.
12. David Hurlbut, "Fixing The Biodiversity Convention: Toward A Special Protocol for related Intellectual Property", 34 *National Resources Journal* 379, (1994) *National Resources Journal.*
13. The New Palgrave: *A Dictionary of Economics,* Vol. 3 at 1014-1018 (J. Eatwell et al. eds, 1987).
14. United Nations Conference Environment and Development; Convention on Biological Diversity, 1992, 31 I.L.M. 818 (1992) at Art. 16.
15. David Hurlbut, "Fixing The Biodiversity Convention: Toward A Special Protocol For Related, Intellectual Property", 34 *National Resources Journal* 379. (1994).
16. Bonnie Teller, "Toward Better Protection of Performance in the United States: A Comparative Look At Performer's Rights in the United States, Under the Rome Convention", 28 *Columbia Journal of Transnational Law* 775, (1990) *Columbia Journal of Translational Law.*

17. Suman Sahai, "Plant Variety Protection and Farmers' Rights Law" *Economic and Political Weekly*, September, 2001; 3338-3342. Dietz, Germany, Federal Republic in M. Nemer and P. Geller, *International Copyright Law and Practice at FRG* 122-130 1 (1989).
18. Cornish, United Kingdom, *id* at UK 62.
19. Herman Cohen Jehoram, Netherlands, id at NETH 20-22.
20. Herman Cohen Jehoram, "The Nature of Neighbouring Rights of Performing Artists, Phonogram Producers and Broadcasting Organisations", 15 *Columbia—VLA Journal of Law and the Arts.* 75 (1990), *Columbia Journal of Transnational Law Association*, Inc.
21. Capital Records, Inc. V. Mercury Record Corp. 221. F. 2d 657 (2d (iv) 1955.
22. WIPO Guide to the Rome Convention and to the Phonogram Convention 12 (Geneva 1981) International Convention for the Protection of Performers, Producers of Phonograms and Broadcasting Organisations (Rome 1961); Article 2; Article 3; Article 4 and Article 5.
23. Bundestagdtucksache 7.7.1989, nr. 11/4929.
24. W.R. Cornish, *Intellectual Property* 275 (1989).
25. Herman Cohen Jehoram, "The Nature of Neighboring Rights of Performing Artists, Phonogram Producers and Broadcasting Organisations: 15 *Columbia—VLA Journal of Law and the Arts* 75, (1990) Herman Cohen.
26. Audio-visual Works and Phonogram, Preparatory Document for and Report of WIDO/UNESCO Committee of Governmental Experts, 22 Copyright 218, 2341 (1986)
27. Nimmer on Copyright 210 (A) (2) (6) (1990)
28. Comn (88) 172 final, Brussels, 7 June 1988.
29. Dworkin "United Kingdom" in S. Stewart, *International Copyright and Neighbouring Rights*, 487 (1989)
30. J.H. Reichman, "Goldstein on Copyright Law: A Realist's Approach To A Technological Age" 43 *Stanford Law Review* 943, (1991) Board of Trustee's of the Leland Stanford Junior Univeristy.
31. Paris Convention for the Protection of Industrial Property (As Revised at Stockholm, 1967) Article 1 (2).
32. TRIPS, Article 14, 1.
33. TRIPS, Article 14, 2.
34. TRIPS, Article 14, 3.
35. TRIPS, Article 14, 6.
36. Bonnie Teller, "Toward Better Protection of Performance in The United States: A Comparative Look at Performer's Rights in The United States, Under The Rome Convention", 28, *Columbia Journal of Transnational Law* 775. (1990) Columbia Journal of Translational Law Association.
37. International Convention for the Protection of Performance, Producer of Phonograms and Broadcasting Orgnisations (Rome 1961), Article 2(2).

38. Rome Convention (1961), Article 15(a).
39. *Ibid.*, Article 7.
40. Werner Rumphorst, "Neighbouring Rights Protection of Broadcasting Organizations", 18 EUPR 339, (1992), Werner Rumphorst.
41. Johnthan Frnaklin, "Pay to Play: Emacting A Performing Right in Sound Recordings in the Age of Digital Audio Broadcasting" *10 U Miami Ent. & Sports L. Rev.* 83 (1993) *Entertainment and Sports Law Review.*
42. The International Convention for the protection for performers, Producers of Phonograms and Broadcasting Organisations, 496, U.N.T.S. at Art. 12.
43. Bonnie Teller, "Toward Better Protection of Performance in The United States: A Comparative Look at Performer's Rights in The United States, Under The Rome Convention", 28 *COLUM. J. TRANSNAT'L, L.* 775. (1990) Columbia Journal of Transnational Law Association, Inc.
44. A Country can either: (1) make a total reservation, treating Article 12 as if it were not part of the treaty: (2) restrict payment for use in broadcasting only (as opposed to use in shopping centers, restaurants, etc). or for use in certain kinds of broadcasts only (cultural or religious, for example); (3) limit its royalty payments only to those situations in which the producer is national of another signatory nation; or (4) demand reciprocity and refuse payment where reciprocity does not exist. Rome Convention. Art. 16.
45. Johnthan Frnaklin, "Pay to Play: Enacting A Performing Right in Sound Recordings in The Age of Digital Audio Broadcasting": *10 U Miami Ent. & Sports L. Rev.* 83 (1993) *Entertainment and Sports Law Review.*

CHAPTER

# 4

# The Protection of Cultural Patrimony

*Where is the wisdom we have lost in knowledge.*
*Where is the knowledge we have lost in information*
*The cycle of Heavern for twenty centuries*
*Take us further from God and nearer to dust.*

—T.S. Elliot

There is an interesting interrelation between a nations culture and the protection it gives to intellectual property. On the one hand, the form, scope and types of intellectual property that a nation chooses to protect are generally determined by that nations own cultural heritage. On the other hand, the existence of intellectual property protection affects the nations ability to protect its won cultural heritage.

This chapter examines the interrelation between intellectual property and the protection of cultural patrimony. We start with a review of the traditional area of perceived intersection between intellectual property and cultural heritage. The traditional view, as we shall see, finds the closest analogue to cultural patrimony in the literary and artistic side of intellectual property, i.e., copyright.

Further we analyse some of the unique problems posed by the protection of cultural patrimony that stem form its dichotomous nature—that it is an amalgam of property values and cultural values.

The Chapter ends with a consideration of the future role of intellectual property law in the protection of all forms of cultural patrimony. This role will undoubtedly be a function of an evolving view of authorship and the creative act. The evolving role of authorship in the protection of intellectual property will be discussed in greater detail in this chapter.

## 1. INTELLECTUAL PROPERTY AS CULTURE

It is accepted beyond peradventure that India's cultural heritage is embodied in its art and literature. Such works fall within the traditional scope of protected intellectual property forms. Culture, however, is not limited strictly to art and literature. To the contrary, monumental architectural works, geographical configurations, unique ecosystems, and religious ceremonies and artifacts are also included within the scope of the term "cultural heritage." Although much of the effort at establishing international intellectual property norms has been directed to the protection of traditional forms of culture, there is little reason why other forms of culture should not be considered when international intellectual property protection norms are being debated.[1]

Like traditional forms of protected intellectual property, cultural patrimony has a dichotomous nature. Traditional intellectual property has a dual nature of intellect (intangibility ) and property. Cultural patrimony is similarly divisible into separate components of tangible property and intangible cultural values. Given the strong role which the protection of culture plays in a country's decision regarding the scope of protection to be afforded intellectual property, an understanding of the issues and positions taken on the interrelated issue of the protection of cultural patrimony can serve to illuminate the debate.

## 2. THE PROTECTION OF CULTURAL PROPERTY

### (a) Art as Cultural Heritage

Artistic and cultural objects began to take on national identities during the Enlightenment, with the rise of nationalism and the creation of modern nations. We can observe during that period the "increase in importance of the monument—the main interest shifted away from the person of the artist to the work of art as such." After the French Revolution monuments were praised for their artistic, historical, and scientific features, People began to conceive of monuments as the "cultural heritage of a nation, an evidence of historical traditions, a historical identity card." This new function of works of art influenced a nations attitude toward its heritage; the protection of cultural property became a goal shared by various societies. As art became closely associated with particular nations, government efforts to protect cultural property were directed primarily toward keeping monuments within the state boundaries. Legislative efforts of this nature were supported by the realization that those objects of out constitute evidence of things other than themselves; they are documents informing us about a certain state of affairs, in particular about social relationships, being at the same time objects of price, exchange, value property, goods which arose from the economic life of a given epoch."[2]

**(b) The Definition of Cultural Patrimony**

Synonyms for cultural property include the terms "cultural patrimony" and "antiquities." Although these words are often used interchangeably, the choice of term often connotes a specific political stance. "Cultural patrimony" implies that an artifact is of such significance to a particular civilization as to be an inalienable birthright of its descendants. For example, Greek nationalists often claim that the Elgin Marbles in the British Museum are the cultural patrimony of Greece. Some cultural activists find even the term "Elgin" Marbles offensive, because the name refers to the British lord who removed the sculptures from the Parthenon in 1816. Accordingly, they generally prefer the term "Parthenon Marbles" for the sculptures now in the British Museum.[3]

**(c) A Second View**

"Cultural objects" are also referred to as "cultural property", "cultural goods", "cultural patrimony", or "national treasures." Some definitions of cultural property are extremely broad, including any cultural significance.[4]

**(d) The Dual Nature of Cultural Property**

The protection of cultural property is developing as a fundamental concern of international law. A growing network of bilateral and multilateral treaties addresses the treatment of cultural property during armed conflict, regulates its import and export, and most recently, governs its repatriation to source countries and peoples. Individual nations have taken measures to protect what they perceive to be their cultural patrimony via state ownership laws and domestic import and export regulations. Indigenous peoples, ethnic and religious groups and organizations, on their own account and through their national governments, are actively seeking repatriation of objects of significance to their respective cultural identities. Although these treaties, domestic laws, and efforts at repatriation have as their goal protection of objects of cultural significance, the legal regime these sources have produced treat such objects primarily as property.[5]

Objects of cultural property can not be stripped of their cultural significance. They are not merely items of property any more than children are the property of divorcing parents. Recognition of cultural significance is an integral part of determining the best means of protecting cultural property.

There are two schools of thought concerning cultural property. The first school of thought, usually identified as cultural internationalism, is primarily concerned with physical preservation of objects. This school articulates concerns in terms of property law principles. The arguments of acquisitive nations, museums, collectors, and archaeologists, all of whom, seek to protect their holding of or access to cultural property for aesthetic, scholarly, educative, or merely possessory purposes, generally belong to this school of thought. The property law principles they espouse include rights of title, possession, conquest, repose, and *bona fide* purchase. The second school of thought, usually termed cultural nationalism, is primarily concerned with the cultural significance of cultural property. Its arguments are often framed in terms of principles of human rights law. The demand is for cultural dignity and cultural self-determination. Arguments for repatriation of objects of cultural significance to source nations or to peoples belong to this school of thought. This argument asserts that the disputes between these schools of thought are really disputes over which aspect of cultural property deserves greater legal protection. Although the common ground between these two camps is concern for preservation of objects of cultural significance, preservation means different things to different interests.

An item of cultural property is an object that is of cultural significance. It therefore has two aspects. The first aspect is the property aspect, which derives from the fact that cultural property consists of tangible, moveable objects. The implication of calling something property suggests that it can be owned, or at least possessed and controlled. The second aspect is the cultural aspect, which derives from the cultural significance of the object. Perhaps the most effective way to demonstrate the two aspects of cultural property is to consider an example of a spefic items of museums, etc. cultural property.[6]

**(e) Cultural Property and Indian Museums**

Being the cultural legacy of the entire mankind, the protection of such property, taken collectively, is the sacred duty of all the nations. That is why the UNESCO in recent years is making all round efforts to save the world's cultural and natural heritage from vandalism, theft, illicit traffic and other menaces which are constantly threatening their existence. According to the recent trends, there is a considerable demand of such objects in the developed countries, and loosers in this bargain are the nations rich in archaeological material and works of art. In different UNESCO documents the term cultural property occurs quite frequently but its use with a definite connotation is only of recent origin. Even today there are only a few national legislations encompassing the whole range of a country's cultural and artistic heritage, for the existing laws in most of the countries cover only a part of a nation's cultural wealth. Yet the museum movement of any country is expected to offer the panoramic view of its cultural property in its various forms of expression. Dose the museum movement in India fulfill that expectation by way of presenting various facets of the country's cultural wealth and traditions—its artistic, industrial and scientific achievements in the past or in the living memory? Does the museum movement offer glimpses of the diversity to which the people often speak of? Before an attempt is made to answer these questions it is necessary to define the term cultural property as given in some of the UNESCO documents. The Convention of the Means of Prohibiting and Preventing the Illicit Import, Export and Transfer of Ownership of Cultural Property adopted by the General Conference at its sixteenth session, Unesco, Paris (14 November 1970) defines it as follows:

For the purposes of this Convention the term "cultural property" means property which on religious or secular grounds, is specifically designated by each State as being of importance for archaeology, prehistory, history, literature, art or science and which belongs to the following categories:

- (a) rare collections and specimens of fauna, flora, minerals and objects of palaeontological interest;
- (b) property relating to history, including the history of science and technology and military and social history, to the national leaders, thinkers, scientists and to events of national importance;
- (c) products of archaeological excavations (including regular and clandestine) or of archeological discovers;
- (d) elements of artistic or historical monuments or archaeological sites which have been dismembered;
- (e) antiquities more than one hundred years old, such as inscriptions, coins and engraved seals;
- (f) objects of ethnological interest;
- (g) property of artistic interest, such as:
  - (i) pictures, paintings and drawings produced entirely by hand or any support and in any material (excluding industrial designs and manufactured articles decorated by hand);

(ii) original works of statutory art and sculptures in any material;

(iii) original engravings, prints and lithographs;

(iv) original artistic assemblages and montages in any material;

(h) rare manuscripts and incunabula, old books, documents and publications of special interest (historical, artistic, scientific, literary, etc.) singly or in collections;

(i) Postage, revenue and similar stamps, singly are in collections.

(j) Archives including sound, photographic and cinemaotographic archives;

(k) Articles of furniture more than one hundred years old and old musical instruments.

It is then evident that the term cultural property has a much wider scope and includes, to put it briefly, objects such as archaeological, botanical, geological, ethnological, zoological, palaeontological specimens, sound archives, cinematographic archives, philaletic items, manuscripts, old books and records, various kinds of works of art and science, musical instruments, furniture and so on. In India, there are only three legislations—Ancient Monuments and Archaeological Sites and Remains Act, 1958, Antiquities and Art Treasures Act, 1972 and Wild Life Protection Act, 1972—which partly cover the items categorized under the definition of cultural property. A point deserving special attention is that the "cultural property" here concerns itself basically with the movable vestiges of the past or even in some measure of the present.

No modern metropolitan city can justify its existence culturally if it has no permanent home for presenting a comprehensive picture of material life and culture as reflected in art treasures. In ancient India, such a home was often the temple; today this important function is largely performed by art museums which is an instrument of audio-visual education. Chennai, Cochin, Delhi, Hyderabad, Kolkata, Mumbai, Pudukkottai, Sarnath, Thiruvananthapuram with their long and varied history, its splendid monuments and historical sites, can boast of such a cultural institution—the

National Museums,[7] Such as Taxila Museum, Peshawar Museum, Kabul Museum, Lucknow State Museum, London British Museum, Edinburgh, Royal Scothish Museum, Kolhapur Museum, Mathura Govt. Museum, Sagar University Museum, Los Angles Country Museum of Art, and Gwalior, Archaeological Museum and Historical Monuments in Maharastra such as, Gokhale's bungalow, Servants of India Society, Tilak Museum, Aga Khan Palace, Empress Garden, Saras Baug, Peshve Park, Dr. Babasaheb Ambedkar Museum, Phule Museum, Parvathi Temples, Pataleshwar Cave Temple, Pune University, Raja Dinkar Kelkar Museum, Rajiv Gandhi Zoological Garden, Shaniwar Wada, Chaturshringe Temple and Shinde's Chhatri,[8] ideally situated at the intersections of their cities. During the years, the National Museum at Delhi has rapidly grown and developed in all their departments. The panorama of Indian art, from prehistoric to modern times, has been attractively presented in their thousands of exhibitions and study galleries.

The collections consist of nearly many lakhs are objects of different categories, acquired through purchase, loan, gift, treasure trove or exchange. These are supplemented each year by way of new acquisitions. The scope of the National Museums are not restricted to the art and culture of India. The institution is making efforts to acquire material from other countries as well as, to help Indians understand their heritage better in the perspective of world art.

A brief survey of the rich, varied collections begins with the archaeological material exhibited on the ground floor of the Indian museum. The Prehistoric and Protohistoric Gallery shows examples of lithic tools of the early, million years; relics of the Copper Hoard Culture of C. 1000 B.C. and examples of the Megalithic Culture of South India dating from C. 700 B.C. to A.D. 300.

A glimpse of the highly developed urban civilization in the third—second millennium B.C., the earliest known on the subcontinent, is provided by the rich finds from Mohenjodaro and Harappa and the recently discovered Harappan culture sites such as Lothal and Kalibangan. These include painted pottery, Terracottas, inscribed seals, votive, objects, Jewellery, copper utensils and small sculptures.

Five other large galleries and the rotunda on this floor illustrate the artistic achievements of the Indian sculptor in stone, clay and stucco, spanning a period form the 3rd century B.C. to the 16th century A.D.

Typical works representing the major Indian schools, such as Maurya, Sunga, Satavahana, Ikshvaku, Gandhara, Kushna, Gupta, Chalukya, Pallava, Chola, Vijayanagara, Hoysala, Kakatiya, Pratihara, Pals and Eastern Ganga, unfold the intellectual properties of India through time and space.

In National Museum, New Delhi gallery, about a hundred fine bronzes, large and small, review the art of metal-casting in India, in the *cire-perduce* process. The inscribed Buddha image of the Vakatakas, the sublime Natarajas and graceful Devis of Chola craftsmanship, the exquisite Pala bronzes from Nalanda are all as pleasing as those of the Chedi, Pratihara and Gahadawala schools are interesting. There are also a few charming examples from Chamba, Kashmir Valley, Gujarat, Rajastham, Orissa and Nepal. Copper-plate grants of varying dates and different dynasties exhibited in this galley are an important source of our intellectual properties, our heritage and history.

On the first floor, there are two Temporary Exhibition Galleries, a reconstructed room with murals from the palace of Chamba and paintings from Ajanta, Ellora and Bagh. A wealth of illustrated and illuminated manuscripts in different languages review the field of Hindu and Muslim literature. The Miniatures Gallery presents a chronological survey of the major schools belonging to different periods and regions. These include typical examples of the Pala period on palm-leaf, and miniatures of the Western Indian, Persian, Mughal, Deccani, Rajasthani and Pahari schools. Their varied themes, dressed in line and colour, are a picturesque documentation of the contemporary religious, social and cultural life of the people. A few *thankas* or temples banners illustrate the art of painting from Nepal and Tibet.

The world-famous collection of Central Asian antiquities, brought together by Sir Aurel Stein in the early years of the Twentieth Century, along the ancient Silk Routes between China and the West, are exhibited here, except for the wall paintings which are in an adjacent building. The antiquities include murals, Buddhist paintings on silk, linen and paper; textiles, sculpture in stucco, carved wood, ceramics, inscribed tablets and documents in the Kharoshthi script dating from c. second through the 11th centuries A.D. The art of Central Asia is important in that it reveals the commingling of diverse traditions from the Western world, Iran, China and India.

The second floor Verandah has the Special Gallery for Periodic Educational Exhibitions and the Study Gallery showing transparent charts on iconography, on coins and on the evolution of Indian and some of the Asian scripts derived from Brahmi. Close by are exhibited a few historical inscriptions on stone.

The anthropological material constituting a great variety of the regional costumes, jewellery, headgear and footwear of India, articles of daily use and the famous collection of tribal arts and photographs assembled by Verrier Elwin are all displayed in a picturesque manner. A brief account of the evolution of man in India and the types of people inhabiting the country is illustrated by explanatory charts.

The Decorative Arts Galleries exhibit textiles and costumes with all their richness of variety and techniques—woven, embroidered, dyed or printed; bidriware, objects in metal, glass, jade, shell and ivory; architectural and decorative wood-car from Kerala temples; south Indian temple chariots; material from Gujarat, Rajasthan and Nepal; weapons of war and hunting, in great variety, some bearing historical inscriptions and other embellished with rich ornamentation; silver objects of daily use; and profusion of gorgeous jewellery of exquisite workmanship.

The Museum has a collection of nearly 60,000 coins of every period and dynasty, documenting the long history of India. Out of this, only a representative selection is exhibited at a time. Some of the coins are as admirable for their fine calligraphy as they are interesting for their art in miniature form.

The latest installation on this floor is the magnificent collection of pre-Columbian art representing the cultures of Mexico, Central America, Peru and the neighboring regions of

South America. This large and fairly representative collection of 355 objects of great intrinsic value in the munificent gift of Mrs. Alice and Mr. Nasli Heeramaneck of New York. It includes pottery in great variety, sculpture in stone, wood carvings, textiles, terracotta's, objects of gold, silver and copper ranging in date from the first millennium B.C. to the 15th century A.D.

The National Museum is not merely a repository of the rich cultural heritage of the country; it also aspires to preserve and present this national wealth of great richness and variety to the Indian public and visitors from abroad for their visual education, intellectual advancement of intellectual properties and aesthetic enjoyment.

These facts demonstrate the property aspect of cultural property. The objects, tangible and movable, are described in terms of shape, size, rarity, and commercial value. The property aspect may be starkly shown by the fact that documentation dating back to the early 2500 B.C. to 1850's shows that anthropologists, archaeologists, geologists, explorers, historians and scholars. Not everything that can be stolen is necessarily property, but most likely these objects were taken because they were valued as property. Thieves foreign to the culture that produced such objects could not understand, or at least did no respect, the cultural significance of the items.

The cultural aspect of cultural property is demonstrated in the cultural significance of such items to the people who created them. The older ones must remain in place, contributing their strength until they decay and return to the earth. Although they can exist as objects, as property, when displayed in a museum, they cannot serve their cultural purpose. Another part of the cultural aspect of these objects is that they cannot be treated as property in the usual sense because no individual can own them.[9] Cultural property is integral to the esteem that people hold for themselves and their past. It is also integral to their identity.

Cultural significance gives particular objects value to a culture or to a collector. Cultural property stripped of cultural significance would be merely property, more or less beautiful or rare and more or less valuable on the basis of that beauty or rarity only. Defining cultural property without reference to its culture is not only foolish, but dishonest. It attempts to strengthen claims of ownership while denigrating the very thing that gives an object some of its value to the holder. Nonetheless, recognition of the cultural aspect of cultural property has rarely been apparent in efforts to define or protect it.

Perhaps the most widely accepted definition of cultural property is found in Article 1 of the UNESCO Convention on the Means of Prohibiting the Illicit Import, Export and Transfer of Ownership of Cultural Property (the UNESCO 1970).[10] The first notable element of this definition is that it consists of a list of categories of property.

The most notable element of the definition of cultural property in UNESCO 1970, however, is that it leaves to the individual states designation of specific items from the various categories as cultural property. The states may restrict the definition. The Government of India for example, has limited the definition of protected cultural property in the 1983 convention on cultural property Implementation Act. Under the cultural definition, objects do not become cultural property unitil they have been removed from or are threatened with removal from their cultural context.

Although UNESCO 1970 emphasizes the property aspect of cultural property, its definition of cultural property is at least partly in terms of cultural significance and cultural context. Recognizing that cultural property can be defined only partially by its age, provenance, category, or threat of pillage, UNESCO 1970 defines cultural property as "property which, on religious or secular grounds, is ...... of importance for archaeology, prehistory, history, literature, art or science."

The definition does not contemplate the designation by indigenous peoples of objects sacred to them as cultural property. The state-centric element is also apparent in that the cultural significance of objects is determined by "importance for archaeology, prehistory, history, literature, art or science", not by importance to the cultural identity of a people or group. The values stated are largely external to the cultural identity of a people or group. Is the judgment that of a living people, defining for themselves their relationship to the world, or the judgment of external academics applying some sort of absolute criteria? The recognition of "religious or secular grounds" upon which to base the importance of cultural property is insufficient entry for the significance of objects to peoples or groups. The Preamble suggests recognition of the importance of cultural property of cultural identity, but even here the nation-state is the unit of identity, not the ethnic group or indigenous people to whom such objects may have the greatest cultural significance.

Setting aside the questions of what is to be protected, and who shall define it, concentration on the property aspect of cultural property inevitably raises the question, "Who Owns The Past?" If cultural property can be properly defined, who may own it? Is "ownership" of cultural property even possible? The problem of ownership has several facets.

A principal text on art law identifies the major problems in protection of cultural property as: (1) illicit trade, and (2) repatriation. Both problems involve questions regarding who may properly own or possess, cultural property. Trade cannot be illicit if it does not dispossess someone of the right to licit trade. Similarly, no one may gain return of cultural property unless they can show "better title."

Reflecting the dichotomous nature of cultural property, the question of ownership might be reformulated in two parts. First, should cultural property be returned to source countries or peoples? This is the repatriation issue. Second, who is a legitimate claimant of and who can legitimately release cultural property to the possession of another? This is the replevin issue. A rough way of classifying these issues is that the first is a human rights/self-determination issue, and the second is a property issue. Repatriation is a moral issue concerned with right treatment of diverse cultures and objects significant to them. Accordingly, the focus of this moral inquiry is on the cultural significance, the cultural aspect of cultural property. Replevin is a title issue, based on who has a superior right to possess particular items of cultural property, defined by objective criteria. Its focus is the property aspect of cultural property.

In addition to the possessory interests suggested by the question of who owns the past, there are myriad interests based on use and enjoyment. These interests may be divided into those of the source nations and those of acquisitive nations, although there is some overlap between them. For source nations, the *first* interest is specific cultural value, or concern over wrenching cultural property away from the culture in which it is embedded. *Second*, there is an archaeological interest in preventing destruction of the records of civilization. A *third* interest is in the integrity of the work of art or object of cultural property, which means simply that is should not be dismembered. *Fourth* is an interest in physical safety of cultural property from deterioration. A *fifth* interest is an economic one, measured in terms of the price the object would bring on an open market (intrinsic value). *Sixth*, cultural property has artistic value independent of its cultural significance. *Seventh*, is the so-called distribution interest. Cultural property may demonstrate to the world the achievements of the culture of a nation if it is disseminated. *Eighth*, there is an interest in mere retention or "hoarding", as the right of source nations and peoples. *Finally*, there is an interest in preserving the national patrimony as a matter of pride and identity, as well as intrinsic and extrinsic economic value.

The interests of acquisitive nations are equally diverse. First is again the interest in preservation, or the physical safety of the objects above. Second, there is an interest among colonial powers and victorious powers in times of conflict in the humiliation of a conquered people by dispossessing them of their cultural and artistic treasures. Third, there is the interest of "good faith purchasers" that their ownership or possession of objects not be unjustly disturbed, or disturbed without compensation. Fourth, acquisitive nations have an interest in enriching their own cultural patrimony by acquisition from external sources. Fifth, like source nations seeking appreciation of their culture abroad, acquisitive nations have an interest in the breakdown of parochialism in a global society. Finally, acquisitive nations have an interest in maintaining access to cultural property for archaeological purposes.[11]

## 3. THE DEBATE OVER CULTURE NATIONALISM

### (a) Lost Treasures Architectual Grandeaur

What constitutes the wealth of our nation? Who generated this wealth ? Whose wealth is it? Can we date its loss? These are difficult and there are no simple answers. Yet, historically speaking one can discern certain phases that saw an unprecedented drain of India's resource: revenues, labour, gold, artifacts, musical instruments such Veena and Nagaswaram jewels and valuable manuscripts containing scientific and religious knowledge about the people of this country. Given the variety of cultural encounters that shaped India's history it is not surprising that attitudes to its wealth varied at different points of time.

As "drain of wealth" came to characterize British power the worst causality was Indian economy and society.

.The Mughal Emperors were patrons of literature, calligraphists, painters, poets, singers and craftsmen. A variety of Persian writing bureaucracy—both Hindu and Muslim—found patronage in their court. Wealth was freely expended to encourage these artists to give their best. The results were soon evident. The Mughal Empire was famous for its beautifully calligraphed and often illustrated manuscripts. The *Ain-i-Akbari* and the *Akbarnama* produced by Abdul Fazl at Emperor Akbar's behest were representative cases in point. Translation of pre-Mughal manuscripts on Indian mythology, religion and sciences was also undertaken on a large scale by the Mughals.

War booty, which included confiscated precious stones and jewels, was an all important source of wealth taken out of the country. Today much of this kind of wealth constitutes the British crown jewels. The famed diamond, the Kohi–i-Noor, now part of the British crown jewels, is an important case in point. The Kohi-i-Noor was confiscated at the conclusion of the Sikh War (1840). The English Company had wanted to keep the diamond to pay for the war, but the Governor-General, Lord Dalhousie, had promised that it would find its "final and fitting resting place in the crown of Britain."

It was, however, the large scale transfer to Europe of precious oriental manuscripts complied by Indian and

Mughal rulers and men of letters that dealt a big blow to India's intellectual heritage. In post Enlightenment Europe the quest for knowledge of "oriental" cultures picked-up and drove many scholar administrators, like William Jones, Charles Wilkins, A.H. Polier to India. Their forays into the oriental book bazaars were inspired by their intellectual curiosity: but knowledge was also essential for a better control of Indian society as well.

It was for this reason that the British scholar administrators were particularly active in the hunt and purchase of Indian texts on governance, law, religion and the sciences. Acquisition of literary arsenals of the vanquished Indians became also the symbol of the superior power of the British conquerors. In this context the plunder of Tipu Sultan's by British armies after the fall of Seringapatnam (1791-2) is noteworthy.

Tipu offered a formidable challenge to the British. His ultimate collapse in 1799 is often described via the British takeover of his rich library. In 1799 a gleeful Charles Wilkins, British Sanskrit's and orientlist, wrote to Warren Hastings, the Governor General, "the papers have told you truly that the captors of Seringapatnam have reserved Tipoo's for the Company repository."

In colonial India the British were not the only ones instrumental in the drain of India's wealth. British power in India, at least in its formative years, rested on a range of Europeans as well. French soldiers, traders, architects and engineers, in particular constituted an informal network of support to British administration in India. The literary wealth of India was shipped to France by soldier trader scholars like A.H. Polier and Jean Baptiste Gentil. Many of their collections are housed in the Bibiliotheque Naionale, Paris. These include priceless Persian manuscripts like the *Shahnama* and the *Akbarnama,* besides the Diwan of famous oriental poets Hafiz and the Gulistan and Bostan of Saadi.

The rich plurality of Indian tradition is a treasured legacy of this historical process.

India is particularly known for such buried treasures. Old Indian coins, jewels and bronze icons packed in mud pots have been unearthed from parts of India. Hoards of ancient Roman coins have also been discovered in certain regions of the country. Some of these hoards such as those from Vellalur and Karur in Tamil Nadu also contain Roman jewellery. These foreign coins and jewels reached India through traders and sailors.

Burial of precious things was not always for the safety of those things. People buried money and wealth for religious and sentimental reasons as well. Many ancient graves and tombs contain coins, jewels, grains, weapons, agricultural tools and other objects used by the deceased during his lifetime. Some of the tombs exhibit sculptures of the servants and slaves of the dead man People believed that the person would need all these forms of wealth including the servants in the other world.

People also deposited coins, gemstones and other precious articles as ritualistic offerings within Buddhist stupas and below the foundations of Hindu temples. Such ritualistic hoards are common in north-west India and Pakistan.

Sometimes money is buried underground not by man but by factors such as earthquakes, floods and sea erosion. Many glorious cities and civilizations with all their architectural, artistic and art factual wealth have simply disappeared below land or sea due to such acts of nature. Present day archaeologists are using modern technological devices to learn more about these hidden civilizations. The cities of Harappa and Mohenjodaro (in Pakistan) that flourished around 2500 B.C. are classic examples of such "Lost Cities" brought to light by modern excavators. In recent years, archaeologists have initiated underwater digging at the ancient port towns of Dwaraka (Gujarat) and Poompuhar or Kaveripattinam (Tamil Nadu) both of which are partially submerged under the sea. Hampi (in Karanataka), the capital of the mighty medieval Vijayanagar empire, is yet another city retrieved from Mother Earth by archaeology.

The British say they have saved the Marbles. Well, thank you very much. Now give them back.—Melina Mercouri.[12]

(The Elgin Marbles were removed from the Parthenon in the Nineteenth Century and were eventually housed and are currently located in The British Museum in London. The removal and retention of these Greek act of that period one result was that Greek antiquities has formed the basis for a bitter and divisive debate over the role of cultural nationalism in the retention, repatriation and protection of cultural patrimony.)

Any estimate of the morality of Elgin's actions has to take account both of his motives and of the results of what he did. His motives, though certainly mixed, included a large element of reverence for the Marbles and the intention of removing them to a safer place. He also wished to bring the marbles to the attention of the world and to see them used to advance the arts. The passion for Greek antiquities was still in its early infancy even in England and France, where the works of the Romans were more highly valued. Elgin's removals focused Europe's attention on the magnificence of the Marbles and other works of Greek art of that period one result was that Greek superseded Roman art as the ideal, both in high and in popular culture. Elgin was convinced of the superiority of Greek over Roman art, and through his actions and the resulting acquisition of the Marbles by the British Museum, the rest of the world came to share his opinion.

Elgin was also motivated by nationalism; he wanted the Marbles for England and feared that they would otherwise go to the French. It is clear that Elgin hoped to advance his own career and may at times have though that the Marbles would help.

We conclude that the legality of the removal of the Marbles is clearly established and that its immorality has not been demonstrated. The Greeks do not have a strong legal or moral case against Elgin. Minister Mercouris and Byrons eloquence and art to the contrary notwithstanding, the British own the Marbles and, on balance, did not wrongly acquire ownership. For those who agree, that settle the legal and moral questions about the removal. There remains, however, the most difficult and interesting question of all; should the British now return the Marbles to Greece? Independent of questions about the legality and morality of the removal is the argument that the Marbles should, on other grounds, be returned. Adequate analysis of this aspect of the case brings a new set of considerations into play, requiring us to consider the relative merits of nationalism and internationalism as guiding principles in the allocation of cultural property.

The discussion up to this point has been retrospective. We have looked at the historical record in order to assess the legality and morality of the British acquisition of the Marbles. What happened in the past strongly affects the present and future, so that one who properly acquired something normally has the legal right to keep and enjoy it and, if he wishes, to dispose of it. Thus if the Trustees of the British Museum became the owners of the Marbles in 1816, they own them today. Still, on no legal system is the right of property absolute; it is possible to establish new rules of property or modify old ones, and although the right of property is respected, it is subject to regulation and even in extreme cases, to expropriation. Even if Britain properly acquired the Marbles, it is still possible to argue for their return to Greece.

The most obvious argument is that the Marbles belong in Greece because they are Greek. They were created in Greece by Greek artists for the civic and religious purposes of the Acropolis of Athens Athens of that time.

In its truest and best sense, cultural nationalism is based on the relation between cultural property and cultural definition. For a full life and a secure identity, people need exposure to their history, much of which is represented or illustrated by objects. Such artifacts are important to cultural definition and expression, to shared identity and community. They tell people who they are and where they come from. In helping to preserve the identity of specific cultures, they help the world preserve texture and diversity. Works of art civilize and enrich life. They generate art (it is a truism among art historians that art comes from art) and nourish artists. Cultural property stimulates learning and scholarship. A people deprived of its artifacts is culturally impoverished.

The cultural nationalist argument is distinct from, but related to, two other arguments, one economic and one political. Economically, whoever has the Marbles has something of value: they would command an enormous price if offered for sale, and their presence in a public collection nourished the tourist industry. Possession is obviously necessary in order to enjoy the economic value, and Britain has the Marbles. We have already seen, however, that the law seems to support the British acquisition and thus to sanction British enjoyment of the economic value. Indeed, providing the basis for allocating things of value is one of the important functions of law, and it is one of the things law seems to do particularly well. If the Greeks were to base their argument on the economic value of the Marbles, they would merely be rearguing a question of property law, claiming that they own the Marbles. As we have already seen, they would probably lose that argument. The applicable law is clear and, on the facts as we have interpreted them, favours the British.

The final component of the nationalism argument is political: the belief that the presence of the Marbles in England, or in any place other than Greece, is an offense to Greeks and to the Greek nation. Here the demand for the return of the Marbles is based on national pride. That sort of sentiment is close to cultural deprivation of the sort just discussed, but it is worlds away from it in a very important sense.

Nationalism in its broader meaning refers to the attitude which ascribes to national individuality a high place in the hierarchy of values. In this sense it is a natural and indispensable condition and accompanying phenomenon of all national movements. On the other hand, the term nationalism also connotes a tendency to place a particularly excessive, exaggerated and exclusive emphasis on the value of the nation at the expense of the values, which leads to a vain and importunate overestimation of ones own nation and thus to a detraction of owners. On this long basic ethics and law. The weight one gives to this kind of argument for the return of the cultural properties depend to a large extent on one s attitude toward political nationalism itself. No candid observer can deny its power in world affairs.

### (b) The Property Aspects of Cultural Artifact

Thieves often take stolen cultural property directly from countries with rich cultural heritages to civil-law nations where the purchaser of stolen property can gain good title. In a civil-law nation, a purchaser of stolen art acquires good title provided that she does not know or learn about the objects illicit removal from its rightful owner. In a common-law country, by contrast a seller cannot transfer better title than she has. A thief in a common-law country thus breaks the chain of good title and any subsequent purchasers can never acquire good title. The original owner can therefore reclaim the object regardless of whether the purchaser knew she had bought a stolen object. Because some EC countries follow the common-law tradition while others have civil-law traditions, art thieves merely need to take a stolen object out of a common-law country and into a civil-law nation to "launder" it.[13]

**(c) Protection Regimes**

Most countries restrict the export of antiquities through a licensing scheme. Great Britain, France, Austria, Canada, and Australia have application procedures for removing an artifact from the country. The licenses granted under such schemes are usually specific to each artifact since each application must be reviewed individually.[14]

The second broad strategy, nationalization of cultural artifacts, operates from the same principle as the nationalization of any other natural resource. Many central American countries, such as Ecuador and Costa Rica, have laws that make all archaeological materials discovered after the effective date of the laws the property of the state. As of 1984, state claims to undiscovered archaeological artifacts could be found in countries of every region and economic and political stratum.

Export restrictions and nationalization laws are sometimes called "blanket" or "umbrella" laws due to their all-inclusive nature. These umbrella laws have been widely criticized because their breadth renders enforcement virtually impossible. As a result, source nations must rely on cooperation at international borders to retain what they have legislated as theirs. However, even this strategy can backfire, since, for example, American courts have refused to return artifacts when the governing national ownership statutes were overly vague.

Enforcement of antiquities laws is a severe, pervasive problem. Most artifact rich countries focus their enforcement measures on the looters of archaeological sites, but these areas are notoriously difficult to police. By definition, many fresh archaeology sites are unknown. The guards at the known sites are frequently underpaid. Corruption at all levels of enforcement adds to enforcement difficulties. In some countries, customs officials can easily be bribed. Corruption can even extend to the highest levels of government. In Greece, for instance, former Prime Minister Constantine Mitsotakis and his deputy police chief were implicated in a scheme to cooperate with an international syndicate of antiquities smugglers.

**(d) The Retention of Cultural Property**

Most nations attempt to retain cultural property.[15] The principal varieties of cultural property for present purposes are works of art and objects of archaeological, ethnological, and historical interest. Any comprehensive definition of cultural property would have to include these objects and many more. Thus, the UNESCO Convention on the Means of prohibiting and Preventing the Illicit Import, Expert and Transfer of Ownership of cultural Property, Nov. 14, 1970, 823 U.N.T.S. 231 (1972), 10 Intl. Legal Materials 289 (1971) [hereafter UNESCO Convention], defines cultural property in Article I to include;[16]

(a) Rare collections and specimens of fauna, flora, minerals and anatomy, and objects of paleontological interest;
(b) property relating to history, including the history of science and technology and military and social history. . .;
(c) products of archeological excavations. . .;
(d) elements of artistic or historical monuments. . .; which have been dismembered;
(e) antiquities more than one hundred yeas old, such as inscriptions, cons and engraved seals;
(f) objects of ethnological interest;
(g) property of artistic interest. . .;

(h) rare manuscripts and incunabula, old books, documents and publications of special interest. . .;
(i) postage, revenue and similar stamps. . .;
(j) archives, including sound, photographic and cinematographic archives; and
(k) articles of furniture more than one hundred years old and old musical instruments.

In some nations cultural objects and environmental treasures (including natural and artificial landscapes and ecological areas plus, in cities, urban structures and panoramas) are treated as fundamentally related to each other.

The entire question of the proper definition of cultural property for legal and policy purposes is there are millions of the original intellctual properties in India which the other illustrates the wonders in the following pages, and the periods of the intellectual properties depending on the political culture. They reflect the saga of the wornders that was India, the the story of the India's intellectual heritage. Theydeclare that cultural objects large and unruly, and fortunately need not be pursued here. Works of art and archaeological, ethnological, and historical objects certainly qualify under any definition; museums acquire and display them, scholars study them, collectors collect them, and dealers sell them. National laws and international conventions provide for their preservation and regulate their trade. A strong international consensus supports their inclusion in any definition of cultural property are state property ("expropriation laws"), or prohibit the expert of cultural objects ("embargo laws"), or give the state or domestic institutions a preemptive right to buy objects offered for export ("preemption laws"). Some laws mix these categories; they may totally forbid the export of particularly important objects; permit the expert, subject to preemptive purchase, of other kinds; and allow the export, with or without a permit, of less important objects. Others indiscriminately retain everything. Elucidated by administrative regulations and administered by governmental officials and agencies, these laws express the intention to keep cultural objects within the national territory. They are a form of export control. We can refer to them generically as "retention schemes."

Many of the most extensive retention schemes are found in nations rich in cultural artifacts but short of foreign exchange. Their development policies normally encourage export trade to earn foreign exchange to pay for imports and to finance domestic growth. But cultural property is an exception: despite a substantial and well-funded market for such objects abroad, export trade in cultural objects is prohibited or restrained. The contrast is striking and seems to call for explanation. What is there about cultural property that produces such an apparently counter-developmental policy?

The practice of national retention of cultural property has a superficial appeal; it seems to many people to be natural and reasonable, a normal expression of the obvious relation between the object and the national culture; Olmec heads clearly belong in Mexico because they are Mexican: classical Greek sculptures are Greek and belong in Greece The retention of cultural property needs no justification; on the contrary, permitting cultural objects to be exported is what seems anomalous. How can one permit the nations "cultural heritage", or "cultural patrimony", to be taken abroad? National cultural objects held (imprisoned?) in foreign museums and collections should be rescued—"repatriated"—returned to their homeland, their *patria*. This concept of a "national cultural patrimony" is frequently cited and treated as an established political and legal category.

This is the basic cultural nationalist position, which has become part of Western culture. Cultural nationalism transcends jurisdiction and sovereignty; even though many "Greek" sculptures Indian sculptures are in the British Museum beyond the reach of Greek laws and Indian laws, they remain Greek and Indian where do these attitudes come from? The major premise is nationalism itself.

European in origin, nationalism is a modern addition to the history of ideas emerging clearly only at the time of the French Revolution as nations become the primary actors in world affairs with nationalism as the supporting ideology. In Enlightenment thought, nationalism had humanist roots; it embodied liberal republican ideas of the kind expressed in the American Declaration of Independence in 1776 and the French Declaration of the Rights of Man and of the Citizen in 1789. But with the rise of romanticism and the relative decline of faith in reason and in the humanist ideal, the content of nationalism changed. Led by German philosophers and poets, such as Fichte, Herer, and Heine, nationalism acquired new premises and a romantic, mystical overlay. Concepts like that of the *Volk* (with *Volksgenosse* and *Volksgeist*) become current.

Under the romantic influence, conceptual distinctions between nationalism, patriotism, and national consciousness blurred. The way was opened to nation-worship, the adoration of national character, national achievement, national culture, national ambitions, and national policies. As each nation preened itself, nationalism became invidious. Patriotism and xenophobia became natural correlates. Nationalism justified violence when employed in the national interest. Nationalism which "begins as Sleeping Beauty. . .[and] ends as Frankenstein's Monster." Romanticism succeeded the Enlightenment; faith in rationalism declined; reason slept. In nationalism, as elsewhere, the sleep of reason produced monsters.

Nationalism in itself is neither good nor bad; the difficulty lies in the tune it has taken and the uses to which it has been put under the influence of romanticism.

The application of these attitudes of nationalism to cultural objects owes much to the English romantic poet George Gordon, Lord Byron. In 1821 the Greeks began their war for independence from four centuries of Ottoman rule. Byron was a powerful publicist for the Greek cause though (sic) his poetry and correspondence (and through his actions, dying of fever at Missolonghi while actively supporting the Greeks). The cause of Greek nationalism captured the Western imagination, where it was seen through romantic spectacles. Byron passionately opposed Lord Eligin s removal of the Parthenon sculptures, the "Elgin Marbles", and wrote about the episode in two poems. The curse of Minerva and childe Harold s Pilgrimage. Although these passages contain some of his least memorable poetry, they were enormously effective as propaganda. The key premise was that of cultural nationalisms the Marbles were Greek and belonged in Greece. Since Byron, that premise has been solidly built into Western thought.

We need a term. The epithet "elginisme", coined by the French to refer to the wrongful (i.e., by persons who are nor French) removal of cultural property from its site, become part of the common language of discourse on cultural property. In a similar spirit we could use the term "Byronism" to characterize the application of romantic nationalism to cultural objects. "Byronism" has dominated post-World War II discourse on cultural property. It is the unexamined premise of much contemporary national and international policy toward cultural property. Let's examine it.

Much of the justification for cultural retention schemes is straightforward Byronism: the romantic attribution of national character to cultural objects, with the corollary that they belong in the national territory. When viewed objectively, this looks more like a statement of faith than a reason. Its effect, however, is no less because of that; it may indeed be more powerful in its candidly emotional appeal than any local argument would be. Consider these statements by Melina Mercouri in her campaign for return of the Elgin Marbles to Athens:

> This is our history, this is our soul . . . you must understand us. You must love us. We have fought with you in the second war. Give them back and we will be proud of you. Give them back and they will be in good hands.
>
> *and*
>
> They are the symbol and the blood and the soul of the Greek people. . . We have fought and died for the Parthenon and the Acropolis..... When we are born, they talk to us about all this great history that makes Greekness.

Such statements appeal primarily to the emotions. They divert attention from the facts and discourage reasoned discussion of the issues.

We turn now to a different group of possible explanations for the existence of cultural property retention schemes based on the familiar power of governments to promote the general welfare of their people. Does the presence of cultural property in private hands in the national territory promote the general welfare? Does export impair it?

There is no serious debate about the proposition that cultural property should be preserved. If the object is damaged or destroyed the opportunity to study and learn from it, to enjoy it, to be inspired by it, is impaired or lost. Public action to protect and preserve cultural property appears to be not only reasonable but laudable. Public action to preserve contextual values also makes sense. To the archaeologist, ethnographer, or historian, an object may derive much of its significance from its context and the context may derive meaning from the object. If a stela is taken from a Mayan temple without full documentation, the value of the stela and the temple are diminished. The act of removal destroys information, impedes learning, and impairs enjoyment. The stela rendered anonymous by the act of undocumented removal, becomes an orphan; the temple, an amputee. "Decontextualization" of this kind is a genuine problem for parts of architectural monuments. Even for unattached works, loss of context can be a serious problem. Consider the case of the removal of a pot from the Etruscan tomb. Unless removal is accompanied by elaborate documentation of the site and its contents and identification of the pots's origin in the site, it leads to the irreparable loss of cultural information. It is a form of destruction, a kind of vandalism.

Loss of integrity is a related problem that is particularly applicable to works of art. A complex work, such as an altarpiece composed of several panels, arguably is greater than the sum of its parts. If one of the panels is removed and sold, both the panel and the remaining part lose something essential. Fidelity to the artist's conception is only a part of the problem; there is also the concern for the object's preservation in its authentic from. The purpose is to preserve the integrity of the culture, to avoid its falsification and decontextualization.

The *troika* of preservation, context, and integrity constitutes a set of higher "public welfare" values that transcend national interests and boundaries. They are concerned with protection of cultural objects, of things that embody or empress or evoke the human record. Such objects, in the words of The Hague Convention of 1954, are "the cultural heritage of all mankind."

We have seen three plausible explanations of why nations try to prevent the export of cultural property: Byronism, i.e. nationalist sentiment, protection, (preservation, context and integrity), and opportunity preservation (i.e., if it stays in the national territory the nation may eventually acquire it at a bargain price or may decide to protect it). Other reasons have been offered and considered, but they do not survive inspection.

### (e) The Problems of the Colonial Era

Prior to 1800, the prevailing "mercantilist" view of international trade assumed that the prosperity of a country could be maximized by policies which ensured a surplus of exports over imports. Since precious metals were used to settle international accounts, this balance would generate a net inflow of gold and silver from the rest of the world. The implicit assumption was that the world's economic pie was of constant size, and therefore any gains experienced by one nation from trade had to come at the expense of its trading partners. In short, international trade was viewed as a zero-sum game.[17]

In 1776, Adam Smith published his now classic work, *Wealth of Nations,* which explained that nations could engage in mutually beneficial trade. This analysis was taken one step further with the formulation of the principle of comparative advantage in the 19th century by David Ricardo and John Stuart Mill. As this theory shows, a nation can benefit from international trade even if it cannot produce any one good more efficiently than its trading partners. If each nation specializes in the production of those products which it can produce with the greatest relative efficiency, and can then trade freely with other nations for the other products it needs; the greater overall efficiency which results from this process increases the size of the world's economic pie, providing a higher standard of living for all. In short, international trade can be a positive-sum interaction.

Although we are familiar today with the economic division between the industrialized countries of the North and the developing countries of the North and the developing countries of the South, the situation was quite different in the immediate Post World War II era. Many countries we know as developing countries today, and most of those in Africa and Asia, had not yet achieved independence from colonial domination in the 1940s.

From the beginning, many in the developing world viewed proposals for a free trade system as a threat to their hopes of rapid industrialization as well as to their independence and sovereignty. They feared an open trading system would make it impossible for the non-industrialization countries of the South to achieve industrialization because any new "infant industries" they might try to create would be unable to compete with the established foreign competition.

The history of relations between North and South has left many in the developing areas of the world with some palpable resentment about international economic relations, and developing countries have tried, with varying degrees of success, to maintain "Third World" political unity within the United Nations system. The nineteenth century "colonial" pattern of trade relations had been typified by a division of labour which prevented the industrial development of the South. The largely industrialized colonial powers had no interest in developing competing industries in their colonial possessions, thus they tapped their colonies as a source of primary commodities. This, in effect, relegated these developing areas to a peripheral role in the economies of their colonizing powers. The economy of the colonial "periphery" was used as a subordinate appendage of the industrial economy of the colonial "center" or "metropolis", supplying commodities to the metropolitan power and also serving as a market for industrialized goods. Those developing areas that achieved political independence sought to sever the economic dependency by establishing their own industries, any they were suspicious that free trade would serve only to perpetuate their underdevelopment.

**(f) Authorship, Cultural Patrimony and Intellectual Property**

In March 1993, a diverse group of educators, scholars and industry experts convened in Bellagio to discuss the relationship between the concepts of authorship, cultural patrimony and intellectual property protection. The Declaration which resulted from the conference highlights some of the future issues to be faced if traditional forms of intellectual property are extended to include objects of cultural patrimony. It sates the following:

> *We,* the participants at the Bellagio Conference on intellectual property, come from many nations, professions and disciplines. We lawyers and literary critics, computer scientists and publishers, teachers and writers, environmentalists and scholars of cultural heritage.
>
> *Sharing a common concern* about the effects of the international regime of intellectual property law on our communities, on scientific progress and international development, on our environment, on the culture of indigenous peoples. In particular,
>
> *Applauding* the increasing attention by the world community to such previously ignored issues as preservation of the environment, of cultural heritage, and biodiversity. But,
>
> *Convinced* that the role of intellectual property in these areas has been neglected for too long, we therefore convened a conference of academics, activists and practitioners diverse in geographical and cultural background as well as professional area of interest.

Discovering that many of the different concerns faced in each of these diverse areas could be traced back to the same oversights and injustices in the current intellectual property system, we hereby.[18]

Declare the following:

*First,* intellectual property laws have profound effects on issues as disparate as scientific and artistic progress, biodiversity, access to information, and the cultures of indigenous and tribal peoples. Yet all too often those laws are constructed without taking such effects into account, constructed around a paradigm that is selectively blind to the scientific and artistic contributions of many of the world's cultures and constructed in *fora* where those who will be most directly affected have no representation.

*Second,* many of these problems are built into the basic structure and assumptions of intellectual property. Contemporary intellectual property's law is constructed around a notion of the author as an individual, solitary and original creator, and it is for this figure that its protections are reserved. Those who do not fit this model—custodians of tribal culture and medical knowledge, collectives practicing traditional artistic and musical forms, or peasant cultivators of valuable seed varieties, for example—are denied intellectual property protection.

*Third,* a system based on such premises has real negative consequences. Increasingly, traditional knowledge, folklore, genetic material and native medical knowledge flow out of their countries of origin unprotected by intellectual property, while works from developed countries flow in, well protected by international intellectual property agreements, backed by the threat of trade sanctions.

*Fourth,* in general, systems built around the author paradigm tend to obscure or undervalue the importance of "the public domain", the intellectual and cultural commons from which future works will be constructed. Each intellectual property right, in effect fences off some portion of the public domain, making it unavailable to future creators. In striking respects, the current situation raises the same concerns raised twenty years ago by the impeding privatization of the deep sea bed. The aggressive expansion of intellectual property rights have the potential to inhibit development and future creation by fencing off "the commons", and yet—in striking contrast to the reaction over the deep sea bed—the international community seems unaware of the fact.

*Fifth,* we deplore these tendencies, deplore them as not merely unjust but unwise, and entreat the international community to reconsider the assumptions on which and the procedure by which the international intellectual property regime is shaped.

*In general,* we favour increased recognition and protection of the public domain. We call on the international community to expand the public domain through expansive application of concepts of "fair use", compulsory licensing, and narrower initial coverage of property rights in the first place. But since existing author-focused regimes are blind to the interests of non-authorial producers as well as to the importance of the commons, the main exception to this expansion of the public domain should be in favour of those who have been excluded by the authorial biases of current law.

*Specifically,* we advocate consideration of special regimes, possibly in the form of "neighboring" or "related" rights regimes, for the following areas:

Protection of folkloric works.

Protection of works of cultural heritage.

Protection of the biological and ecological "know-how" of traditional peoples.

*In addition* we support systematic reconsideration of the basis on which new kinds of works related to digital technology, such as computer programs and electronic data bases, are protected under national and international intellectual property regimes. We recognize the economic importance of works falling into these categories, and the significant investments made in their production. Nevertheless, given the importance of the various concerns raised by any such a regime—concerns about public access, international development and technological innovation—we believe that choices about how and how much to protect databases should be made with a view to the specific policy objectives such protection is designed to achieve, rather than as a reflexive response to their categorization as "works of authorship."

*On a systemic level,* we call upon states and non-governmental organizations to move towards democratization of the fora in which the international intellectual property regime is debated and decided.

*In conclusion,* we declare that in an era in which information is among the most precious of all resources, intellectual property rights cannot be framed by the few to be applied to the many. They cannot be framed on assumptions that disproportionately exclude the contributions of important parts of the world community. They can no longer be constructed without reference to their ecological, cultural and scientific effects. We must regimagine the international regime of intellectual property. It is to that task this Declaration call its readers.

## Notes and References


1. Doris Estelle Long and Anthony D' Amato. Copyright 1996 by Doris E. Long and Anthony D'Anthony D' Amato.
2. Halima Nice, "Legislative Models of Protection of Cultural Property" 27 *Hastings Law Journal*, 1098, (1976) Halina Nice.
3. Lisa J. Borodkin "The Economics of Antiquities Looking and a Proposed Legal Alternative", 95 *Columbia Law Review* 377, (1995) Lisa. J. Borodkin.
4. Victora J. Vitrano "Protecting Cultural Object in an Internal Border—Free E.C: The EC Directive and Regulations for the Protection and Return of Cultural Objects", 17 *Fordham International Law Journal.* 1164 (1994) Victoria J. Victrano.
5. Roger W. Mastalir, "A Proposal for Protecting the "Cultural" and "Property" Aspects of Cultural Property Under International Law," 16 *Fordham International Law Journal.* 1033, (1993) Fordhan University School of Law.
6. The UNESCO Convention on the means of Prohibiting and Preventing the Illicit Import, Expert and Transfer of Ownership of Cultural Property, Nov. 14, 1970 823, U.N.T.S. 231 (1972); H. Sankar (1981) Museums and Protection of Monuments and Antiquities in India (New Delhi Sundeep Prakashan) 14-17.
7. G.D. Khullar "The National Museum" *Illustrated Weekly of India,* June 22, 1969.
8. *One India One People*: "Lessons from History" June 2001.
9. S.F. Markhan and H. Hargreaves, *The Museums of India* (London 1936); H. Sarkar, "Museums in Archeological Remains Monuments and Museums (New Delhi, 1964) C. Sivaramamoorthy "Directory of Museums in India" (New Delhi 1959.)
10. John H. Merryman, "Thinking about the Elgin Marbles", 83, *Michegan Law Review* 1881 (1985), (1985).

11. Seema Alavi "Lost Treasures" *Welath Folio The Hindu Suppliment* 22, August 2000.
12. *Sunday Times* (London), May 22, 1983 at 15, Col. 2.
13. Victoria J. Vitrano, "Protecting Cultural Objects in an Internal Border—Free E.C. The EC Directive and Regulations for the Protection and Return of Cultural Objects", 17 *Fortdham International Law Journal*, 1164. (1994).
14. Lisa J. Borodkin, "The Economics of Antiquities Looting and a Proposed Legal Alternatives" 95 *Columbia Law Review* 377, (1995).
15. For a discussion of folklore as cultural property, see *Glassie, Archaeology and Folklore: Common Anxieties, Common Hopes, in Historical, Archaeology and the Importance of Material Things* 23 (L. Ferguson ed. 1977).
16. John Henry Merryman "The Rentention of Cultural Property" 21 *UCLA DAVIS LAW Review* 477 (1988).
17. Bartram S. Brown, "Developing Countries in the International Trade Order", 14 *Northern Illinios University Law Review* 347. (1994).
18. The Bellagio Declaration March 11, 1993, *The International Journal of Cultural Property* (1995).

CHAPTER

# 5

# The Protection of Authorship as a Cultural Value

*As the pleasure of learning increase by constant application.*
*So the friendship of the worthy increasath by constent intercourse.*

—Thiruvalluvar, Thirukkural 783

*All books are divisible into two classes the books of the hour and the book of all time*

—John Ruskin

## I. AUTHORSHIP AS A CULTURAL VALUE

Regardless of the form, all intellectual property, as "products of the mind", must be created by human intervention (even if that intervention is the creation of a machine which then creates the intellectual property in question). The decision to protect intellectual property, and the nature and scope of such protection, reflects the value that a particular culture place upon the creative act. The role of the author/artist becomes imbued with a variety of historical, philosophical and cultural values that have a direct bearing on the amount of protection afforded the author's work. This phase begins with an examination of the evolving view of "authorship" in the pantheon of protection-worthy values. In order to highlight the cultural value issues behind the protection of authorship, we then turn to the philosophical historical and economic underpinnings behind the debate over the protection of *droit morale* (moral rights). *Droit morale* are rights granted to authors in compensation and protection of the act of creation. These rights generally exist in addition to any copyright or neighboring rights granted. Droit morale consists of four basic rights—the right of publication, the right of paternity, the right of integrity, and the right of withdrawal. This phase explores the precise grant of rights provided under various moral rights regimes. It also includes discussions regarding the role which moral rights protection plays in the censorship of "undesirable" creations and the impact of moral rights on diverse categories of protectable works. Since a natural corollary to the issue of an author's "moral" rights is an artist's right to enjoy the economic benefits of resale royalties (droit de suite), it includes several excerpts discussing *droit de suite* and the Visual Artists Act. legislation. We end with a brief discussion of the role of intellectual property in protecting "culture".

## 2. THE PROTECTION OF AUTHORSHIP PERSONALITY

It is said that the overarching object of the international copyright laws is to encourage the widest possible production and dissemination of literary, musical, and *artistic works.*[1] This theme, sounded repeatedly by the modern Supreme Court, was also the basis for pre-constitutional copyright statutes enacted by the original states. Those statutes were intended to "encourage persons of learning and genius to publish their writings, which may do honor to their country and service to mankind."[2] By conferring the privilege of a limited term monopoly on creators of literary and artistic works, copyright law seeks to afford them a fair return on their creative efforts. This should, in turn, increase the likelihood that they will produce and disseminate those works. Copyright is thus a mechanism for strengthening our society by encouraging the free flow of ideas. It is intended to guarantee, rather than thwart, public access to the thoughts and expressions of others. As noted by the late Professor Melvile Nimmer, "implicit in this rationale is the assumption that in the absence of such public benefit the grant of a copyright monopoly to individuals would be unjustified. "After this "monopoly" has lapsed, creative works enter the public domain and are free for all to use or reproduce as they choose.

In furtherance of this dissemination-oriented policy, the law provides that almost all interests in copyright are fully alienable. Furthermore, the employers (or certain commissioning parties) of creative artists are deemed to own all copyright interests in works made for hire from the moment of their creation. This thorough system of alienability of copyright interests ensures that the progress of creative expression into the marketplace will be unimpeded when a willing buyer encounters a willing seller.

The rights of publication are multidimensional. They include the right to refuse to create, and the "absolute right to decide when (and whether) a work of art is complete, and when (and whether) to show it to the public.[3] With this "divulgation" right, "the author [has] complete authority over the decision to publish, sell, unveil, or by any other means make his work public."[4]

The sovereignty of the artist over a work until she chooses to disclose it under French law is best illustrated by *L'affaire Rouault,* a case in which an art dealer kept 806 canvasses of the painter Rouault locked in his room. From time to time, Rouault would visit to put finishing touches on the paintings. Upon the dealer"s death, his heirs claimed ownership of the works, but because Rouault claimed the works to be unfinished, the court held that ownership had never passed to the dealer. Stating that "the painter remains master of his work, and may perfect it, modify it, or even leave it unfinished if he loses all hope of making it worthy of himself", the court ordered that the paintings be returned to Rouault provided he repay to the heirs advances the dealer had paid him.[5] The divulgation right has been expanded in recent decades in France, Germany, and Japan for example, to encompass the positive right of an author to prevent others from suppressing her work against her will.

Opponents of "moral rights" argue that these European doctrines are, in general, "alien" ideas fundamentally inimical to the purposes and foundations of American copyright law. While "moral rights" doctrines are based on natural law principles and are designed to protect the personality interests of the creative artist, American copyright law is "not primarily designed to provide a special private benefit" to creative artists, but to encourage the dissemination of these works to the public. Opponents claim that the adoption of moral rights doctrines would. Upset the intellectural property and tangible property interests of non-creator copyright owners and skew the natural balance of risk and reward between creative and financial contributors to creative works. They are particularly troubled by the right of withdrawal and the right to object to the contet in which an artist's work is presented. Recognition of the latter, for instance, could permit artists to prohibit "improper interpretive borrowing and adaptation of their creations." In short, opponents argue that recognition of the "moral rights" of artists in the developed as well as developing countries would ultimately discourage the dissemination of creative works to the public.[6]

The economic reasoning supporting this conclusion is straightforward. If authors retain inalienable personal rights in their creations, buyers will pay less for the works because they are restricted to purchasing a truncated bundle of property rights in those works. This reduced remuneration would not only injure artists, but would also, the reasoning goes, have the aggregate effect of reducing incentives for artists to create, thus reducing the availability of creative works to the public. The wholesale adoption of "moral rights" doctrines could therefore tremendously destabilize the country's very lucrative, yet very risky, entertainment industries.

Professor Robert Gorman sets forth the critics' position on this issue most persuasively:

> The principal entertainment and cultural industries of the United States are highly collaborative. They contemplate and depend upon a wide variety of derivative forms in their

> distribution to the public, and are historically regulated by individually and collectively negotiated agreements. The introduction into these industries of a right—exercisable by any one of a host of collaborative contributors—to protest the alleged distortion or modification of a particular literary or artistic contribution is extremely problematic. At best, it introduces an element of instability and uncertainty, as well as the frequent possibility, because of the increased threat of litigation, of delay in public access to and enjoyment of entertainment vehicles. At worst, it threatens to prevent altogether the dissemination to the United States and international public of a host of cultural and entertainment materials in forms that are varied, appealing and affordable. Any significant limit upon the ability of producers and publishers to disseminate works in these secondary markets—dissemination which commonly can mean the difference between a losing and a profitable business venture—runs a substantial risk of chilling investment in the arts and entertainment fields. This may in turn reduce the financial support of an innovative creative endeavour—a result that will obviously be harmful to the public interest. Introduction of moral rights into these industries (particularly if these rights are statutorily declared to be inalienable and non-waivable) will also unsettle the network of contractual agreements that have been developed over many years in the various industries and that appear on the whole to be working quite successfully and fairly.[7]

Other critics object to the expansion of moral rights in this country on non-economic grounds. Many moral rights advocates wish to protect not only the physical integrity of artworks, but also the contextual "integrity" of literary, musical, and dramatic works by preventing "improper interpretive borrowing and adaptation of artists' intellectual creations."[8] Critics consequently charge that "moral rights advocates are taking, if unwittingly, a position of cultural conservatism, inhibited expression, and unnecessary deference to creators' intensions."[9] Moral rights could be used as "a charter for private censorship,"[10] in direct conflict with the purposes and functioning of the American copyright system.

## 3. THE US VIEW OF AUTHORSHIP

There is precedent in American law for singling out artistic works for special treatment. Even though American law has generally viewed artistic works as property, it has treated them as a special kind of property. The United States Supreme Court made this point as early as 1834 in *Wheaton* v. *Peters*. When it held that an author's natural property right to the fruits of his labour was realized by the sale or transfer of the material object when it was first published, and that any property rights held by the author there-after derived from federal statutory protection under the copyright clause of the United States constitution. The constitution provided for and congress enacted legislation to confer property status in products that had no claim for such protection under the leading theory of the day. Not only were products of the mind treated specially, but distinctions were made within this category that resulted in separate branches of the law, such as copyright and patent law. Thus, "writings" were distinguished from "discoveries." Indeed, a legislative distinction was made between "works of authorship" and useful articles. These distinctions reflect the view that different principles are at work and that not al products of the human mind need be included in the right of personality.[12]

The Copyright Act of 1976 manifests the unique nature of "original works of authorship" even when they are considered aspects. Despite the fact that copyright is classified as personal property, it is a peculiar form of personal property indeed.

The reason for the special treatment accorded "original works of authorship" is traceable to the promotion of artistic creativity, and it has been traditionally recognized that personality protection has been an important factor in this regard. The right of disclosure is a case in point. As early as 1849, in *Prince Albert* v. *Strange,*[13] the personal aspect of the right of first publication in common law was noted. In the 1969 case if *Estate* of *Hemingway* v. *Random House,*[14] the New York Court of Appeals not only reaffirmed this principle but also noted the link between personal and economic interests. Despite the virtual abolition of common-law copyright by the 1976 Act, the United States Supreme Court recently reiterated in *Harper & Row* v. *Nation Enterprises*[15] the personal aspect of the right of first publication and pointed out the interrelationship between the economic and the personal aspects of the right and freedom of speech.

## 4. THE EC VIEW OF AUTHORSHIP

On 29 October, 1993, the Council of Ministers adopted a Directive harmonizing the term of protection of copyright and certain related rights. The Directive fixes the duration of protection to the highest existing level in any Member State: life of the author plus 70 years for most copyright works, and 50 years from execution, fixation or publication for performers and producers' rights. It contains special provisions regarding films in it Articles 2 and 3.[16]

Article 2, headed "cinematographic or audio-visual work," specifies that the principal director of such work is to be regarded as its author or one of its authors, Member States being free to designate other co-authors [Article 2(1)].

The Present assumption under UK copyright is that the producer is the sole author of a film.

Cinematographic and audio-visual works are not given protection as such, but through the copy right on their recording, that is, the "film" under Section 5(1) of the Copyright, Designs and Patents Act, 1998. The producer is granted authorship of this film by Section 9(2) of the Act. Accordingly, since the author of the film is the "person by whom the arrangements necessary for the making of the film are undertaken," the question of joint authorship in the film can only arise among co-producers. In other words, the director and authors of the component elements (script, scenario, music, decor and soon) are deprived of any copyright interest in the final cinematographic or audio-visual work.

Creators of the contributory works are nevertheless given separate copyrights in their contributions, each measured by reference the life of the individual author.

Who then should be considered the author of the dramatic audio-visual work embodied in the film? Under Section 9 of the CDPA, the author of the dramatic work is its creator. In this respect, UL law is back to its pre-1956 state. It seems clear that the director will qualify as author of the audio-visual work: "Since a director is almost always responsible for the manner in which a film is shot, it is he would supply the film with its original character and therefore be the author of the dramatic work." The Question of the other contributors is too complex to be fully answered here, but I would argue that being the creator of a component of a larger composite work is not sufficient under UK copyright to claim joint authorship in the whole, roughly, joint authorship implies that contributors work in collaboration and the part contributed by each author is not distinct in the final work. Hence the script or scenario writer is probably the only contributor who will almost always meet these conditions. According to the same principle, it is unlikely that under UK copyright the musical composer or the creator of the decor would be considered as a co-author. The question of there contributors like the editor or the director of photography remains to large extent open, their situation depending on their input in the final work and on the creative freedom they are given by the director.

### (a) The Moral Rights Debate

France is normally held up as the model for moral rights law, but many Western European civil law countries espouse the doctrine, with some variation. The doctrine's origin is entirely judicial, perhaps unusual in a legal system that stresses legislative over judicial lawmaking.[17]

There are four basic rights that constitute the droit moral; not all systems recognize all of them. They are: the right of publication (droit de divulgation), the right of paternity (droit de paternite or droit au respect dunom, the right of integrity (droit de respect de l'oeuvre), and the right of withdrawal (droit de repentir or de retrait). Each of these rights is compound, each consisting itself of a small bundle of rights.

The right of publication is the right of the author to choose whether or not to present her work to the public. As one author notes, it protects the artist from having her "lack of inspiration considered to be a breach of contract."[18]

The right of paternity is the right to claim authorship of one's work, to prevent others from unjustly claiming authorship, and to prevent having one's name falsely associated with another's work. The right of paternity includes the right to publish pseudonymous.

The right of integrity includes the "right to authorize or prohibit any modification of [the author's] work",[19] and to protect against distortion of the work. It also includes the right to prevent mutilation of or derogatory action toward the work. This was the right at issue in the Buffet case, where the buyer of a refrigerator painted by Bernard Buffet attempted to sell the individual painted panels of refrigerator separately; the court enjoined the sale.

The right of withdrawal is the least exercised moral right. Its formal existence is rare outside France and countries that derive their law from France. There is wider recognition of a right to make corrections, particularly in later editions. The author may be required to pay damages when he withdraws a work from circulation, as is clearly the case in Spain. The right of withdrawal may exist in common law countries, but only under compelling circumstances and in very limited cases. Even French commentators question the efficacy of the right of withdrawal.

While there is universal recognition of the author's right "to affirm his paternity in a work, or to defend his integrity in it," there are two approaches to enforcement of these rights. The civil law countries of Latin America, Africa, and East Asia spell out the right with particularity in their copyright laws, while the common law countries generally leave moral rights to the protection of the courts. Statutory recognition of moral rights has grown, however, in India, Israel, and other nations have adopted moral rights legislation within their copyright law, which the United States has adopted the Visual Artists Rights Act, and Australia has undertaken consideration of moral rights.

The countries that protect the right of divulgation as part of copyright law are civil law counties and countries whose law derives from the civil law. The right is apparently widely respected, with variation as to extent and statutory wording. Common law countries provide or secrecy, and through the refusal to specifically enforce personal service contracts.

Fewer countries, as noted above, recognize the right of withdrawal. Only France and countries deriving their law from France protect it extensively. Some other countries, including Spain, which historically adopted the French model in many respects, adopt a more limited right to make changes or corrections. Moreover, some countries only require the publication of a new edition.

The right of retraction, to fully cancel an assignment of rights to publish, is the least recognized of the four moral rights. The method of executing the right is seldom detailed in statutory law. In all countries recognizing the right, the author must pay full compensation. Indeed, in Spain, for example, if the author later decides to publish the work, she must offer it to the original assignee on the original terms.

### (b) Human Rights Bodies Gear-up on TRIPS

There has been a flurry of activity by international human rights bodies on the issues of intellectual property rights and the WTO-TRIPS Agreement—the agreement on Trade-Related Aspects of Intellectual Property Rights, which entered into force in 1995 as part of the World Trade Organization (WTO) Agreement. In recent months, the following events have occurred:

At its sessions in August 2000, the UN Sub-Commission on the Promotion and Protection of Human Rights adopted a resolution on "Intellectual Property Rights and Human Rights" (E/CN.4/Sub. 2/2000/7);

At that same session, the Sub-Commission reviewed a preliminary report presented by its Special Reporters on globalization and its full impact on human rights; in the report, state that the implications of patenting, especially of plant varieties and life forms, are serious for the issue of food security and represent "outright piracy and appropriation of nature's bounty which has been designated for the whole of humanity and not for a privileged and technologically advanced few";

On 19th August, 2000 a joint informal workshop was held by the UN Committee on Economic. Social and Cultural Rights (CESCR) and the International NGO Committee on Human Rights in Trade and Investment (INCHRITI) which dealt, in part, with intellectual property and human rights, focusing particularly on the TRIPS Agreement;

The CESCR has committed itself and held a general discussion on intellectual property and human rights on 27 November 2000, in Geneva, and led to the drafting of a "General Comment" by the Committee on this topic. A "General Comment" by the Committee is an authoritative legal interpretation of the relevant articles of the International Covenant on Economic, Social and Cultural Rights (ICESCR).

In a paper presented at a panel discussion on "Intellectual Property and Human Rights", Organized by the World Intellectual Property Organization (WIPO) in November 1998, Dr. Peter Drahos had already made the observation that Intellectual Property Rights (IPRs), being subject to adjustment according to economic circumstance and generally limited in duration, lack the characteristics of fundamental human rights. As subordinate or "instrumental" rights.

Dr. Drahos suggested that IPRs "should serve the interest and needs that citizens identify through the language of human rights as being fundamental. On this view, human rights would guide the development of intellectual property rights; intellectual property rights would be pressed into service on behalf of human rights. "It is precisely because information has become the primary resource, he said, that exploitation of information through the exercise of IPRs affects interests that are the subject of human rights claims.

Dr. Drahos concluded by noting that "the development of intellectual property policy and law has been dominated by an epistemic community comprised largely of technically minded lawyers", and he called for a dialogue between the human rights community and the intellectual property community.

The extraordinary level of activity by international human rights bodies on this rather technical aspect on international economic law is founded on increasingly widespread concerns in human rights circles abut the social impacts of the enhanced regime of intellectual property rights protection under TRIPS.

Other aspects of the TRIPS Agreement which have raised serious human rights concerns are the following:

1. The implementation of the TRIPS Agreement has resulted in the restriction of access to patented pharmaceuticals for citizens of developing countries, as has been highlighted by analysis by the World Health Organization, Medicines sans Frontiers and others, raising obvious implications for the enjoyment of the right to health.
2. The "pirating" of indigenous and traditional knowledge and designs for commercial exploitation by others pursuant to intellectual property rights, shown to be contrary to human rights law in established jurisprudence, is nevertheless flourishing under the TRIPS regime. Unlike the Convention of Biological Diversity and the ICESCR, the TRIPS Agreement does not explicitly protect the interests of indigenous and local communities.
3. The establishment and expansion of plant variety rights and intellectual property protection of genetically modified organisms hold serious implications for food security, and the enjoyment of the right to food.
4. Stronger intellectual property protection under TRIPS also tends to impede technology transfer to developing countries, particularly through the

imposition of higher prices for protected technologies, thereby presenting an obstacle to the universal right to enjoy the benefits of scientific progress and its applications, and to the realization of the right to development.

5. The larger ethical issues surrounding human genome mapping and patenting also carry implications for the human right to self-determination.

Intellectual property law is founded upon the attempt to balance the interests of the originator/author—or Intellectual Property Rights (IPR) holder—with those of the consumer and the general public. A human rights analysis help to sharpen the view, shared by some sectors of the intellectual property law community, that implementation of the TRIPS Agreement has upset that balance in favour of IPR holders. A human rights analysis also assures that the differential impact of the TRIPS Agreement (which is largely gender insensitive) on men and women will be taken into account, as will the impacts on vulnerable sectors of society such as children, indigenous people, marginal farmers and rural agricultural labourers.

The current levels of activity on this issue in the UN human rights bodies and civil society organizations shown that they are intent upon making their voices heard, initiating monitoring mechanisms of the TRIPS impacts and review and injecting a human rights perspective into this policy discussion.

We are hopefully moving towards a time when there will be more coherent international policy making agenda, for all areas that have human rights and environmental implications. In such a context the active participation of the international human rights community, in the ongoing review of the WTO agenda, is a welcome development.[20]

## 5. INCLUDED RIGHTS

### (a) The Right of Disclosure

The right of disclosure is based upon the notion that

only the artist can possess any rights in an uncompleted work. This right therefore gives the artist control over his work from the time of creation. Furthermore this right encompasses the artist's right to decide whether a work corresponds to the artist's original conception, at what moment the work is completed, and whether the work is worthy of the artist. The American analog of this right is found in copyright law, which protects the "right of first sale" and the "right of first publication" as soon as the work is fixed in any tangible medium of expression.[21]

**(b) The Right of Paternity**

The right of paternity safeguards a creator's right to have name attached to her work. The derivation of this right is founded upon the injection of the artist's creative personality into her work, thus vesting her right to claim authorship. Generally this right is perpetual, unassignable, and is not barred by statutes of limitation. Moreover, the right of paternity protects against falsely attaching an artist's name to a work she did not create. American courts have not expressly recognized the right of paternity but have granted similar relief on other theories.[22]

**(c) The Right of Integrity**

The right of integrity is also known as the right to modify and to prevent deformation. This right prohibits the modification, alteration, or distortion of an artist's work without her permission. The right of integrity, just as the right of paternity, is generally perpetual, unassignable, and free from any statute of limitation. The laws of the United States do not expressly protect an artist's right to integrity. However, American legal protection has been found in the Lanham Act and specific state statutes.[23]

**(d) The Right of Withdrawal**

The right of withdrawal permits the author to retrieve her work even though it has been sold or published. When this right is granted, an artist can recall her creation if she experiences a change of heart from that which originally provided her inspiration for the work. However, the artist will usually be required to compensate the individual in possession for any loses that the renunciation might cause. The right of withdrawal is founded on the assumption that the public will forget works to which it has previously been exposed. This assumption has caused many commentators to doubt the viability of this right. Where the right of withdrawal is recognized, however, it is generally limited to literary works. The United States does not recognize the right of withdrawal in any form.[24]

## 6. THE BERNE DEFINITION

Article 6bis of the Berne Convention of 1886 provides *linter alia*:

> Independently of the author's economic rights, and even after the transfer of the said rights, the author shall have the right to claim authorship of work and to object to any distortion, mutilation or other derogatory action in relation to, the said work, which would be prejudicial to his honour or reputation.[25]

Paragraph 1 of Article 6bis of the Berne Convention protects the rights of paternity and integrity. Moral rights protection was introduced into the Berne Convention in 1928, and was slightly amended in 1967. While the rights are separate from and not transferred with the copyright, they are not clearly inalienable. The rights of divulgation and withdrawal are not included in Berne. Under the second paragraph of Article 6bis, moral rights must last at least as long as the economic rights, but countries that did not provide moral rights protection prior to acceding to the convention are excepted from this requirement. In those countries, protection need only last until the author's death.

The third paragraph of the article provides that enforcement of the provision is to be through the national law "of the country where protection is claimed." Thus, an American being sued for violation in Israel of moral rights should be subject to Israeli law. An American being sued in

Israel for a violation of American copyright law should be subject to American law.

One can envision a number of moral rights regimes, each allocating the costs and risks differently. A system that does not recognize moral rights imposes the cost by default on the author, who takes the risk that an unscrupulous user will damage her reputation by misattribution or by distortion of her work. This does not allow risk-averse authors to accept lower sums for a guarantee of no infringement of moral rights. A system that provides uncertain recognition (as in the United States) allows some degree of bargaining over risk; but in all probability, except for authors with substantial bargaining power, the risk will non-etheless be placed on the author, who will be insufficiently compensated for accepting it. A system that allows for full-recognition of moral rights but also for assignment or waiver by contract would similarly keep risks on authors who lack sufficient bargaining power to refuse waiver or those who seek increased payment for shouldering the risk. However, the costs to the user, both in compensation to the author and transaction costs, will be somewhat higher, since such waiver must be bargained for expressly. Finally, a system that provides inalienable and unwaivable moral rights places the cost of violation squarely and solely on the user, but does not allow the possibility of increased rents for the risk-accepting author.

Where moral rights are a default rule subject to negotiation and the parties have equal bargaining power, the author will demand a higher price for assuming the risk of violation, or accept a lower one for placing the risk on the user. The price will reflect the cost of the possible damage and the degree of risk.

Most authors, however, probably do not possess bargaining power equal to that of the user. In that case, as also where such rights are uncertain, the user can force the author to bear a disproportionate part of the risk and cost of violation. Thus, it would seem that, in the absence of equal bargaining power between authors and users, inalienable and unwaivable moral rights are the only ones that fully prevent users from externalizing the costs of infringement. However, while inalienable and unwaivable rights protect the weak or risk-averse author, they reduce the possible return to the risk accepting author. It may be that allowing waiver or alienation of the moral right would result in the greatest net gain over all authors, risk-accepting and risk-averse.

Many non-European countries, developing or newly industrialized, joined the Berne Union shortly after gaining independence. Several commentators suggest, however, that the decision to accede to Berne was frequently the result of pressure to join from former colonial rulers. These countries only belatedly realized that the high level of protection that the Berne Convention required was ill-suited to their needs for, among others, inexpensive educational material. Their concerns led to the negotiations that culminated in the Appendix to the Berne Convention adopted in Paris in 1971. However , they apparently never objected to the moral rights provisions of the Berne Convention.

Moral rights laws serve to protect national authors against damage by other nationals, as in Mannu Bhandari, and by foreigners, as in Qimron. Moral rights require indigenous industries to operate at a higher level of sophistication that would otherwise be the case. Although the cost of producing works thereby increases, suggesting lower production, the lower risks to authors might induce more to publish for reduced payment demands. In addition, some exteralities might also be viewed as justification, such as improved reputation of indigenous authors and publishers outside the country. It seems likely that the importance of the indigenous protection rationale increases in proportion to the growth of copyright industries.

## 7. HISTORICAL AND PHILOSOPHICAL DEVELOPMENT

### (a) Monist *v.* Dualist

The history of moral right in copyright statutes does not much antedate the 1928 Rome Revision of the Berne Convention on copyright. Until that time moral right was judge-made law. Most legal scholars begin their discussion of moral right's genesis by referring to French judgments of the nineteenth century. Some scholars go further in their investigation of moral right, tracing the principle's history from pre-Christian times to the present day. Until the end of the Middle Ages, however, author's rights generally were limited to a ban on plagiarism and it was not until the eighteenth century that the notion of moral right as it is now understood even began to be discussed.[26]

In France, prior to the French Revolution, virtually all rights in intellectual property were conferred by the Sovereign. The revolution led to an abolishment of this royal privilege and the French copyright laws of 1971 and 1793 affirmed the existence of writers' pecuniary rights as distinct from an authors' pecuniary right, did not receive statutory recognition; however, it arose from the spirit of these laws and from the philosophy of individualism which infused the French Revolution particularly, and Romanticism Generally.

In German, during the nineteenth century, a debate arose between Joseph Kohler and Alfted Gierke as to the composition of moral right. Kohler argued that moral right was distinct from the exploitative rights an authors had in his or her work, while Gierke argued that moral right was an aspect of the exploitative right. The former "dualist" view prevailed in France to be embodied in the law of 11 March 1957. The latter "monist view triumphed in Germany and is now articulated in the West German law of 9 September 1965. Nevertheless, the thrust of both these laws is a comprehensive protection of both the author's rights are inalienable.

Neither England nor the United States accord express recognition of moral right in their respective copyright acts.

### (b) Natural Rights Economic Rights and Personality

One can hardly begin a study of droitmoral without pausing to observe the inexhaustible reverence with which French jurists approach the subject of author's rights. Pierre Recht accurately has observed, "When droit moral fanatics discuss moral rights, they take the attitude of a religious zealot talking of sacred things, or a Girondin reading the Declaration of the Rights of Man."[27] Perhaps one reason for this sentiment is that French scholars regard the droit d'auteur as a natural right, deeply rooted in the principles of the French Revolution from which modern French jurisprudence emerged. Indeed, scholars have sought the origins of droit moral in the earliest periods of recorded history. Until the end of the Middle Ages, however, recognition of authors' rights generally was limited to a ban on plagiarism, and it was not until the eighteenth century that the notion of *droit d'auteur,* as it is now known, came into being.

During the Ancient Regime virtually all rights in an intellectual work were conferred by the sovereign, and generally were bestowed upon printers. Rights in books went scarcely beyond a monopoly on the reproduction of the work for a fixed term, and did not even include a right to sell the work. Voltaire, in 1769, grumbled that druggists, by comparison, at least could sell their own concoctions freely.[28]

Yet, even before the French Revolution and its emergent "natural right" concept of droit d'auteur, important principles of modern civil law were debated in France. As early as 1725, it was argued that an author had a perpetual property interest in his unpublished manuscript. Consequently, in the two decades preceding the French Revolution, various ordinances and decrees were published, which defined more explicitly the prerogatives of editors and publishers, and affirmed the existence of perpetual interests of writers 'emanating from the Creative activity of the author."[29]

During the French Revolution, jurists sought to abolish any notion that *droit d'auteur* was a royal privilege. Early legislation eased the freedom to perform plays in public, and confirmed the authors' exploitative rights, based on the notion that these rights were inherent in the artist. The *droits patrimoniaux* at last were enunciated in the law of 19-24 juillet 1793. Although they—like American copyright—were primarily pecuniary rights, they expressed the principle that *droit d'auteur* was not merely a privilege of the sovereign, as in the Ancient Regime, but it was, rather, a natural right, arising simply from the authors' act of creation.[30]

*Droit moral,* on the other hand, emerged not from statute, but from judicially created doctrines, which developed slowly in the nineteenth century, and more rapidly in the twentieth. But droit moral, too, arose from the spirit of these laws, and from the philosophy of individualism which accompanied the French Revolution.

Scholars divide the history of droit moral into three periods; the first from 1793 to 1878; the second from 1878 to 1902; and the third from 1902 to 1957. During the first period, French scholars began to debate the "property" nature of an author's rights. Gastambide and his followers in the 1830's held to the traditional notion that *droit d'auteur* was a property right, albeit a temporary one. On the other hand, Renouard and his school, influenced by Kant, preferred to dislodge author's rights from the notion of property, and considered them instead to derive from a more abstract "right of personality. Recht observes that opposition to the "property" characterization of *droit d'auteur* grew even stronger with the early influence of Marx in the 1840's and 1850's, and by the 1860's, a generation of "personalist" writers emerged, who strongly discredited the idea that *droit d'auteur* was a from of property.[31]

It should come as no surprise, than that during this first period, the notion that there may exist non-property "moral" rights could easily gain acceptance in French courts. By 1880, the foundations had been laid in French jurisprudence for *droit de divulgation, droit a lapternite,* and *droit au respect del'oeure.*

The doctrine of *droit moral* received even greater development in the second period, from 1878 to 1902. In this period, the application of traditional notions of property to *droit d'aiteir* was virtually abandoned, and scholars continued to search for a more precise characterization of droit moral, and of its place in the larger *droit d'auteur*. Some French scholars, led by pouillet, tended to hold into fragments of the property notion of *droit d'auteur,* and developed a theory of "intellectual property," by which *droit d'auteur,* combined certain elements of property with elements of purely personal or intellectual rights.

However, the central debate over the nature of authors' right arose in Germany. Joseph Kohler developed a theory of "Doppelrecht," which considered an intellectual work to be a "been immaterial," from which various rights of personality arose.[32] These personal prerogatives could be separated into two distinct categories of either a patrimonial or a moral nature. The other principal view, advocated by Alfred Gierke, considered both personal and patrimonial rights to be inseparable parts of a single *"personlickkeitsrecht.*[33]

It was in the third period, from 1902 to 1957, that the debate over these two views became resolved. Kohler's "dialist" view triumphed in France, where to this day, *droit d'auteur* is considered to be a right of *"propriete incorporelle"* separable into moral and patrimonial rights. In Germany, the monist school prevailed, and as a result, moral rights ("Urheberpersonlickkitsrecht") and exploitative interests form a single rights, which expires seventy years after the author's death.

We see, then, that *droit d'auteur* is part of a larger debate over the meaning of "property" and "personality" rights in the Civil Law system. The debate, in fact, engendered two systems of authors' rights with different characterization of *droit moral*—each purporting to be as vigilant of the authors' well-being as the other.

One the whole, however, artists' rights receive less respect under the American system than they do in France. *Droit de retrait* and *droit de repentir,* although their value is at best questionable, barely exist at all in the United States. The first category of *droit a la paternite*—the right to claim authorship of one's own creation—is underdeveloped in this country, and *droit au respect,* which is considered by the French to be the very essence of an artist's prerogative, is only in its infancy.

Furthermore, whatever moral rights do exist in the United States receive for less weight than they do in France, and although this difference ultimately may reflect only a discrepancy in social status between French and American artists, it also is rooted in legal realities. In the United States, author's rights may more readily be waived, and they generally cease to exist upon the author's death. This contrasts markedly with the "personal, perpetual, inalienable and unassignable" character of *droit moral.* And in the United States, a contract between the artist and the transferee of his rights is presumed to be the repository of all of the artist's remaining rights in his work; French law will more readily look beyond contractual obligations in order to assert the artist's moral rights.

Thus, the French concept of *droit moral,* indeed all of *droit d'auteur,* is for more idealistic than any Americannoytion of author's rights. It proceeds from a romantic idea of the artist and his work; it treats artists as a special class of laborers, and art works as a special category of property; and at least in theory, it defends artist's rights even against the contract or property interests of third parties.

Within the conception of *droit d'auteur,* droit moral takes on a transcendent, even spiritual quality, which even its own name reveals.

In the United States, on the other hand, the protection of artist's rights beyond copyright has developed on more pragmatic and democratic basis. American law refuses to recognize artists as a special class, and insists on a more equitable balance between the interests of artists and the interests of others who are involved in the exploitation, publication, or adaptation of works of art. Furthermore, American law characterizes the artist's work more as an object of commerce than as a product of the spirit and the artist's rights of personality in his work generally must be protected by the same legal language which would be applied to any commercial venture.

**(c) Alienability and the Marketplace**

The French Law provides for the author's right of divulgation or first disclosure and the right of withdrawal or modification of an already disclosed work in addition to the . . . rights of "paternity"[34] (attribution and integrity).

"Only the author can decide whether his work corresponds to his original conception, at what moment it is completed, and whether it is worthy of him."[35] Under the French statute the right of first disclosure is included in the moral rights regime; because moral rights are inalienable and perpetual in French law, this obtains even where economic rights or the material object itself has been transferred and can be enforced by the author's successors.

French law provides that despite a work's completion and a full assignment of rights or reproduction, exhibition, and performance he author retains "right of modification or withdrawal as against the assignee."[36] This right is subject to indemnification for authors to invoke the right, since it applies only to publishing contracts (i.e., it is "incorporeal" and does not attach to a physical object transferred).

French law protects the right to be recognized as the creator of a work, or to have it discloses anonymously or under a pseudonym. The author has a right of action against false attribution of her work to another, and a right to prevent use of her name on work she did not create or on works she did create but which have been mutilated.

The right of integrity arises when the work is marketed, sold or is subject to a contract or publication or performance. "From that time on the author has the right to insist that its integrity must not be violated by measures which could alter or distort it.[37] Special problems arise in the case of adoption of a work, e.g., for film or television, where the adaptor's original creation is itself protected. Outright destruction of the work has been found within the scope of the right in France. The French law succinctly requires "respect for [the author's] name, his authorship and his work.[38]

The right of action under the moral rights regimes has traditionally been limited to the author or her successor, even though a public interest in maintaining the integrity of cultural works in often given as one rationale for protection. The French law extremely "personalist", specifying that the right is attached to the person of the author Italy's 1941 statute provides for enforcement by "competent State authority, "while Germany eschewed such a provision in its post-war legislation apparently out of nervousness about state supervision of culture.[39]

California pioneered a public interest regime for moral rights protection with its art preservation enactments of 1979 and 1982.[40] The Preamble to California Art Preservation Act cites both protection of the author's reputation and preservation of the integrity of cultural and artistic property as objectives. It protects rights to claim or to disclaim authorship and prohibits alteration or destruction, limiting this protection to "fine art" or "recognized quality," as in the opinion of expert witnesses including "artists, art dealers, collectors of fine art, curators of art museums, and other persons involved with the creation or marketing of fine art." The 1982 enactment provides for litigation of the rights by public or private non-profit interest groups. The regime permits an express written waiver of the rights by the artist, and it does not extend to an injurious association of the work or other "derogatory action." "New York's law is oriented primarily to the protection of the artist's reputation and is limited to public display. It does not contain the controversial "recognized quality" requirement.[41]

Different national legislatures have resolved the issues differently. France and the United States have formulated their copyright legislation on the property analogy, while moral rights are grounded in the theory of personality rights. This resulted in a "dualist" theory with both philosophical and practical ramifications. Germany, apparently for purely philosophical reasons, adopted personality rights as the single basis for both its copyright law and creator's moral rights; a "monist" legal framework.

As a practical result, French dualism freed the judiciary to develop the droit moral in comparative isolation from contractual and public policy issues arising from the grant of exploitive rights. Thus moral rights in France are, in theory at least "personal perpetual, inalienable, and unassignable." The rights inhere in the natural person of the creator of the work, and not in the work itself. Inalienability is considered by some proponents to be the transcendent principle of moral right, so that any contract for transfer of them will be in principle unenforceable, Perpetuity is accompanied by providing that the moral rights which do not require the author's personal will and judgment, such as modification, may be passed by will to the author's heirs. The foundation of the moral rights in the creative personality.

> Is a profoundly romantic characterization of the artist, perhaps conjuring-up visions of poets in garrets, burning their lyric masterpieces for heat in the icy Parisian winter, or of Walt Whitman, crying out to the corporeal world, "I celebrate

> myself, and sing myself." Yet it is because of this characterization of the author and his at that French law feels a need to protect the honor of the author's personality and the integrity of his work. The author has, in a sense, made a gift of his creative genius to the world; in return, he has a right—a moral right—to expect that society respect his creative genius.[42]

By contrast, German theory rejected the essential distinction between exploitation rights and moral rights, building its entire copyright regime on the Kantian theory of expressive work as an extension of the creative personality. Where the French law provides for unqualified transfer of copyright as a form of "property" and maintains droit moral as perpetual and inalienable rights of personality. German monism required tailoring both moral rights and contractual assignment of commercial rights to fit a unified legislative scheme. German law compromised perpetuity of the moral rights by limiting them to its "life plus seventy years" term of copyright protection, and it compromised the free alienation of pecuniary rights by restricting inter vivos transfer to specific editions or series of performances rather than outright assignment of a copyright.

To bring the idea of culture into *the theory of moral rights* requires reexamining its premise that source of creative work is in the "inviolable personality." The right of personality describes creative activity in terms of an entirely private expression of the self in the material object. Creative activity is considered the physical embodiment or result of the exercise of the individual will, whether formulated in terms of Romantic enthusiasm of Kantian principle. The expressionist theory leaves the source, the motivation, and the structure of "creativity" in the realm of subjectivity, consistent with the abstract freedom of choice of the free subject in liberal social theory. What is missing in this characterization of creative activity—as purely private in its expressive aspect and purely commercial in public exchange—is the essence of the work as communication, as involving an exchange of communally accessible and valuable meaning, i.e. as symbolic exchange.

The law posits the created art work at a point of intersection between the inalienable right of the artist, for whom creation is a permanent and almost sacred self-expression, and the system of market exchange demanding that products be freely available for efficient allocation.

In effect, the theory of personal rights purports to give artists a special exemption from the exigencies of the market system. Yet, in so doing, these "legalized" moral rights seem to evoke and protect many important characteristics of the gift. The right of disclosure acknowledges the tactical significance of giving or withholding a gift at a particular time. The rights of attribution, anonymity and pseudonymity recognize the creator's perennial entitlement to the intangible cultural debt owed for the work. Rights of modification and retraction are also consistent with the continuing claim of the giver over the gift. Finally, legal protection of the work's integrity ensures that the "honour and reputation" of the giver will not be depreciated by mutilation of the work, maintaining the gift's "simultaneously material, social, and spiritual."[43] Nonetheless, these non-pecuniary interests in creative work, which were rooted in a rich collective appreciation of art work as a unique cultural gift, have been transplanted to the less nourishing soil of the general law. Now they take the form of the set of universal and abstract "moral rights," entitlements to which "everyone" is equally entitled in theory. The case law indicates they are highly problematic in practice. The difficulty in integrating moral rights with copyright within modern legal doctrine arises from the larger problem of defining the status of "art" and other creative work in our culture, and whether vesting moral rights exclusively in the author really address the ancient, prescriptive, public interests in authenticity and orthodoxy.

The theory of gift exchange defines the importance of the work in terms of the community's acknowledgement of a cultural contribution. As the law moves toward the recognition of public interest reflected in the California art preservation legislation, it inevitably moves away from the Kantian theory of moral rights as an aspect of the creator's freedom to define and pursue ends. In this view, moral rights reflect "economic" values which are embodied in cultural status entitlements rather than the paradigm of market relationships. Thus we can understand the intuition that some cultural products are "priceless", irreducible to the abstract equivalences of market valuation.

## 8. MORAL RIGHTS AND CENSORSHIP

### (a) Editorial Control

The principle of moral rights does not pertain to morality, instead, it defines a regime of legal rights that attach upon the creation of a copyrightable work by, among others, authors, photographers, illustrators, song writers, directors, and screenwriters. The Berne Convention describes moral rights in Article 6bis as: (1) the right to claim or disclaim paternity (attribution) of a work; (2) the right to object to distortion or mutilation of a work; and (3) the right to the creator's honor or reputation. Moral rights supplement existing economic rights which permit creators to profit from the performance, reproduction, or distribution of their works.[44]

Editorial control will be jeopardized by the ability of creators to object under Article 6bis to any editorial modifications. Newspaper and magazine editors must edit articles, crop photographs, and adapt illustrations extensively to conform with specified view-point, context, or space requirements. This process is undertaken within tight deadlines that demand instantaneous decisions Thus, editors can afford neither the time to obtain consent for specific uses of works nor to hesitate on decisions out of concern that they may subsequently be second-guessed in litigation. Broadcasters face similar challenges in the preparation of news programming. Broadcast and video editors must edit for content, advertising, time, sizing, and colorization reasons. The moral rights prohibition of distortion without the author's consent would ruin these industries and their ability to remain economically viable.

The radio and textbook publishing industries face a comparable but different moral rights dilemma under Article 6bis, the right to attribution. This requirement would obligate radio stations to credit composers and lyricists in addition to performers. The enormous encroachment on available airtime would impede programming and, at a minimum, irritate listeners. Textbook publishers have the same problems. Textbooks are generally researched, developed, and written by a team of scholars, writers, and editors. Each individual has a potential claim under the moral rights proviso to attribution. Thus, the added acknowledgement requirement undermines a carefully developed scheme.

The permutations and combinations of potential moral rights claims that confront these businesses is staggering. While a host of claims may not arise, it will take very few to claims may not arise, it will take very few to upset a complex and stable set of copyright relationships developed over two centuries. This disruption and uncertainty will inevitably cause editors and copyright owners to slow or change their procedures to the industry and public's detriment. In addition, they will be forced to accommodate challenges, or face subsequent objections in court at great expense and time. The litigation threat cannot be underestimated. The litigiousness of the United States is well-known and far greater than any Berne member nation. Furthermore, the prospect of litigating the highly subjective and volatile issue of what constitutes a moral rights violation is daunting.

The non-existence of legal standards for the moral rights question imposes an arduous burden on the courts and the media industry. The courts will have the unenviable task of determining whether an alteration to a film or manuscript is a mutilation or a judicious edit. The uncertainly and threat of inconsistent judicial outcomes, due to the lack of legal standards, will destroy the editing process. Additionally, as is the case with libel challenges, media attorneys will review editorial work for moral rights violations. Unlike libel law, however, with its clearly delineated, judicially mandated tests, practitioners will have to basis for determining moral rights violations and will rely on ad hoc subjective interpretations. The unpredictability of the outcome will chill editorial freedoms, and therefore presents an unacceptable proposition.

### (b) The Aesthetic "Veto"

Though surely the exception rather than the rule, the

suppression of creative works against an artist's will is not a purely hypothetical problem. The ongoing debate about the level of protection creative artists "moral rights" (recognized under the laws of many European nations) do and should receive under American law has brought to light the accounts of writers, photographers, and film-makers whose works have proven very susceptible to suppression by others. These stories indicate that not only are the moral rights" of artists—specifically, the right to divulge or to choose to make a work public—ill-protected under our copyright system, but that the distributional goals upon which that system is predicated are being thwarted.[45]

As a general matter, the owner of an object or "the owner of the copyright, if he pleases, may refrain from vending or licensing and content himself with simply exercising the right to exclude others from using his property."[46] The arbitrary exercise of this right could lead to suppression of creative works in a wide array of situations such that the work would never be seen by the public.

Legislatively mandating that such a broad "aesthetic veto" be placed in the hands of the artist, especially in the context of multiple artists engaged in collaborative works, would therefore mean that moral rights could be used as "a charter for private censorship.[47] Such results would conflict directly with the purposes and functioning of the American copyright system. Thus, these adverse consequences ought to be guarded against even if that entails the continued sacrifice of artists' noneconomic interests to the brutalities of the marketplace and the continued appearance, to other Berne nations, that the United States is less than enthusiastic about adherence to the Convention.

## 9. THE TREATMENT OF MORAL RIGHTS IN SELECTED COUNTRIES

### (a) The United Kingdom

"Moral rights" were never expressly incorporated into UK law until the Copyright, Designs and Patents Act, 1988 ("the 1988 Act") which, as for as "moral rights" are concerned, came into force on 1 August, 1989. Until that time there were one or two provisions in UK law (such as—43 Copyright Act, 1956) concerning "false attribution of authorship" which touched upon the subject matter of "moral rights," but nothing comprehensive or too specific. It was argued that torts, such as defamation or passing off, as will as contractual rights, were sufficient to protect authors in these circumstances, It has now been accepted, however, that these generalized protections are not enough.[48]

Chapter IV pt I of the 1988 Act identifies four kinds of "moral right."

(1) the right to be identified as author of a copyright literary, dramatic, musical or artistic work, or, as, the case may be, as the director of a copyright film (77);
(2) the right for such an author or director not to have his work "subjected to derogatory treatment" (80);
(3) the right in certain circumstances for a person not to have a literary, dramatic, musical or artistic work (whether or not a copyright work) falsely attributed to him as author or to have a film (whether or not a copyright film) falsely attributed to him as director (84);
(4) the right for a person in certain circumstances who for private and domestic purposes commissions the taking of a copyright photograph or the making of a copyright film not to have copies of those works issued to the public or exhibited or shown in public or broadcast or included in a cable programme service ($85).

The law has at last recognized that there my be many circumstances where the author or the director of the work no longer owns the copyright in that work but should still be entitled to public recognition for his or her creative association with the work.

There are a significant number of exceptions to what has been called this "right to paternity," and in particular the right does not apply to computer programs, designs of typefaces or to any computer-generated work. It also does not apply where the author or director in question is an employee and the copyright automatically vests in his employer by virtue of a 9(2) (a) ("person to be treated as author of film") or 11(2) ("Works produced in course of employment") of the 1988 Act, as the case may be.

For the purposes of 80, "treatment" of work is defined to mean: any addition to, deletion from or alteration to or adaption of the work, other than—

(a) a translation of a literary or dramatic work, or
(b) an arrangement or transcription of a musical work involving no more than a change of key or register . . .

The treatment of a work is stated to be "derogatory" if the treatment "amounts to distortion or mutilation of the work or is otherwise prejudicial to the honour or reputation of the author or director."

It is clear that the necessarily subjective nature of establishing what is "derogatory" in a particular instance may lead to much fervent argument; particularly from a civil rights standpoint where one might be concerned as to whether this so-called right of integrity would limit legitimate freedoms of expressions such as satire or parody. In this context, there are a number of exceptions to the right of integrity, and in particular 81(3) states that the right is not to apply in relation to any work made for the purpose of "reporting current events:"

Whilst the so-called "moral rights" are included within the part of the 1988 Act generally entitled "Copyright" these rights are not really rights of copyright in the pure sense.

Section 86 provides that the rights conferred by 77 ("to be identified as author or director"), 80 ("to privacy of certain photographs and films") last as long as the copyright lasts in the work in question. The 84 right ("false attribution") on the other hand is expressed to last for a period of 20 years after a person's death—this is a necessary distinction since, as mentioned earlier, the right to be protected against false attribution of a work does not merely apply to copyright works.

Section 87 of the 1988 Act drives a veritable "coach and horses" through the defenses of the legislation by providing that a person may give up all his moral rights by consent or by waiver and it may be expected therefore that the force of bargaining power may cause authors and directors to give up their rights unless and until a suitable code of conduct can be agreed.

Section 94 makes it clear that moral rights are not assignable but 95 of the 1988 Act does enable moral rights to be transmitted on death to the heirs of the person in question.

Section 103 of the 1983 Act provides that an infringement of these moral rights is actionable as a breach of statutory duty owned to the person entitled to the right and goes on to provide specifically that, in relation to the 80 right (the right to object to derogatory treatment of work), the court may grant an injunction. It is not clear from this provision whether the Act is intended to exclude rights of injection in relation to other kinds of moral right and one cannot immediately see why such rights of injunction should be so excluded.

The writer cannot say that the existence of these new moral rights shows, as Dr. Pangloss would have it, that everything is for the best in the best of all possible worlds or that, as Mr. Gradgrind would have it, these moral rights can be justified on a factual utilitarian basis because "facts alone are wanted in life." The writer also cannot say whether the easing of the author's lot will in any way dilute the essence of pure artistry which flows from the tormented minds of a Balzac or a Mozard but what the author can say is that these new moral rights may well produce some interesting legal arguments in years to come. With that thought, the writer intends to "go and work in the garden" (with respect to Voltaire).

**(b) Australia**

Australia is bound by the Paris text of the Berne convention, Article 6bis of which is the same as the text adopted at Stockholm in 1967. What is required under this article can be stated as follows:

*1. Independence of Mmoral Rights*

It is clear that moral rights are independent of author's economic rights. That is, their exercise cannot be tied to, or made dependent upon, the ownership or exercise of economic rights. This notion of independence is, of course, basic to the whole conception of moral rights.

*2. The Rights required to Protected*

Only two moral rights require protection: those of paternity and integrity. Proposals to protect rights of disclosure were made and rejected at the time of the Rome Conference in 1928 and, in any event, are largely covered by the rights of first publication and distribution which are recognized as part of authors' economic rights in many countries.

*3. Duration of Protection*

The basic principle established under para. (2) of Article 6bis is that the period of protection should be at least for the duration of the author's economic rights. Accordingly, the Convention adopts a neutral stance on the juridical nature of moral rights, that is, the monist and dualist theories referred to above. It also gives member countries flexibility in the way in which they protect these rights after the death of the author: national laws may stipulate the persons or institutions who are to exercise these rights in that country. This may well be the heirs of the author, but it would be equally open to a member country to entrust the exercise of these rights post mortem auctoris to a government or public agency charged with the promotion of national culture or to some other analogous body. The latter course of action would be particularly appropriate where moral rights were protected after the expiry of the economic rights as any heirs of the author would be then be for removed form him or her.

*4. Mode of Protection of Moral Rights*

Although Article 6bis contains no specific reference to this, it has been accepted from the start that Unison countries are not obliged to protect moral rights as part of their copyright laws. This was the historic compromise which enabled the inclusion of moral rights in the first place of Rome in 1928, and was confirmed at the time of the Stockholm Conference in the general report of Main Committee I. Countries are therefore free to adopt other means of protection for the rights specified in para. (1). Para. (3) further makes it clear that the "means of redress for the safeguarding of these rights" is a matter for the laws of the country where protection in claimed. This is the same as for the economic rights protected by the Convention, and means that the remedies available in each Berne country may vary considerably.

It is important to reiterate the obligatory nature of Australia's obligation to protect the two moral rights mentioned in Article 6bis (1). As a matter of treaty interpretation, there can be little doubt about this. The first task in treaty interpretation is to do so "in accordance with the ordinary meaning to be given to the terms of the treaty in their context and in the light of its object and its purpose." in this regard, the language of Article 6bis (1) is clear and unambiguous: the rights mentioned in that paragraph must be protected by each member country of the Berne Union.

The obligations under Article 6bis only exist with respect to foreign authors and works claiming protection in Australia pursuant to the provisions of the Convention. There is nothing in the article which concerns the protection to be given to Australian authors and works. On the other hand, as a matter of practical politics, it is difficult to conceive of a situation where the Australian Parliament would wish to treat foreign authors more favourably than Australian authors.

Australia is not a country where treaty obligations are directly implemented into municipal law, so that they can be directly invoked in our courts by foreign claimants. Specific legislative measures must be taken in order to give effect to treaty obligations.

In the event that Australia fails to accord the protection required under Article 6bis, it stands in breach of its obligation under Article 36 (1) of the convention "to adopt, in accordance with its constitution, the measures necessary to ensure the application of this convention." This is then raises the question of what, if anything, can be done to ensure compliance with the convention by as errant member state.

Protection under current Australian law for the rights of authorship and integrity is to be found across a wide range of statutory, common law and equitable provisions:

*(i) The Right to Claim Authorship*

Under statute, this is dealt with partially by the false attribution of authorship provisions of Part IX of the Copyright Act 1968. These impose a number of duties on persons not to make false claims of authorship of works or of altered versions of works.

*(ii) The Right of Integrity*

This is protected only in small measure under the Copyright Act, in two provision that have limited application and have never been the subject of judicial consideration. The first is sub-section 35(5), which gives the authors of certain commissioned artistic works a veto over uses for a purpose other than the originally contemplated at the time of the commissioning of the work. The second is sub-section 55(2) which provides that the compulsory license under that section in respect of the recording of musical works does not apply in relation to an adaptation of a musical work that debases the work. Apart from these provisions, the protection of the right of integrity in Australia is left to contractual arrangements where possible or the common law action of defamation.

In the light of the above, it may be concluded that Australian law probably provides sufficient protection for the right of integrity referred to in Article 6bis (1), but only very partial protection for the right to claim authorship. In so far as these protections only survive the author in very limited circumstances, there is a clear breach of para (2). These matters point then to the need for specific legislative action in order to achieve compliance with Article 6bis.

Are there any defenses or justifications for non-compliance that can be advanced? It could be argued that the subsequent practice of Berne Union countries establishes that there is agreement between them that the protection presently accorded under Australian law complies with the requirements of Article 6bis. Under the rules of treaty interpretation, it is possible to the account of any subsequent practice "in the application of the treaty which establishes the agreement of the parties regarding its interpretation." In this instance, the argument would be that the practice of Berne Union countries clearly established that the present forms of protection available for moral rights in common law countries such as Australia suffices for the purposes of Article 6bis. However, to establish such a practice, it is necessary to point to some positive agreement or understanding between the parties to the treaty in question: it is not possible to infer such an agreement form the mere absence of compliant. In the case of Article 6bis, it is impossible to establish such a positive agreement.

If it is accepted that Australia stands in breach of its international obligations under Article 6bis of the Berne Convention, what flows from this in legal terms? The Convention contains no specific provision dealing with its enforcement and has no sanctions against non-compliance.

A moral rights approach explicitly appreciated the value of parody to democracy and artistic progress by weighting the balance in favour of the secondary users. It casts the onus on the original author to prove infringement only where he or she can show that the secondary work so distorts the original creation as to harm his honor or reputation.

The economic rights approach to copyright law in Australia and other English speaking countries is wholly inappropriate to the protection of parody. It wrongly perceives parody as an attack on the copyright owner's economic interests whereas what this genre potentially undermines if any thing is the original author's moral right to the integrity of his work, and to honor and reputation.

By contrast the moral rights approach is uniquely suited to parody because the peculiar problems posed to copyright law by parodies and burlesques are fundamentally ethical and not economic. There is inevitable tension between a law which professes to further humankind's creative endeavours by protecting the extent to which works may be copied, and the need to encourage derivative literary forms whose intrinsic value lies in their unique critical and humorous purpose but which rely on heir works for inspiration. The dilemma is not an economic one: it is a moral one which necessitates adjudication between conflicting public interests—the freedom of expression, creativity and humor represented by parodies and burlesques on the one hand, as opposed to the protection of the personality or integrity of authors' original works.

Mark Twain once Wrote that "Only one thing is impossible to God, to find any sense in any copyright law on this planet." If "any sense" is to be made of the copyright law relating to parody, it will be through the belated adoption of Australia's Berne Convention obligations relating to moral rights; and to see the protection of the original work's integrity and its author's honor and reputation as the only legitimate trammeling of the creation of the best (true) parodies.

**(c) Musical Works**

Since moral rights exist independently of "economic rights," the author retains a degree of control even if he commercially exploited the creation by transferring his economic interests in the work. For example, a song's composer could invoke his moral rights to ensure that he is named as the author, or even to prevent the performance of the song in a form which he perceives as a "distortion, mutilation or other modification" that could damage his "honor or reputation." With the advent of music videos, digital sampling techniques and increasing popularity of music that incorporates sampled sounds, recognition of moral rights in the countries like India would empower composer to assert some control over the post-release use of their works by music publishers or other musical artists.

The Berne Convention expressly provides that moral rights are independent of "economic rights are independent of "economic rights" in the works created by an author. Thus, an author's moral rights are unaffected by the transfer of the underlying work. Moral rights under Berne can be broken down into two categories: attribution and integrity.

Attribution refers to the creator's right to claim authorship of the work, securing the fame (or notoriety) of the work to his credit. Integrity is the power to prevent an unauthorized, derogatory alteration of the work, enabling the author to prevent an undesirable use of the work which could impair his "honor or reputation."

These rights have broad ramifications. The Berne Convention takes an expansive view of the literary and artistic works it protects, and encompasses "every production in the literary, scientific and artistic domain, whatever may be the mode or form of its expression." Berne then lists examples of works, specifically including "dramatico musical works," and a myriad of other works. Thus, the rights of attribution and integrity are intended to ensure to composers of musical works under Berne.

France is considered the birthplace of the moral rights concept. The doctrine of "le droit moral" reflects the notion that an artist has a natural right to the fruits of her creativity which cannot be conveyed away through licensing or transfer of the economic interest. A recent decision involving the colorization of the film "Asphalt Jungle" illustrates the modern French view of the right to integrity. The Cour de Cassation, France's highest civil court, emphatically reinforced moral rights, holding that the integrity rights of the film's American director, the late John Huston, had been violated by the conversion of the film from black-and-white to color. This case also stands for the proposition that moral rights should be evaluated according to the law of the country in which a claim is heard, not the country in which the author actually acquired the rights by creating a work.

In upholding the plaintiffs' moral rights claim, the Cour de Cassation cited a French law which bars infringement of integrity and attribution in countries whose domestic law fails to provide sufficient or effective protection to works produced by French artists. It therefore appears that despite its accession to the Berne Convention and the implementation of Section 106A, the Cour de Cassation believes that the United States in-adequately protects moral rights.

Users, those whose business entails the consumption of the artistic works produced by others, have two intertwined concerns. First, they fear that the recognition of moral rights in authors will disrupt existing contractual arrangements involving intellectual property. Users undoubtedly wish to avoid a situation like the "Asphalt Jungle" case, where no mention of moral rights was made in the contract that assigned the author's copyright interests, as no such right existed in the United States at the time, but the court retroactively superimposed moral rights on the contract, frustrating the user's expectations.

A second problem is users' reluctance to have their future transactions complicated by creators' interests in attribution and integrity, as moral rights in the artist by definition divest the copyright owner of some discretion to subsequently use the work. Essentially:

Film producers didn't want interference from directors and writers, television wanted to be able to slice up programs any way it saw fit, owners of old movies wanted to "colorize" them, publishers and editors wanted to remain free to edit manuscripts before printing them, and owners of works of art wanted to retain the right to display them in their bathrooms, alter, or even destroy them if they so chose.

These attitudes reflect the intrinsic conflict between moral rights and the economic interests in intellectual property in the United States. The American value structure accentuates economic rights rather than personal interests like attribution and integrity. This emphasis is perhaps a reflection of the United States' Anglo-Saxon antecedents. The notion that one who produces a good shares an interest in that good with the person to whom she has conveyed title is alien to our concept of property, as our culture tends to consider property in more absolute terms. As a result, copyright protection in the United States "continues this country's tradition of safeguarding the pecuniary rights of a copyright owner, . . . ensur [-ing] the copyright owner's receipt of all financial rewards to which he is entitled . . . by virtue of ownership."

Two years after acceding to the Berne Convention, Congress codified limited moral rights in federal law with the Judicial Improvements Act of 1990. In enacting Section 106A, The Visual Rights Act, the United States did little to advance the interests of the intended beneficiaries of moral rights—creators of intellectual property. Because of its very narrow parameters, Section 106A fails to meet the moral rights mandate conferred by the Berne Convention.

First, section 106A only applies to some creators of "work[s] of visual; art." Second, while the Berne Convention extends moral rights beyond the life of the author, under Section 106A allows the author to waive his moral rights, in contrast to the French position, albeit extreme, that moral rights are inalienable interests in the author's creation.

Even visual artists may be adversely affected by this development because in enacting Section 106A, Congress probably decreased the moral rights protection available under state law to many visual artists. Section 301(f)(1) of the Copyright Act provides, "all . . . . rights conferred by Section 106A . . . . are rights that are equivalent to any of the rights conferred by Section 106A 106A," thereby preempting state statutes that confer moral rights to creators of visual art.

To assess the impact of inadequate moral rights protection on composers of musical works, it will be instructive of discuss several cases that deal with moral rights issues in practical terms rather than in the abstract.

Shostakouich V. Twentieth Century Fox Film Corp. involved a moral rights claim brought by prominent Russian composers who objected to the use of their music in a film that had an anti-communist theme. The court collapsed the plaintiffs' moral rights and tort claims, and found that there was no "clear showing of the infliction of a wilful injury or of any invasion of a moral right." Thus, while recognizing the theoretical existence of a moral rights claim, the court chose not to provide a remedy on the facts of the case, citing the conflict between the moral right and the societal interest in using works in the public domain, and the lack of standards by which to determine whether or not such rights were violated. In contrast, the same facts, litigated simultaneously by the plaintiffs in France, resulted in a verdict in their favour. The French court held that there was "undoubtedly a moral damage."

Shostakovich raises the question of whether a composer's integrity can be impaired by a faithful rendition of his song in an objectionable context. A composer who conveys his economic interest in a work could find that their transferee has licensed the song for use in a manner which the composer deems derogatory reflecting poorly on the composer and thus prejudicing her "honor or reputation." Hypothetically, a composer who enjoys the reputation of providing musical scores for serious dramatic works could find her song licensed for use in a pornographic movie. Would the composer have a cause of action based on violation of her integrity? What if instead of a pornographic movie, the song was performed as a pornographic movie. Would the composer have a cause of action based on violation of her integrity? What if instead of a pornographic movie, the song was performed as a music video pursuant to a license from the copyright owner: would this violate the composer's integrity, as it "distorts" the personality that the composer injected into her song? Under the French holding in Shostakovich, the answer would probably be yes (or oui) in either instance, but the composer's success in such an action in the United States is far more dubious.

A supermarket tabloid provides an even more extreme example: what if a composer's song is used as background music for a scene depicting the rape of a child? while the licensing of the song "Honey Don't" was beyond the control of composer Carl Perkins, he would ordinarily consider its use in a film, to be "great." However, says Perkins, in the context of Prince of Tides, "people are asking me, 'Carl, why would you have a song in such a filthy place in a movie?' They are shocked, especially since they all know I started [a] child-abuse center. I am very damaged by this and very hurt." If Perkins were to bring suit for infringement of his integrity rights because he feels the use of his song in this context harmed his reputation, the central issue would be whether the use of "Honey Don't" damaged his honor or reputation as a songwriter, not his reputation in the community as a children's advocate. It thus seems that Perkins could not prevail in the United States or in France.

Digital sampling is another practice unique to the music industry which has potential moral rights implications. For the first time, a district court recently ruled that sampling constituted copyright infringement, issued a preliminary injunction to cease the sale of the infringing work and referred the matter to the United States Attorney for possible criminal prosecution for copyright infringement. The case concerned the unlicensed use of a sample form Raymond "Gilbert" O'Sullivan's 1972 hit Alone Again (Naturally) in rapper "Biz Markie's" 1991 song Along Again. Though this case could foreshadow subsequent decisions fovorable to composers, the holding seems limited to instances where the composer is also the copyright owner, as it focuses on the copyright owner's proprietary rights and not on the creator's moral rights. As such, it has no direct hearing on the composer's moral rights of attribution and integrity.

A possible defense to sampling that constitutes infringement is the Copyright Act's fair use doctrine. In Acuff-Rose Music, Ins. u Campbell, the rap group "2 Live Crew" successfully invoked the fair use defense to an infringement action based on the group's parody of the Roy Orbison song "Oh Pretty Woman." Recognizing the commercial nature of 2 Live Crew's parody, the court nonetheless found that the character of the use supported the defendants, members of "an anti-establishment rap group [that used the song to] demonstrate how bland and banal the Orbison song seems to them." The court also noted that even though parody usually only permits the infringer to copy the amount necessary to conjure up the original work, the nature of a musical composition means that a parodist should be afforded more leeway. Finally, the court found that there will be no diminution of the value of "Oh Pretty Woman", since the intended audience of the 2 Live Crew version is entirely different from the Roy Orbison original.

While this case was a victory for rap artists, it vitiates composers' rights of integrity. Orbison's original "pretty woman" was transformed from "a pleasing image of feminity to bald-headed, hairy and generally repugnant [,] . . . completely inconsistent with the tone and story of the romantic original." Furthermore, the "off-color" content and context of the 2 Live Crew version could be construed as objectionable. While finding that "2 Live Crew's version is neither obscene nor pornographic," the court noted that "[e]ven if the work included pornographic references, that does not necessarily preclude a finding of fair use."

It therefore appears that the moral rights protection available to composers in the United States is inadequate to meet the guaranteed level of protection contemplated by the Berne Convention.

The legal system has a valid interest in judicial economy. Congress should not "open the floodgates" to allow every disgruntled artist to assert a claim sounding in moral rights. To assuage fears of frivolous litigation in hopes of a large monetary reward, Congress could limit damages for moral rights violations to actual damages or unjust enrichment or, in the alternative, to statutory damages, and exclude punitive damages. This is consistent with the notion that moral rights are personal and not pecuniary in nature.

On the other hand, there should be enough substance to moral rights that users will be encouraged to respect authors' rights of attribution and integrity. As a disincentive to the violation of moral rights are personal and not pecuniary in nature.

On the other hand, there should be enough substance to moral rights that users will be encouraged to respect authors' rights of attribution and integrity. As disincentive to the violation of moral rights, Congress could provide for fines to be levied against wilful infringers. Also, artists could be awarded the costs of bringing suit to vindicate their moral rights. Finally, criminal liability could be imposed on infringers in extreme cases.

**(d) Works-For-Hire**

The laws of several EC Member States create problems for Americans who wish to exploit works made for hire in the EC. Foremost among these problems if the disparate treatment that Member States Accord to authors whose status as author does not stem form creating a copyrighted work, but from the legal fiction supplied by work-for-hire rules. This legal fiction posits that when a creator constructs a copyrightable work in the context of certain employment relationships, authorship vests in the person for whom the creator works.[49]

The dilemma posed by these divergent approaches was played out most recently in the French Supreme Court decision, *Huston* v. *La Cinq*. In Huston, John Huston's heirs sough and obtained an injunction barring the broadcast of the colorized version of the film "Asphalt Jungle." Despite the fact the Metro-Goldwyn-Mayer studios owned the original copyright law the heirs possessed the separate moral rights of paternity and integrity that the colorized. Even assuming Huston purported to transfer or waive his moral right by contract, French law, and the law of eight other EC Member States, would invalidate such contractual efforts. Despite the warm reception Huston's heirs received in France, the United Kingdom, Ireland, and the Netherlands would not recognize their claimed moral right subsequent to a contractual transfer or waiver.

The conflict Huston addressed illustrated a significant inconsistency in EC copyright law, which greatly impacts the US work-for-hire doctrine. Copyright laws in the EC and those of the United States represent two different copyright traditions—the civil law dualistic system and the common law monistic system. The dualistic system consists of "two essential components, each with a different nature: moral right and economic right." On the one hand, "Moral right is a right of personality that protects the person of the author." The right enables an author "to maintain respect for his work and, thereby, for his reputation. This right is perpetual and inalienable." On the other hand, "the economic component of copyright is the right to exploit a work and draw profits from it and is by nature transferable."[50]

Under the monistic system, copyright as a whole safeguards "both the financial and intellectual interests of the author." The monistic structure, unlike the dualistic structure, views authors' financial and intellectual interests as complimentary and therefore permits authors to profit from both. Thus, the United Kingdom, Ireland, and the Netherlands—all of whom adhere to the monistic system—allow authors to transfer or waive their moral right. The dualistic system of all other EC civil law countries affects US work-for-hire owners most severely.

Because the work-for-hire doctrine inverts the concept of "creator as author" to "employer or principal as author," the doctrine is averse to many signatories' the doctrine is averse to many signatories' the doctrine is averse to many signatories' notions of author's rights. Those countries who feel that author's rights are strictly personal are offended by the prospect that one who pays for a creator's rights are strictly personal are offended by the prospect that one who pays for a creator's work in the course of employment or pursuant to contract acquires the copyright in that work.

The Berne Convention does not define the term "author." Instead, the Berne Convention leaves the concept to the ordinary meaning it has in each signatory.

In general, countries that unconditionally adhere to the "creator as author" concept do so on the premise that authors can only be natural persons.

Just as the Berne Convention omits any definition of "author" it also does not explicitly address the work-for-hire doctrine.[51]

The Berne Convention's moral right provision however, places a significant stumbling block between an employee's work and an employer. In addition, because the Berne Convention never affirmatively recognizes contractual waiver or transfer of moral right, it creates the same morass the French Supreme Court addressed in *Huston* v. *Lacinq*.[52] Overall, the Berne convention furthers the dual copyrights, and forgoes committing to the monistic view that copyright should only protect authors' commercial interests "for limited times."

Like the Berne Convention, the UCC relies on a policy of reciprocal national treatment. But, unlike the Berne Convention, it focuses on protecting authors' economic rights and does not explicitly address moral right. It does, however, tacitly approve of Contracting States adopting moral right under certain conditions.[52] Undoubtedly, the UCC's most significant departure from the Berne Convention is in the copyright for-malities it imposes.

Like the Berne Convention, the UCC does not define "author." Several passages in the Convention, however, demonstrate a less strict approach to the "creator as author" rule than appears in the Berne Convention. For example, Article IV prescribes the minimum term of protection as the life of the author plus twenty-five years after her death. Following this prescription, the Convention addresses those Contracting States that compute duration "from the first publication of the work," and authorizes those states that do not use such a durational method to adopt such a method. This broad recognition of a "date of publication" measure diverges from the Berne Convention, which only applied such a measure to anonymous and pseudonymous works. Because work-for-hire is the other primary class of works that uses a "date of publication" measure, and because of employers and principals who acquire authorship status in such works are frequently corporate entities, the UCC could be read to approve of granting author's rights to non- natural persons. The fact that the United states was the motivating force for the UCC further supports this suggestion; US copyright law does not distinguish between natural and non-natural persons for authorship purposes and uses the date of publication as the alternative measure for works-for-hire.

The "Berne Safeguard Clause prohibits a Berne Convention country form denouncing Berne and relying on the UCC in its copyright relations with members of the Berne Convention. Because all EC Member states belong to the Berne Convention's preeminence undercuts the protection that the UCC theoretically affords to work-for-hire copyright holders. As a result, persons asserting rights as work-for-hire copyright holders in the EC must turn either EC or national copyright law.

National copyright protection is almost divided evenly between a strict author's rights approach and a common law-oriented, economic rights approach. Member States utilizing a strict author's rights approach protect creators through a rigid moral right regime that, by definition, also restricts ownership rights in works made for hire. Member States employing an economics rights approach allow contractual relations to control the extent to which moral right may apply and, consequently, support ownership rights in the works-for-hire.

*Belgium*

Belgian employees who create works in the scope of their employment acquire the copyright in the work. Belgian law regards employees as authors who may then transfer their copyright interest to their employers.

Employee-employer transfers, however, do not give employers unfettered discretion in exploiting the work. "Moral right remains vested in each author even after full conveyance of all copyright-based economic interests." Furthermore, the law does not permit authors to transfer or waive the moral right of integrity contained in Article.

*Denmark*

A composite of two statutory provisions suggests that Denmark also adheres to the civil law custom of separating copyright economic and moral rights. First, Section I employs a· strict "creator as author" rule: "The person producing a literary or artistic work shall have copyright therein.

Second, Section 3 gives the author several moral right protections: [including the rights of paternity and integrity.] Because no EC Member State (except Germany) prevents copyright transfers, Danish law would presumably permit an author to transfer her copyright to an employer if she created the work in the scope of employment. Such a transfer would not, however, create any limi on the employee's moral right. Since Section 3 prohibits an author from waiving her moral rights of attribution, paternity, and integrity in most circumstances, it is unlikely that a contractual effort to transfer these rights would succeed.

*France*

France's copyright law specifically addresses the work-for-hire doctrine. The first article of France's copyright statute establishes rules governing works-for-hire. The first paragraph provides: "The author of an intellectual work, shall, by the mere fact of its creation, enjoy an exclusive incorporeal property right in the work, effective against all persons." It also states in part: "The existence, or the conclusion by the author of an intellectual work, of a contract shall imply no exception to the enjoyment of the right recognized in the first paragraph."

In the employ-employee context, French courts have interpreted these provisions to give employers the economic component of copyright and employee-authors the moral right component. The employer need not secure a separate transfer of copyright since she "acquires the economic component of copyright upon execution of the employment contract." Because the economic component vests in the employer by virtue of the employment relationship. French law partially follows US work-for-hire rules.

French copyright law diverges from US law in the principal-independent contractor context. This context usually involves commissioned works or works that will constitute part of a collective whole. In France, authors of commissioned works retain both the economic and moral right to the principal. The United States, in contrast, does not require any transfer between the creator and the principal, provided (1) the parties have an express writing describing the work as one for hire, and (2) work falls into one of nine categories. Once the principal satisfies both these requirements, she acquires the same rights that an employer has over works created in the scope of employment.

A significant exception to general French work-for-hire rules exists for computer software. For these works, French law-for-hire in that employers acquire both the economic and moral right component of the copyright. By amendment in 1985, French copyright law now provides: "Unless otherwise stipulated, software created by one or more employees in the exercise of their duties shall belong to the employer together with all the rights afforded to other authors." This provision represents a radical departure from France's strict moral right regime.

### *Germany*

The concept of work-for-hire is entirely absent from German copyright law. German law adheres to the basic principle that only the natural person who creates a work can be the work's author. In the employment contest, "the initial owner . . . of a work made for hire or of a commissioned work is . . . always the author . . . who actually created the work" by vesting ownership in the employee or the independent contractor, the law requires employers to acquire copyright interests by contract.

German moral right provisions imply that an author may waive her moral right. Article 39 of the German Copyright Act states that "in the absence of any contrary agreement, a licensee may not alter the work, its title or the designation of the author." These alterations concern the moral rights of integrity and attribution, The fact that this article refers to a "contrary agreement" indicates the copyright Act recognizes contractual waivers of moral rights. As one commentator has suggested however even though an author can waive her moral right of integrity under Article 39, the beneficiary of such a waiver does not have unlimited freedom to alter the work. Alterations are limited to those which do not constitute a "gross distortion" of the work.

*Greece*

Work-for-hire rules do not exist under Greek copyright law. Like most civil law countries, Greek law vests initial copyright ownership in the human being who actually created the work. Employers cannot alter this principle by contract. Instead, employers must acquire copyright interests in works made in the scope of employment in the same manner as any person or entity would acquire a copyright interest—by transfer from the author.

Employers must also contend with potential moral right claims. The Greek Copyright Act expressly provides for the right of attribution or paternity and the right of integrity. Greek law also generally recognizes two other moral right provisions: the rights of divulgation and access to the author's work.

Greece, like Germany, France, Denmark, and Belgium, adheres to the civil law notion that moral right is personal to the author and therefore nontransferable. Yet, despite the nontransferability of moral right, Greek law recognizes a narrow moral right waiver. A waiver could arise in relation to the rights of divulgation and paternity where an author contractually renounces her power to decide when to publish her work and agrees to publish without mentioning her name. A waiver of the right of divulgation would provide some relief to publishing houses that hold copyrights in books and other media and wish to time publication themselves. Similarly, an employer who holds the copyright in a work an employee created and who seeks to label the work as her own may benefit from a right of attribution waiver. In sum, although Greece does not preclude employers from disarming their employees of their moral right, Greek copyright law places significant hurdles in the way of unlimited economic exploitation of works-for-hire.

#### *Luxembourg*

The fact that Luxembourg is a civil law country and civil law countries (except for the Netherlands) uniformly follow the "creator as author" rule would indicate that only creators can secure copyright interests under the statute. BY implication, this position precludes employers from acquiring copyright interest upon creation as work-for-hire rules generally dictate.

Employers and principals must acquire copyright interests by contractual transfers from employees or independent contractors. The interest that either may acquire is limited to the economic right of exploitation.

The fact that moral right "attaches to the author personally," indicates an author cannot alienate the right through an inter vivos transfer. Moreover, in view of Luxembourg's overall scheme, the personal nature of moral right also precludes moral right waiver. These prohibitions are consistent with most civil law countries and embody the usual limitations on works-for-hire that can potentially impair the economic exploitation of these works.

#### *The Netherlands*

The Netherlands is the only civil law country that has incorporated the work-for-hire doctrine into its copyright law. Three separate provisions from the basis of the Dutch work-for-hire scheme. First, Article 6 provides. "If a work has been produced according to the plan and under the guidance and supervision of another person, that person shall be deemed to be the author of the work. "This article would apply if, for example, an artist employs several artists at his or her studio to execute works. Article 7 is the second Dutch work-for-hire provision. In the event another person employs the supervisor and the latter oversees the creation of a work in the course of his or her employment Article 7 indicates that the supervisor's employer is the work's author.

In the Netherlands, employers' work-for-hire rights only arise in instances in which an employer "factually" addresses an employee to produce certain works. Article 7 will "not apply where the employee produces other works on his own initiative, whether in the time of his employer or even with the mere consent of his employer."

Therefore, if an employee creates a work on his or her won initiative, even while using her employer's facilities, receiving payment from her employer, following her employer's instructions, and even if the work is the type of work that the employer generally produces, the employee will be the work's author and will acquire all copyright interest in the work.

Article 8 is the third provision addressing the work-for-hire doctrine. It states: "Any public institution, association, foundation or partnership which makes a work public as its won, without naming any natural person as the author thereof, shall be regarded as the author of the wok, unless it is shown that making the work public in such manner was unlawful. "This article covers work created in the course of a principal-independent contractor relationship. It also applies to all other works not covered by Articles 6 and 7 where an entity has contracted for the right to publish the work as its own. In theory, this provision greatly exceeds the scope of US work-for-hire rules since it permits an entity to acquire authorship status and all appurtenant copyright interests by publishing a work in its own name pursuant to contract. Article 8, unlike US law, does not require an agency relationship nor limits itself to particular categories of works.

*The United Kingdom*. The United Kingdom fully recognizes work-for-hire principles. Section 11 sets forth the work-for-hire rules that apply to works created on or after August 1, 1989:

(1) The author of work is the first owner of any copyright owner of any copyright in it, subject to the following provisions.

(2) Where a literary, dramatic, musical or artistic work is made by an employee in the course of his employment, his employer is the first owner of any copyright in the work subject to any agreement to the contrary.[54]

This section gives employers the status of authors and vests initial copyright interests in them absent any contrary agreement. Because employers acquire their interests upon creation and the employment relationship alone determines this interest, the British rule closely resembles the US approach. Similar to the CCNV "scope of employment" analysis, British work-for-hire interests depend on whether an employment relation-ship exists.

To determine whether such a relationship exists, the British. . . . focus on "whether the work forms an integral part of the business."[55] This analysis depends on:

> Whether the typical attributes of employment are present: whether regular sums are paid as wage or salary; whether income tax deductions are made on the "pay-as-you-earn" basis used for employees; whether there is a joint contribution to a pension scheme; whether national insurance contributions are paid by both parties as for an employee.[56]

Assuming some or all of these attributes are present, an employer will acquire the copyright interest in the work. Even if the employment relationship does not satisfy this test, an employer could nonetheless acquire a copyright interest unimpaired by moral right. Unlike most EC countries, the United kingdom permits moral rights waivers.

The above overview of EC Member States' national work-for-hire rules reveals three interrelated problems. The first problem is that the Member States differ over how copyright ownership in works-for-hire may arise. At one extreme, Belgium, Denmark, Germany, Greece, and Luxembourg only allow creators to have the initial ownership interest and require employers to contract for copyright licenses or transfers. Simewhere towards the center, France requires principals to contract with independent contractors, but employers need not contract with employees. Similarly, Italy and Spain permit copyright ownership to flow directly to the employer in some instances,[57] but not in others.[58] At the othe extreme, Ireland, the Netherlands, and the United Kingdom nearly always vest copyright ownership in employers and principals upon creation. In essence, no single copyright ownership rule prevails in the EC for works-for-hire.

The second problem is that the Member States disagree over who may be the author of a work-for-hire. This issue is significant since only an author can claim moral right. As a general rule, all EC Member States consider the natural person who created a work as the work's author. In relation to authors of works made for hire, however, two distinct approaches emerge. These approaches break down according to the civil and common law traditions. On the one hand, the civil law countries, except for the Netherlands, adhere to the general rule almost without exception. On the other hand, Ireland, the Netherlands, and the United Kingdom deviate from the general rule and recognize employers and principals as authors of works made for hire.

The third problems arises from the divergent moral right treatments existing within the EC. The discrepancies characterizing moral right proceed directly form the problem of determining authorship in works made for hire. That is, the same civil law countries that strictly follow the "creator as author" rule also forbid moral right transfer and waiver. The identical common law countries (and the Netherlands) that part from the "creator as author" rule also permit moral right transfer or waiver. Because these latter countries' work-for-hire and moral right regimes most closely resemble the US system, US work-for-hire copyright holders can expect the same treatment under these countries' laws as they would receive in the United States.

**(e) Patents**

The traditional view of the institutions grouped in the category of intellectual property adopts a distinction between works of creativity, where attention is focused on the personality of the author, and technical accomplishments, where attention falls on the discovery. The first category relates to the domain of art, the second gives importance to the utilitarian aspects of the work. Such a bipolar view, based on an idea of the work of intelligence and creativity, seems to have been called into question by the latest technological and social developments. The consequence of any decline in such a view would be to sweep away the distinction between artistic property and industrial property.[59]

Moral rights probably embody the essence of the right of authorship, that is, that very strong bond which links the author to his or her work, since the author is the subject whose personality is impressed on the work in an indestructible way. This justifies the fact that moral rights are not transferable, not renounceable, autonomous from financial rights and accompanied by a right of action aimed at their defence which is absolutely without limitation. These peculiarities represent one of the most pronounced differences from the monopolies which derive from patent protection. The figure of the inventor compared to that of the author loses centrality, since the invention, even if it gives prestige and reputation to the inventor, does not have any moral or personal implications for him or her at the moment of its realization by third parties. In a society dominated by technology, the position of moral rights becomes uncertain. If they are left untouched, this leaves copyright basically unprejudiced. However, if moral rights are affected, then this classic division of intellectual property will begin to show its limitation.

The realisation of systems able to carry out intellectual activities formerly considered the exclusive domain of man has reached a very advanced phase. Often the creative activity is the result of the collaboration between one or more human workers and an intelligence system and it is not always possible to distinguish the contribution of the man from that of the machine. In these case, one wonders who should be regarded as the author of the work, and who as the owner of the moral rights, assuming that they exist. The more obvious problem is the fact that, in principle, the present laws on the right of authorship require human origin in order for a work to be protected. The first legislators to overcome this imapasse were the British legislators of the 1988 Act who expressly provided for the protection of works made by computer, that is, in circumstances where it is not possible to trace a human author, treating the author as the person who undertook all the preparation necessary for the creation of the work. It is very interesting to note that, with regard to moral rights, the British legislators inserted the first moral rights of the author in copyright, but the options open to authors are limited to the right of paternity, the right of integrity and the right not to be falsely attributed as the author of a work, and in many cases such rights are not applied. Such partial acknowledgment shows the existence of some gaps, or at least of some differences within the system.

Where computers, even if simplifying the activity of the author, do not bring any creative assistance to the realisation of the work, we have a traditional situation, because the computer's contribution is not conceptually different from that made by more traditional instruments, like paper and pen. Very similar is the case where man teaches the computer his ideas and his methods, which the computer then applies to real situations which are supplied to it later Actually the intelligence system carries out mediation activity only, and if one excludes the temporal indications which arise from the fact that the machine can postpone, for ap potentially unlimited time, the expression of the creation, one can understand that the moral rights concerned in no way differ from those of traditional authors.

When an intelligence system is endowed with the capacity to learn and to synthesize, allowing it to have creative skills, it is no longer possible to trace an author in the classic sense of the word, since the umbilical cord which traditionally links man to his creation is irreparably cut.

It does not seem possible to attribute any rights, either moral or economic, to the computer, which, even if it is responsible for the creation, is still a machine without a personality (in the legal or in the psychological sense of the word). The problem of identifying an author arises principally in connection with economic rights; it is not possible to enlarge on this here, but whatever direction is followed, moral rights will probably take their won path. This is because moral rights from part of the more generic right to personality, and, as already mentioned, in creations realized by a machine the umbilical cord which traditionally joins man, and thus his personality, to the work is irreparably severed. Therefore, until such time as artificial intelligence systems come to be regarded as endowed with their own personality, it does not seem possible to find a place for moral rights.

New technology has not altered, at least for the moment, some of the traditional aspects of intellectual and industrial property. The different identities of these two categories are confirmed by the growing interest shown in common law countries in moral rights. However, these institutions are undergoing a profound transformation. New technology has led to enormous financial investment in a field traditionally not involved in entrepreneurial activity—that of the right of authorship. Until this revolution affects works created according to traditional criteria, such trends do not seem to undermine the traditional centrality of the author, who sill has all moral rights. However. for technological means, the object of protection changes; this is not loner the personality of the author but economic investment. The personality element of the creation is seriously compromised, if not lost, either because of the manner of the creation, or because of the use of technology in the creation process. Every time that the work is realized by a team of experts who use the technology and the capital put at their disposal by an entrepreneur, the frame of reference changes appreciably. When one or more computers participate, sometimes exclusively, the frame changes completely.

One will always be concerned with creations, but only because of an objective creative value, the meaning of which inevitably approaches the well-known concept of inventive originality. With this concept of inventive originality. With this conceptual change, the first legal aspect to disappear would certainly be that of moral rights. That would be justified not only by the absence of an object to protect, that is, the personality element, but also by the increase of dominant economic interests, which are at the root of the creation. The English legislation on copyright recognizes the new industrial face of the rights of authorship, because, even though introducing some moral rights, it provides that these are not applicable in cases in which either there is an insufficient personality factor, or this personality factor is dominated by the entrepreneurial factor. Therefore, the Anglo-Saxon system, showing that some cases exist in which the person of the author loses that absolutely pre-eminent position which, traditionally, they have always had. This revels movement away from the subjective aspect, neglecting continental system, showing that some cases exist in which the person of the author loses that absolutely pre-eminent position which, traditionally, they have always had. This reveals movement away from the subjective aspect, neglecting continental theories which assess the possibility of protecting the work only because of the personal imprint which these works received, and leading the assessment to a more objective originality.

The second aspect which has declined, or will soon decline, concerns the direct acquisition of the right. The requirement of industrialization in copyright has been pointed out by the EEC Directive on Software, which provided clearly for the possibility of a legal person to the rights of authorship directly, and which left single Member states the option of implementing such provisions. Italy, for example, did not implement this possibility, and left the old regulations unchanged, regulation which provide that rights of authorship could only arise in favour of the intellectual creator, while the employer could only obtain the exploitation rights by way of a derivative title. It seems necessary to allow a legal person separate from the creator to have the original economic rights to a work, for at least two reasons. *First,* it seems justified by the transformation of the creative action which, becoming personalised, could easily refer to a subject which is not the creator. *Secondly,* it seems equally important to allow the protection of works created by computer, on its own or with the aid of one or more persons, because if the old personality concept is adhered to, such works would not obtain protection until the time that computers endowed with their won personalities were produced.

In conclusion, the difference between the right of authorship and the patent system is no longer so well-defined as it was at the time of its origin. New technology inevitably leads to the painful abandonment of the view of personality which was at the root of right of authorship. It therefore leads likewise to a partial abandonment both of moral rights, the greatest expression of the personalization of the work, and of that intimate author-work bond which forced the absolute denial of the possibility of allowing original rights of exploitation of a work in favour of a third person, with regard to the author, or to a legal personal and it leads finally towards the recognition and the protection of works realized not by people, but by machines.

## 10. MULTINATIONAL TREATIES AND THE PROTECTION OF "CULTURE"

### (a) Culture as Commodity

What if one day you woke up, turned on the radio and could not find an American song? What if you went to the movies and the only films were foreign? What if you wanted to buy a book, and you found that the only American works were located in a small "Americana" section of the store? Furthermore, what if you came home to find your kinds glued to the television for back-to-back reruns of a French soap opera and two German police Dramas? It sounds foreign, even silly, to an American. Ask a Canadian, a German, or a Greek the same question, however, and you will get a different reaction. Europe faced an inversion of this hypothetical scenario. At one point in the late 1980, The Cosby Show was the top rated sitcom in both France and Germany. Even today, evening television in France includes reruns of Hogan's Heroes and Dynasty.

The European Community (EC) reacted to this predicament by passing a Directive—a law—requiring that its members dedicate at least one-half of their television air time to European-made programs. The Directive was the European answer to the fear that European culture was being assimilated into the "Great American Melting Pot." A fear corroborated by numbers, statistics, and trends. The tentacular American intrusion seemed to undermine the cultural autonomy (and in so doing stifled the cultural creativity) of the European countries. The experience was especially galling to the "old world" precisely because it was old and took pride in its multi-secular capital of culture. It was one thing for the United States to purvey jeans and Coca-cola; it was wholly another, and far more ominous, to commodify culture.[60]

**(b) The Canadian Free Trade Agreement**

Both international copyright conventions and domestic copyright laws may conflict with the concept of free trade. Free trade among nations is a concept which has increased in importance over the last several decades as has been shown by the proliferation of multinational trading organizations such as the European Community (EC) and by free trade areas created by agreements (CFTA) and the North American Free Trade Agreement (NAFTA). The increasing incidence of international trading areas and organizations indicates that trade protectionism is on the decline as the interdependence of nations increases.[61]

The concept of free trade focuses on the reduction of trade barriers. Actions by a state which restrict the flow of goods or services infringe on free trade. One of the more transparent restrictions of trade is a cultural exclusion, also known as a cultural exemption. Cultural exclusion, which exist in virtually all trading agreements, allow a state to limit the trade of goods and services involving that state's culture. Cultural exclusions severely limit or even prohibit cultural industries from competing in a free trade area. Although no trade agreement refers to them as such cultural industries are essentially synonymous with copyright industries, which are defined as industries that produce copyrighted goods or provide copyrighted services. Some trade agreements seem to encourage the free trade of copyrighted goods through provisions in-creasing copyright protections for creative works. The holders of the copyright will therefore be inclined to introduce their creative works into the market. Cultural exclusions, however, severely diminish the effect of these provisions by restricting the entry of many copyrighted works into the international marketplace.

The Canadian Free Trade Agreement, signed by Canada and the United States, specifically excludes cultural industries from application of the treaty provisions. That section of the CFTA agreement, Article 2005, has been called the "cultural exclusion" or "cultural exemption" provision. Cultural industries have been defined as those involving the publication, distribution, or sale of books, magazines, periodicals or newspapers, film or video recordings audio or video music recordings, and music in print. Direct transmission of radio and all radio, television, and cable broadcasting services, as well as satellite programming and network broadcast services, are also included in the cultural industries exclusion. As in most trade agreements, the terms "cultural industry" and "copyright industry" are virtually synonymous.

Cultural exclusions are promoted by states as a means of protecting their cultural integrity. In the case of Canada, many Canadian citizens feel very strongly that their culture is distinct from the culture of the United States and thus deserves recognition on its own merits. To Canadians cultural exclusions prevent an amalgamation of American and Canadian culture. However, the fact that Canada is the largest single importer of American intellectual property reflects the potential blurring of American and Canadian cultural boundaries.

The Canadian government has made the protection of Canadian culture and cultural industries a priority, with the creation and maintenance of the Canadian Broadcasting Corporation (CBC) as the most visible sign of the social policy. Television has also been the battlefield for a number of conflicts between the United States and Canada regarding programming and satellite transmissions, and as such is a prime example of .the cultural exclusion at work.

The Canadian government uses the CBC as a means to

promote uniquely Canadian values through various production subsidies and programming restrictions. However, the Canadian viewing public has clamored for American television programs, threatening the viability of Canadian programs. As the popularity of television viewing in Canadian daily life has increased, there has been a corresponding increase in American influences in spite of government subsidies of Canadian television. Some observers believe that vital information about Canadian cultural and political issues may no longer be available to segments of the Canadian public due to the predominance of American television programming.

CFTA's cultural exclusion may seem attractive in the short run, but the long-term effects could harm the Canadian economy and cultural industries as we as the economy and industries of the United States. In the near future, the Canadian government could continue to subsidize what is seen as a struggling domestic industry, thus protecting Canadian culture. Eventually, however, Canadian cultural industries will become less competitive on the global market and will continue to lose their audience members to readily available American books, movies, and television shows. Government assistance, such as subsidies, will not make Canadian cultural industries more competitive, and will not result in the kind of cultural protection that is envisaged by the exclusion, namely the increased availability and production of culturally significant goods and services. Because the cultural exclusion cannot effectuate either of its goals, it appears to be disguised restraint of trade used to protect Canada's cultural industries for economic, not cultural, reasons.

NAFTA in essence has duplicated the cultural exclusion provision of CFTA. Unlike CFTA, however, trade between Mexico and the United States is free of cultural exclusions. [T]he absence of a cultural exclusion will allow Mexican copyright industries to target the Hispanic population which is often ignored by, or even currently closed to, mainstream United States industries, resulting in a potential tidal wave of cultural trade. In addition, once United States industries see the profit-making potential from this largely untapped market, they will begin to target more products to that market, products which will be exportable to Mexico and South and Central America. This type of trade expansion benefits both states and is the result that free trade agreements are intended to produce; it would not be possible, however, under a trade agreement containing a cultural exclusion provision.

**(c) "Television Without Frontiers"**

*1. The Directive*

Article 6 [of the EC "Television Without Frontiers Directive"] defines a European work as follows:

> (a) works originating from Member States of the Community . .
> (b) works originating from European third States party to the European Convention on Transfrontier Television of the Council of Europe [Council of Europe, May 5, 1989, reprinted in 28 ILM 857 (1989)] and fulfilling the conditions of paragraph.[62]

**(d) 2(c) works from other European third countries**

It further provides that

The works [must be] works mainly made with authors and workers residing in one or more States referred to in Paragraph 1(a) and 1 (b) provided that they comply with one of the following three conditions;

1. they are made by one or more producers established in one or more of those States;
2. production of the works is supervised and actually controlled by one or more producers established in one or more of those States; or
3. the contribution of co-producers of those States to the total co-production is preponderant and the co-production is not controlled by one or more producers established outside those States.

If unable to attain a majority proportion of European

Works it is stated that where the majority cannot be attained, "it must not be lower than the average for 1988 in the Member State concerned." *Id.* Art. 4(2).

In direct reference to the quota system, Community Vice president Martin Bangemann, in charge of internal markets, made it clear that the Commission did not regard it as a legally enforceable commitment, but a "political obligation."

The Commission is convinced that increased activity in the cultural sector is a political and socio-economic necessity given the twin goals of completing the internal market by 1992 and progressing from a people's Europe to European Union . . . The essential aim of the general guidelines proposed is to facilitate complementary action by the Commission and the Member States within the Community system and coordination and cooperation between the Member States consistent with Treaty rules.

In relation to the US the other production communities around the world have had limited success distributing mass media products internationally. In 1991, US-based productions accounted for 81% of all EC screenings (raising to a level of 90% in states such as the UK, Greece, the Netherlands and Ireland), 70% of all European box-office receipts, and 54% of all comedies and dramas broadcast on television.

Witness, for example, the decision by the French film industry to exclude all non-French speaking films from the Cesars (the French Oscars). Intellectuals fear that the French language, long under siege by English, needs defending . . . French film industry officials, supported by Tack Lang and his Ministry of Culture, worry that French films are being swamped at the box office by Hollywood, products. The language issue has never arisan with the Oscar because Hollywood can rightly assume that its national products will also be international hits.

## 11. CULTURAL DIVERSITY[63]

The controversy [regarding the "Television Without Frontiers"[64] Directive] focuses on two issues: *first,* whether Europe can legislate its culture (legally and practically): and *second*, whether there is a need for Europe to do so. In its broadest sense, this problem is linked to the enormous political stakes—identity, sovereignty, and independence—and the secondary, but still important, economic stakes-survival of the national industry. In a narrower sense, the dynamics of this issue are played out in the arena of European audio-visual communication. The rapid and widespread demographic and technological changes in Europe in the 1970s and 1980s set the stage for a virtual invasion of American culture. The EC responded in the form of the "Television Without Frontiers" Directive. Simply put, it was an attempt to regulate culture in Europe. The Directive presents an opportune case study in which to explore the issue of whether in fact a state can legislate culture or whether cultural protectionism is nothing more than economic self-promotion cloaked in cultural language.

Two theories explain the attraction of the European state to its present system of audio-visual media. One theory is political, entitled la television toute-puissante (the all-powerful television. This theory embraces the practical strengths of television as a means of communicating with vast numbers of people. The second theory, labeled cultural uniformity, emphasizes the cultural link between television and the masses. Although there are two separate approaches, both theories recognize the connection between the cultural domain and political sovereignty.

The European state has been an active participant in its audio-visual landscape since the inception of advanced technological communication. Governments commissioned studies, funded research, allocated Hertzian frequencies, set national standards, and generally kept a paternal hand on the media with their economic and political potential in mind. The end product of a state-subsidized and state-controlled audio-visual communication industry was a well-founded and highly successful television and radio system. Broadcasters successfully created quality programs with cultural and political influence. These broadcasters played important roles in strengthening democratic values and in encouraging the arts. Because of the successful relationship between state and artist, the state scaffolding that held the industry together earned a place in the public eye as the natural order of things.

Television, therefore, has taken on a particular role in European society. It is an institution charged with upholding the fundamentals of democracy. For television networks, information is the cardinal obligation, the core of their activity. Networks criticized for the mediocrity of their programming nonetheless will concentrate their financial means on broadcast news rather than on entertainment programs. This phenomenon expressed itself recently in France in the confrontation between the partially-privatized network TF1 and its private rival La Cinq.

It is fair to conclude that the non-English-speaking European countries always have been intent on protecting their national sovereignty and culture. In many western European nations, government ownership of the media evolved as a way of protecting national culture from a flood of programs from nations with more sophisticated production capabilities. Despite an initial flirtation with free enterprise, most of these states adopted government-run systems instead of allowing private ownership. States routinely adopted strict regulatory barriers against foreign ownership and investment, and against foreign-produced programming. Similar restrictions also exist presently in commercial advertising, ranging from total bans in Denmark to content and time limitations in Germany.

In recent years, European countries watched as their sovereignty became undermined by the globalization or Americanization phenomenon. This invasion was at once egregiously apparent the presence of American shows) and insidiously subtle (the way in which American values, images, and assumptions infiltrated the minds of both old and especially young viewers.) The American programming market slowly invaded the markets of each European nation. The closer Hollywood came to dominating the market in Europe, the more the economic aspect of television programming extended from the cultural domain into the realm of political sovereignty

"Television without Frontiers" was the coined name for the European Council Directive adopted on October 3, 1989 "on the coordination of certain provisions laid down by on regulation or administrative action in number States concerning the pursuit of television broadcasting activities." This Directive was secondary piece of legislation offered to the Member States whose task was to implement the Directive into their own legal systems to make them effective.

*Grosso modo,* the Directive, outlined standards, rules and regulations touching on such areas as transfrontier broadcasting, advertising, the intra-EC flow of programs and information, and program content, The most important and controversial standard was the last, a mandatory program content quota. The quota required members to implement rules obliging public and private networks to earmark at least fifty percent of their total airtime for "European works." From a practical standpoint, this quota translated into a trade restriction on the amount of foreign (American) films and shows that could be broadcast in EC Member States. The quote made international waves because due to its potential to dramatically affect American and Japanese imports into Europe.

At the center of the debate surrounding the directive was justification of the quota system. None of the parties involved in the debate (i.e., the United States and the EC) denied the importance of culture, and none denied that culture was worth protecting. The focus of this debate was whether there was a genuine need for Europe to protect its culture in this particular situation.

The Preamble outlined the purposes, aims, and goals of the Directive:

It is essential for the Member States to ensure the prevention of any acts which May prove detrimental to freedom of movement and trade in television programmes or which Amy promote the creation of dominant positions which would lead to restriction on pluralism and freedom to televised information and of the information sector as a whole.

The acts which "may lead to restriction on pluralism," referred, of course, to the dominant position held by imported American television programs. The goal in preserving pluralism in television programming was to ensure "the independence of cultural development in the

Member States and the preservation of cultural diversity in the Community." These two goals combined to provide a cultural foundation on which the directive's justification was to stand. "Pluralism" and "diversity" were the key words. They stood in the face of the prime timeslots in Europe that had been dominated by American shows like Dallas, The Cosby Show, Baywatch, and, most recently, Quantum Leap.

The Directive provided that these policies and goals were to be implemented in the form of a quota, or minimum broadcasting requirement Article 6 contained the language of the controversial cultural quota itself.

In layman's terms, the quota required that European broadcasters earmark more than fifty percent of their entertainment, education, and documentary programming for "European works." The practical effect was to reduce the quantity of foreign imported programs that dominated prime time slots in the European programming grids. More specifically, in practice, the quota would diminish the amount of American programs broadcast on networks of Member States.

## 12. THE "AMERICANIZATION" OF CULTURE

The Television Without Frontiers; Green Paper on the establishment of the Common Market for Broadcasting, recognized a need to protect European culture form invasion; "Frequent warnings are heard about the dangers of cultural domination of one country by another in the cinema, although this is not a problem between Member States." The attack, however, was directed outwards, in particular at the United States dominance of the media. According to the Commission "[t]he creation of a common market for television production is . . . . one essential step if the dominance of the big American media corporations is to be counterbalanced."

The general feeling among the Community members according to the Community members according to the Commission is that the "Americanization" of Europe being Kentucky Fried and Coca-Colonized out of existence—must be reversed.

The controversy surrounding the Directive involves, in particular, the European Quota and content provision in Member State programming. Member States shall ensure where practicable and b appropriate means, that broadcaster reserve for European works, within the meaning of Article 6, a majority proportion of their transmission time, excluding news, sports events, games, advertising and teletext services. This proportion, having regard to the broadcaster's informational, educational, cultural, and entertainment responsibilities to its viewing public, should be achieved progressively, on the basis of suitable criteria.

The EC subsequently established incentive programs in an attempt to promote European-wide production and distribution networks. These incentive programs, collectively referred to as the MEDIA program, provide for a wide range of incentives, which include the promotion of business partner ships as well as providing for tax benefits for program producers.

In justifying protection, French President Francois Mitterand warned that all of Europe may soon be watching American programs on Japanese televisions. However, the motivation behind the Community adopting of the directive is clear from the various debates on the subject in the European Parliament. Representative Schinzel, Socialist party member from the Federal Republic of Germany, stated in the European Parliament that television broadcasting, in particular, is a critical cultural asset of the EC and is "of major significance to our democratic way of life and our cultural and social coexistence within the EC." Representative Kuijpers, a Rainbow Party member from Belgium, noted that the Directive was to be implemented not only to protect community and European broadcast markets, "but also and above all of protecting Europe's cultural heritage, which—far more than we realize—is the victim of increasing Americanization." Actively supporting the implementation of a Community-wide 60% quota of European works, Representative Roelants Du Vivier, Rainbow Party member from France caustically stated:

We want—to guarantee the diversity of cultures and their identity, to guarantee pluralism of expression, to protect copyright and to avoid an influx of cheap productions primarily from the USA—and I have no hesitation in taking about American cast-offs here-we have to act and provide adequate protection for/community works. Protectionism? Who is being protectionist if it isn't the United States, where the market is protected from productions from elsewhere?

The community further justifies its zealous position by identifying measures within the US legal system. US law forbids any foreign government or their representatives to own broadcast stations. This restriction is extended to any alien or representative, and any alien-affiliated foreign corporation. If an alien or foreign-controlled corporation chooses to buy into the US market, they must first comply with the restrictive provisions imposed by Section 30 of the Communications Act of 1934. These restrictions relate to stock ownership, management control and citizenship requirements for foreign individuals and corporations. The policy and underlying justification for this legislation dates back to the Radio Act of 1912, which contemplated that a foreign-controlled radio station could seriously threaten national security by potentially interfering with American communications. The Community stresses that these US laws, as well as the FTA Exemption Clause, explicitly recognize culture as a separate and distinct animal from other goods and services, thereby warranting the restrictions.

The American reaction to the inclusion of the Exemption clause was swift. Jack Valenti, President of the Motion Picture Association of America, noted that if NAFTA is left unchanged, it will cause the film, TV, and video industry severe injury, putting its 3.5 billion trade surplus at risk. Jay Berman, President of the recording Industry Association of America, stated. "The Canadians have deliberately confused commerce and culture. For the Canadians, culture is used to mask a real commercial interest. Most often this type of commercial self-interest will result in discriminatory treatment for United States copyright industries." For these reasons, the US entertainment industry has repeatedly called for renegotiation of the NAFTA Exemption clause.

The EC did not escape criticism. Mr. Valenti, in response to the Directive, wondered whether "the culture of any European is so flimsily anchored, so tenuously rooted, that European consumers and viewers must be caged and blinded else their links with their historic and distinguished past suddenly vanish?"

However, despite all the criticism, the US still does not seem to recognize that there is a genuine problem. The United States domination of global entertainment markets has caused visible resentment.

## Notes and References

1. Paul Goldstein (1991), *Copyright: Principles, Law and Practice,* 1.
2. Library of Congress, *Copyright Enactments, 1783-1900* (Copyright Office Bulletin No. 3) 10-11 (1900).
3. John H. Merryman, "The Refrigerator of Bernard Buffet", 27 *Hastings law Journal,* 1023, 1028 (1976).
4. Russell J. Da Silva, "Droit Moral and the Amoral Copyright", 28, Bull. Copyright Society, 1, 17 (1980).
5. Judgement of Mar. 19, 1947, Courd' appel, Paris (1949) D.P. 20.
6. Sony Corporation of America, V. Universal City Studies, 464 U.S 417, 429 (1984).
7. Robert A. Gorman, "Federal Moral Rights Legislation: The Need for Caution", 14 *Nova Law Review,* 421, 423-24, (1990).
8. *Ibid.*
9. *Ibid.*
10. Peter Jazsi, Toward a Theory of Copyright: The Metamorphoses of "Authorship," 1991 *Duke Law Journal,* 455, 497.
11. Wheaton V. Peters, 33 U.S. (8.Pet.) 591 (1834).
12. Edward J. Damich, "The Right of Personality: a Common-law Basis for the Protection of the Moral Rights of Author 23 *Georgia Law Review* 1 (1988).
13. DeG. & Sm. 652, 64 Eng. Rep. 293 (1849) affd, 1 Mac. & 6. 25, 41 Eng. Rep. 1171 (1849).
14. 23N.42d341 NE2d 250, 296 N. 45. 2d. 771. (1968).
15. 471 U.S. 539 (1985).
16. Pascal Kamina, "Authorship of Films and Implementation of the Term Directive: The Dramatic Tale of Two Copyrights", 8 E.I.P.R. 319 (1994).
17. Jeffrey M. Dine, "Authors" Moral Rights In Non-European Nations: International Agreements, Economics, Mannu Bhandari, and the Dead Sea Scrolls", 16 *Michigan Journal of International Law* (1995) 545. Copyright © 1995 University of Michigan Law School.

18. Raymond Sarraute, "Current Theory on the Moral Right of Authors and Artists under French Law", 16 *American Journal of Comparative Law* 465, 468 (1968)
19. Stephen Stewart International *Copyright and Neighboring Rights* 73, 7374 (2d ed. 1989). Jack. A. Cline, "Moral Rights: The Long and Winding Road Toward Recognition", 14 Nova Law Reveiw 435, (1990) Jack A. Cline.
20. *Human Rights Tribune*, Vol. 7 No. 2&3, September 2000, 11-12.
21. Jack. A. Cline, "Moral Rights: The Long and Winding Road Towards Recognition", 14 *Nova Law Review* 435, (1990).
22. Jack. A. Cline, "Moral Rights: The Long and Winding Road Towards Recognition", 14 *Nova* Law Review 435, (1990).
23. See, E.g. Ellies *v.* Hurst, 66 Misc. 235, 121 N.Y. Supp. 438 (Sup. Ct. 1910 (utilizing the right to privary); Clemens *v.* Press Publishing Co., 67 Misc. 183, 122 N.Y. Supp. 206 (Sup. Ct. 1910) Contract rights); Fischer *v.* Star Co., 231 N.Y. 414 132 N.E. 133 (1921) Unfair Competition.
24. Jack. A. Cline, "Moral Rights: The Long and Winding Road Towards Recognition", 14 *Nova Law Review* 435, (1990).
25. Jeffrey M. Dine, "Authors' Moral Rights in Non-European Nations: International Agreements, Economics, Mannu Bhandai and the Dead sea Scrolls", 16 *Michigan International Law* 545 (1995), University of Michigan, Law School.
26. Christopher Aide, "A more Comprehensive soul: Romantic Conceptions of Authorship and the Copyright Doctrine of Moral Right." 48U, *Toranto Faculty Law Review* 211, (1990).
27. Russell J. Dasilva, "Droit Moral and the Amoral Copyright: A Comparison of Artists," Rights in France and the United States," 28 Bull. (1980).
28. P. Recht, le Droit D'Auteur, Une Nouelle Forme De Propriete 281.
29. 1 S. Stromholum, 1 *Droit Moral de L'Auteur* 159-53 (1996).
30. *Ibid.*, at 154-56.
31. P. Recht (*Supra* note 45) at 58-60.
32. *Ibid.* at 78.
33. *Ibid.* at 84.
34. Jeff Berg, "Moral Rights; A legal Historical and Anthropological Reappraisal." 6I. P.J. 341 (1991).
35. Reymond Sarraute, "Current Theory in the Moral Rights of Authors and Artists under the French law" 16 American Journal of Comparative Law 465 (1968)
36. Article 32 of the French Law of March 11, 1957.
37. Sarraute *Supra* note (35) at 480.
38. French law of March 11, 1957.
39. J. Merryman & A. Elesen, *Law, Ethics and the Visual Arts* 147 (2d ed. 1987).
40. California Art preservation Act. cal. Civ. code 987, 989.
41. New York Arts and Cultural Affairs Law, 14. 51-14, 59 (1983).

42. Dasilva, "Droit Moral and the A Moral Copyright: A Comparison of Artists' Rights in France and the U.S." 28 Bull. Copyright Soc'y 1, 12 (1980).
43. L. Hyde, "The Gift: Imagination and the Erotic Life of Property", (vintage 1979).
44. Arthur B. Sackler, "The United States should not Adhere to the Berne Copyright Convention, 3 *Journal of Law and Technology* 207 (1978).
45. Carl H. Settlemyer III, Between Thought and Possession: Artists "Moral Right" and Public Access to Creative Works" 81 Georgia Law Journal 2291 (1993).
46. Fox Film Co. *v.* Doyal, 286 U.S. 123, 127 (1932)
47. Peter Jazsi, "Toward a Theory of Copyright: The Metamorphosis of "Authorship," 1991 *Duke Law Journal.*
48. Sam Ricketson, "Is Australia In Breach of Its International Obligations with Respect to the Protection of Moral Rights?" 17 Melbourne University Law Review 462 (1990).
49. Robert A. Jacobs, "Work—for Hire and the Moral Right Dilemma in the European Community: A U.S. Perspective", 16 B.C. *International and Comparative Law Review* (1993).
50. Judgement of May 28, 1991 (Huston *v.* La clinq) Cass. Civ. 1991 Bull;. Civ. No. 89-19. 522 (Fr.).
51. However, Article 15(2) Implicitly Recognizes the Doctrine since it addresses Corporate authorship of a Cinematographic work: The Person or body Corporate whose name Appears on a Cinematographic work in the usual manner shall, in the absence of proof to the contrary, be presumed in the absence of proof to the contrary, be presumed to be the maker of said work" Berne Convention, at Article 15(2). Corporate authorship can only arise by treating the corporation as author. A corporation, in turn, can only be an author through its employees, and only by virtue of work for hire principles. Hence, Article 15(2) incorporates work-for-hire, albeit implicitly, only in the context of cinematographic works.
52. Judgement of May 28, 1991 (Hustron *v.* La Clinq) Cass. Civ. 1991 Bull. Civ. No. 89-19, 522 (Fr.).
53. After setting forth specific economic right that the Convention protects in Article IV bis(1), Article IV bis(2) states the following: 2. However, any Contracting State, may by its domestic legislation, make exceptions that do not conflict with the spirit and provisions of this Convention, to the rights mentioned in paragraph I of this Article. Any State whose legislation so provides, shall nevertheless accord a reasonable degree of effective protection to each of the rights to which exception has been made.

    Universal copyright Convention, at Art. IVbis (2). By Juxtraposing the exceptions that paragraph (2) authorizes with the term "(H)owever", the UCC impliedly sanctions moral rights so long as it does not hinter exploitation of economic right. In theory and sometimes in practice (as in Huston) this hindrance is inevitable.

54. United Kingdom Copyright Designs and Patent Act, 1988, Sec. 87(2).
55. William R. Cornish, "United Kingdom" in *International Copyright Law and Practice* (1991) at 31.
56. *Ibid.*
57. See, eg. Italian Copyright Law, at Arts. 38, 45, 88 (publishers of collective works), all obtain economic copyright interest); Spanish Copyright Law at Arts, 8.51 (Publishers of collective works acquire both economic and moral right copyright interest and employers acquire limited economic interest without contract).
58. See Fabiani, *Supra* note 156, at 38 (in most contexts employers and principals must contract for copyright interest); del Corral, *Supra* note 182, at 25 (s)ince. . . only natural persons can be authors . . . legal entities normally acquire copyright from such persons by contract.").
59. Mario Franzosi and Guistino de Sanctis, "Moral Rights and New Technology: Are Copyright and Patents Converging?" 2, EI.P.R. 63 Copyright 1995 Mario Franzosi and Guidstino de Sanctis.
60. Laurance G.C. Kaplan, "The European Community's "Television without Frontiers" Directive: Stimulating Europe to Regulate Culture" 8, *Emory International Law Review* 255 (1994).
61. Stacie I. Strong, "The Cultural Exclusion: Free Trade and Copyrighted Goods", 4 *Duke Journal of Comparative and International Law.*
62. Stephan A. Konighsberg, "Think Globally, Act Locally: North American Free Trade, Canadian Cultural Industry Exemption and the Liberalization of the Broadcast Ownership Laws" 12 *Cordozo Arts Entertainment Law Journal.*
63. Lawrence G.C. Kaplan, "The European Community's Television without Frontiers Directive: Stimulating Europe to Regulate Culture," 8 *Emory International Law Review*, 255 (1994).
64. See for details and discussion, Pradip N. Thomas and Zaharom Nain (Editors) (2004) Who owns? *The Media?—Global Trends and Local Resistance* (Malaysia South Bound? Sdn. Bhd. Suite 20 Fordham Northam House.

CHAPTER

# 6

## Major Themes under Discussion

*The Wise is rich,With every blessing blest;*
*The fool is Poor, of everything Possessed.*
—Thiruvalluvar Thirukkural 430.

When a distinct class of disputes arise and recur among a group of nation, sooner or later they entertain the idea of entering into treaty that could make it possible to avoid further disputes. Treaties are broadly classified as bilateral or multilateral. Bilateral treaties often include a more disparate set of provisions than do multilateral treaties. This follows from the fact that two nations, A and B, may have a number of contentious issues between them, and the treaty conference is a handy vehicle for horse-trading among issues and resolving all of them. Thus, a bilateral treaty might have provisions favoured by A on matters of copyright, and provisions favoured by B on a distinct issue such as a most-favoured-nation customs agreement. In the Nineteenth Century, such omnibus bilateral treaties were often called treaties of Amity, Commerce and Navigation. Today, it is more likely that the treaty conference between A and B might result, in the example above given in two separate bilateral treaties: One on copyright and the other on most-favoured-nation status.

As soon as three or more states come to a treaty conference, the resulting treaty is likely to be a single-issue treaty. It could be a huge issue (like the law of the sea), but it is nevertheless single-minded. This again is a function of the kinds of issues that tend to be resolved when three or more states meet. State A might have a particular claim against State B, which in turn might have a different claim against state C; it would be difficult and frustrating to get these separate matters resolved in a single treaty because the unaffected party would not necessarily know where is future interest may lie. Thus, multilateral conferences tend to be called with respect to a single issue. Copyright has its own multilateral treaties; patents its own; and recently there have been off-shoot multilateral treaties (TRIPS is an off-shoot of GATT).

This Phase of arguments begins by looking at the bilateral and multilateral approaches to dispute avoidance by treaty. It continues with a discussion of treaty interpretation and treaty reservations (reservations only apply to multilateral treaties; there is no such thing as a reservation to a bilateral treaty).

Often the treaty that emerges from a multilateral treaty conference is noticeably shaped by the organization that provided the forum for the conference. A treaty that results from a UNESCO initiative thus might be different from a treaty that comes out of a conference sponsored by GATT or WIPO, even if the state participants are the same and issues are the same. Much of the debate going into the initial choice of forum centers on the perceived status of the sponsoring organization. is it political or neutral, pro-developed nations or pro-developing nations? This Phase examines some of these issues, with a particular focus on the debate during the Uruguay Round Negotiations of GATT over the appropriateness of utilizing GATT as a forum for intellectual property concerns.

We conclude with a closer look at the major intellectual property treaties; The Paris Convention for the Protection of Industrial Property,[1] the Berne Convention, the Universal Copyright Convention[2], the Agreement on Trade Related Aspects of Intellectual Property Rights[3] (TRIPS), and the

North American Free Trade Agreement (NAFTA)[4]. . . . we will take a closer look at Trademark and Patent registration treaties[5], including the Madrid Agreement and Protocol and the Patent Cooperation Treaty.

## I. MULTINATIONAL OR BILATERAL SOLUTIONS TO INTELLECTUAL PROPERTY PROTECTION

### (a) Bilateral Agreements[6]

The existence of differing legal regimes complicates intellectual property protection. A reasonable standard for one country may not be similarly viewed by another. Whether a country follows case law, as opposed to a civil code, may be highly determinative of the type of legal standard that country is willing to embrace.

Bilateral agreements provide the most workable vehicle for addressing the contentious issues surrounding intellectual property protection. Unlike multilateral agreements, bilateral agreements are country specific and thus may provide more protection for owners of foreign rights.

The Government of India has recently enacted a number of Legislation in Indian Parliament agreements that take a hard line against intellectual property piracy. These Legislations that take a hard line against intellectual property piracy.

> In a Country that has a more- than-a-century-old tradition of strong legal protection for innovation in technology and processes (through grant of patents) and systems of registration of copyrights (for works of literature and arts) and trademarks (for symbols of merchandise and trade names) such confusion should be a matter of serious concern. The public doubts about the value of IPRs have been influenced by the 1994 GATT agreement on Trade -related Aspects of Intellectual Property Rights, which has compelled India to amend the Indian Patents Act of 1970. The 1970 Legislation, which permitted only process and not product Patents for foods, drugs

> and agrochemicals, facilitated the production and availability of Pharmaceutical and other products at prices highly advantageous to Indian consumers. The benefits experienced in the health care filed were particularly significant.

Some agreements are usually subsequent to a US threat of trade sanctions pursuant to "Super 301" of the 1988 Omnibus Trade and Competitiveness Act.[8] These bilateral agreements have generally encouraged speedier and more substantial changes in suspect nations, as failure to comply might result in immediate trade sanctions.

For example, the People's Republic of China amended its intellectual property laws pursuant to a Memorandum of Under-standing it concluded with the United States in January 1992. This document was drafted in direct response to threatened retaliation by the United States.

A bilateral approach can recognize and incorporate into the agreement the developing country's stage of development and genuine efforts to improve the system of intellectual property protection. In addition, bilateral negotiations present a workable environment in which the developed country can introduce the developing country to the benefits of protecting intellectual property.

**(b) Special 301**

Strong international protection of copyright removes the incentive of states to employ unilateral measures to ensure protection of works produced by their nationals. US trade sanctions against China were proposed because there was no other effective remedy available to the United States. Specifically, there were no international mechanisms in place to compel China to enforce its copyright laws.

The criticisms leveled at the United States for its use of the Special 301 procedures focuses not on the ends, but the means. The protection of intellectual property is supported by the majority of nations, although many express displeasure with the unilateral nature of "Special 301" actions. If successful, US judicial extension of extraterritorial jurisdiction would likely elicit a similar reaction.[9]

Uniform standards are indeed difficult to attain when nations pursue bilateral agreements, each with its own terms. The threat of trade sanctions, moreover, is always accompanied by risk. The United States-China trade impasse may have been triggered by copyright negotiations, but its resolution involved political issues that are far afield from intellectual property.

**(c) Multinational Treaties: An Overview**

Multinational treaty regimes include both regional agreements, such as The Treaty of Rome (establishing the European Union) and NAFTA, and broad based, multination agreements such as the Berne Convention and the General Agreement on Trade and Tariffs ("GATT"). In the area of intellectual property protection the major multinational treaty regimes are administered either by WIPO (the Berne and Paris Conventions, among others), the WTO (the TRIPS Agreement) or UNESCO (The Universal copyright Convention). Differences in the methods for altering these agreements and in their enforcement mechanisms often dictate which forum is selected. Regardless of the forum selected the goal of these agreements is similar—to achieve a multinational solution to the problems caused by inadequate international protection of intellectual property rights.[10]

**(d) WIPO and UNESCO**

The World Intellectual Property Organization is a specialized agency of the United Nations having its headquarters in Geneva. WIPO's General Assembly is a representative body having delegates from each of its 116 member states. The General Assembly appoints WIPO's Director General, currently Director General Bogsch, who is in charge of the International Bureau (Secretariat). The objectives of WIPO are to promote the protection of intellectual property throughout the world and to administer the international intellectual property unions, such as the Berne and Paris Conventions.[11]

The four major multinational unions that WIPO administers are the Paris Convention, the Berne Convention, the Madrid Agreement and the Rome Convention. The Paris

Convention, which is over 100 years old, contains provisions relating to inventions, trade names, trademarks industrial designs, utility models, indications of source, appellations of origin, and the repression unfair competition.

The Paris Convention grants the rights of priority and national treatment. National treatment requires that a country cannot provide less favorable intellectual property treatment to foreigners than to its citizens. National treatment of the Paris Convention is often criticized—if a country chooses to provide no intellectual property protection for its citizens, the Paris Convention does not require it to provide intellectual property protection for foreigners either.

The Patent Cooperation Treaty ("PCT") implements the Paris convention's right of priority, by providing a one year grace period from the date of the filing of a patent application in the home country to the filing in another member country.

The Berne Convention [which contains Provisions relating to copyrights] receives much less criticism than the Paris convention. Berne requires minimum standards of protection in addition to national treatment. Perhaps the reason for the minimum standards in Berne, but not in the Paris Convention, is because Berne applies special rules to developing countries. The Berne Convention has 88 members.

The Universal Copyright Convention ("UCC"), which is administered by UNESCO, is an alternative copyright treaty for non-members of Berne at its inception such as the US, Soviet Union and China. The foundation of the UCC is also national treatment. While the UCC provides minimum standards of protection, the standards are lower than those of Berne. Since the US and the former Soviet Union acceded to Berne, Berne has taken the primary role in formulating international copyright policy.

The Madrid Agreement, another WIPO agreement over a hundred years old, simplifies the procedures for filing trademarks and service marks in different countries. The US is not a member of Madrid, but is actively seeking accession to the Madrid Protocol.

The Rome Convention requires international protection for performers, producers of phonograms and broadcasting organizations; i.e., neighboring rights. The Rome Convention provides for national treatment and specifies minimum rights. As of January 1, 1990, the Rome Convention had 32 members. The US was not a member.

#### (e) WTO

The World Trade Organization ("WTO") is the successor organization to GATT and is charged with overseeing the TRIPS Agreement. TRIPS utilizes the Paris, Berne and Rome Conventions to establish minimum standards of protection in addition to national treatment. It also establishes multinational enforcement standards for intellectual property rights.

## 2. THE ENFORCEMENT OF TREATY OBLIGATIONS

#### (a) Treaty Interpretation[12]

The defining issue in both legal and literary interpretation can be characterized as follows; to what extent does the text have a determinate meaning, and to what extent is the reader free to interpret it as he or she chooses? This question is especially relevant to treaty interpretation where, more often than not, the contracting parties themselves have the final say about the meaning of particular provisions of the agreement in question (a phenomenon that can be labeled "auto-interpretation") Because many international instruments do not provide for the submission of disputes to impartial tribunals, interpretation is a responsibility of domestic officials who are institutionally predisposed to interpretations preferred by their State and government.

Skepticism about the determinacy of meaning combined with the absence of an impartial interpreter can lead to the discomforting conclusion that treaty auto-interpretation is an unconstrained activity determined entirely by short-term national interests and power politics. In this article, this author seeks to counter that perception by positing the existence of a structure of constraints embedded in the process of treaty interpretation despite the absence of a disinterested interpreter. Interpretive authority, it will be argued, resides in neither the text nor the reader individually, but with the community of professionals engaged in the enterprise of treaty interpretation and implementation. This "interpretive community: is defined and constituted by a set of conventions and institutional practices that structure the interpretive process.

Of primary importance is the notion that treaties, unlike works of literature, embody a commitment to a distinctive process of interpretation. This commitment is rooted in the fact that a treaty is the product of the consensual activity of two or more States, and its terms embody the collective expectations and interests of the parties. Because the parties to the treaty comprise the collective norm-creating body, the competence of authoritative interpretation is vested in the composite organ they form rather than either of them individually. If the treaty does not provide for a dispute resolution procedure, then an authoritative interpretation can only result from a process that embodies this notion of the parties as a composite lawmaking entity in some other way. In entering into a a treaty, a State binds itself not only to the terms of the instrument (however interpreted) but also a process of intersubjective interpretation; the interpretive task is to ascertain what the text means to the parties collectively rather than to each individually. The activities and perspectives of the interpretive communities associated with this enterprise render treaty auto-interpretation something other than the exercise of unilateral political will.

The interpretive process, then, must be understood as part of an ongoing relationship in which the parties generate, elaborate and refine shared understandings and expectations.

The parties can be viewed as having implicitly agreed to a process of intersubjective interpretation because, while they expect disagreement over the meaning of terms, they do not expect every disagreement to signify a desire on the part of one or the other to revoke the treaty or terminate the relationship embodied in it. States comply with treaties primarily because they have an interest in reciprocal compliance by the other party or parties.

In understanding how treaty auto-inter-pretation is constrained, two interpretive communities can be identified;

the community interpreters directly responsible for the conclusion and implementation of a particular treaty, and a broader, international community consisting of all experts and officials engaged in the various professional activities associated with treaty practice. The conventions and institutional practices of both interpretive communities have constraining effect, although the contribution of the latter is derivative in that its authority can be traced to the implicit a agreement between the parties to engage in intersubjective interpretation.

*I. The Narrow Interpretative Community*

The exercise of formulating, negotiating, ratifying, and implementing a treaty generates an interpretive community of individuals within each contracting party who share what Fish calls "assumed distinctions, categories of understanding, and stipulations of relevance and irrelevance."[13] That is, the process of producing and living under a treaty generates a community (not out of whole cloth but out of already existing communities with an elaborate web of relationships to the new community) of people and institutions associated with the treaty. These people are the officials within each State (from the leader down) who have or had responsibility for any of the various steps involved in producing the treaty.

The Constraining effect of this narrow interpretive community is felt, in part, though the expectations and beliefs controlled by the agreement. In the period prior to the making of an agreement, some sort of relationship exists or the agreement would not have been possible that generates a body of knowledge shared by the parties. Officials within each State learn about the others' interests, values and assumptions, as well as their perspectives on the various components of the relationship. An agreement "crystallizes the learning of the particular period"[14] and the" learning of a particular period" and the contacts made help spread common understandings about the precise terms of the agreement as well as its significance to the broader relationship. The agreement becomes a focal point around which expectations converge. Furthermore, by communicating and exchanging information the governments come to know their partners in the agreement and not merely know about them. The participants in the enterprise come to inhabit a common world—a world that does not simply come out of the shared beliefs and attitudes of it inhabitants but in fact generates those beliefs and attitudes through common participation.

*2. The Broader Interpretive Community*

Beyond the immediate interpretive community centered abound the treaty itself, interpretation in constrained by an amorphous community of all those regarded as possessing the knowledge of an expert or professional in the relevant field. As Oscar Schachter explains, governments cannot escape legal appraisals of their conduct by other governments. (expressed either individually or in collective bodies), political parties, international lawyers, non-governmental organisatios and other organs of public opinion.[15] In the ream of military security, this community judgment is influenced by the opinions of governmental and non-governmental experts on international law, world politics and strategic affairs. The competency or expertise comes from training and immersion in some feature of the enterprise in which the experts and immersion in some feature of the enterprise in which the experts are engaged. As participants in the field of practice, they have come to understand its purposes and conventions, learned not merely as a set of abstract rules but through the acquisition of know-how, a mastering of the discipline or technique. Having participated in the techniques and discourse of international law, treaty interpretation and or the subject matter of the treaty, they have become competent in the field.

The outlying interpretive community represents the institutional mechanism closest to an impartial arbiter that the structure of treaty auto-interpretation provides. It constrains interpretation primarily because States have an interest in maintaining a reputatiosn for good faith adherence to treaties. As Louis Henkin states:

> Every nation's foreign policy depends substantially on its "credit"—on maintaining the

> expectation that it will live-up to international mores and obligations. Considerations of "honor," "prestige," "leadership," "influence," "reputation," which figure prominently in governmental decisions, often weigh in favour of observing law. Nations generally desire a reputation for principled behaviour, for propriety and respectability.[16]

This interest combined with the implicit agreement between the parties to engage in intersubjective interpretation means the outlying interpretive community effectively checks and structures the interpretive activities of the parties.

## 3. RESERVATIONS

### (a) Definitions[17]

The three major classifications of treaty qualifying unilateral statements are reservations, understanding, and declarations. A reservation is a formal declaration made by a state when it joins a treaty, a declaration that acts to limit or modify the effect of the treaty in application to the reserving state. A reservation is external to the text of the treaty and is an attempt to alter the negotiated package. Because reservations are made outside of the treaty negotiations, their amendment to the multilateral treaty may conflict with the original text of the treaty. The ultimate effect of the reservation will depend on the practice or rule of reservations applied and the existence of nonexistence of special provisions within the treaty governing inclusion and effect of reservations.

The term "understanding" is used to designate a statement not intended to alter or limit the effect of the treaty, but rather to set forth a state's interpretation or explanation of a treaty provision. In practice, understandings are sometimes used to provide a memorandum of the nation's interpretation at the time of signing in case of future judicial or arbitral proceedings.

A declaration is a unilateral statement of policy or opinion that, like an understanding, is not intended to alter or limit any provision of the treaty. It is considered to have the least effect on the original treaty text and is used primarily to articulate a signatory's purpose, position, or expectation, concerning the treaty in question.

### (b) The Vienna Convention

The Vienna Convention on the Law of Treaties defines a "reservation" as "a unilateral statement, however, phrased or named, by a State, when signing, ratifying, accepting, approving or acceding to a treaty, whereby it purports to exclude or modify the legal effect of certain provisions of a treaty in their application to that State." Among the pertinent provisions of the Vienna Convention regarding the force and effectiveness of a reservation are the following:

*Article 19*[18]

A State may, when signing, ratifying, accepting, approving or acceding to a treaty, formulate a reservation unless:

(a) the reservation is prohibited by treaty;
(b) the treaty provides that only specified reservations, which do not include the reservation in question, may be made; or
(c) in cases not falling under subparagraphs (a) and (b), the reservation is incompatible with the object and purpose of the treaty.

*Article 20*

1. A reservation expressly authorized by a treaty does not require any subsequent acceptance by the other contracting States unless the treaty so provides.
2. When it appears from the limited number of the negotiating States and the object and purpose of a treaty that the application of the treaty in its entirety between all the parties is an essential condition of the consent of each one to be bound by the treaty, a reservation requires acceptance by all the parties.

3. When a treaty is a constituent instrument of an international organization and unless it otherwise provides, a reservation requires the acceptance of the competent organ of that organization.
4. In cases not falling under the preceding paragraphs and unless the treaty otherwise provides:
   (a) acceptance by another contracting State of a reservation constitutes the reserving State a party to the treaty in relation to that other State if or when the treaty is in force for those States;
   (b) an objection by another contracting State to a reservation does not preclude the entry into force of the treaty as between the objecting and reserving States unless a contrary intention is definitely expressed by the objecting State;
   (c) an act expressing a State's consent to be bound by the treaty and containing a reservation is effective as soon as at least one other contracting State has accepted the reservation.
5. For the purposes of paragraphs 2 and 4 and unless the treaty otherwise provides, a reservation is considered to have been accepted by state if it shall have raised no objection to the reservation by the end of a period of twelve months after it was notified of the reservation or by the date on which it expressed its consent to be bound by the treaty, whichever is later.

*Article 23*

1. A reservation, an express acceptance of a reservation, and an objection to a reservation must be formulated in writing and communicated to the contracting States and other States entitled to become parties to the treaty.

2. If formulated when signing the treaty subject to ratification, acceptance or approval, a reservation must be formally confirmed by the reserving State when expressing its consent to be bound by the treaty. In such a case the reservation shall be consideredhaving been made on the date of its confirmation.
3. An express acceptance of, or an objection to, reservation made previously to confirmation of the reservation does not itself require confirmation.
4. The withdrawal of a reservation or of an objection to a reservation must be formulated in writing.

*Article 21*

1. A reservation established with regard to another party in accordance with Articles 19, 20 and 23:
   (a) modifies for the reserving State in its relations with the other party the provisions of the treaty to which the reservation relates to the extent of the reservation; and
   (b) modifies those provisions to the same extent for that other party in its relations with the reserving State.
2. The reservation does not modify the provisions of thetreaty for the other parties to the treaty inter se.
3. When a State objecting to a reservation has not opposed the entry into force of the treaty between itself and the reserving State, the provisions to which the reservation relates do not apply as between the two states to the extent of the reservation.

Although the United States has not acceded to the Vienna Convention, it has relied upon it as an authoritative text for treaty interpretations in state Department communiqués and in cases before international tribunals.

### (c) Desirability of Reservations

Conceptually, the issue of the desirability of reservations is straightforward. Most arguments in favour of the liberal use of reservations have as their cornerstone the belief that the liberal admissibility of reservations will encourage wider acceptance of treaties.

The other edge of the sword, as it were, is that reservations necessarily reduce the uniformity and consistency (if not the integrity) of a treaty.

The exact nature of the balance between uniformity/ consistency and universality may be complex. For example, it is possible that a point exists in the liberal use of reservations beyond which participation will be reduced as those states satisfied with a treaty feel its integrity is being stretched to the breaking point by the permissibility of reservations. This problem may be both latent and practical, i.e., perceived because the treaty does not restrict the use of reservations, and an actual reaction to reservations that have been made The point is that a direct proportionality between the liberal admissibility of reservations and wider acceptance of a treaty cannot be assumed.[19]

## 4. THE ABSENCE OF HARMONIZATION STANDARDS

Article 10bis includes a general obligation to member countries "to assure to nationals of the Paris Convention for the Protection of Industrial Property effective protection against unfair competition." However, this provision has not afforded a meaningful guarantee, for the treaty's definition of unfair competition leaves too much room for inconsistent and uncertain application.[20]

The text prohibits "any act of competition contrary to honest practices in industrial or commercial matters." [Article 10bis (2)] The two key terms are "act of competition" and "contrary to honest practices.:" These terms, however, refer to different legal regimes. According to a leading commentary on the treaty, the national law of each member country will determine what acts constitute "acts of competition", while international trade norms will determine the meaning of "honest practices."[21]

The treaty's failure to give content to these terms seriously weakens article 10bis. Consider the unauthorized adaptation of a computer program to a "hardware platform" for which it was not originally designed. Reference to a given member country's law may yield different responses as to whether the unauthorized transporting of the program would constitute "competition." If it would not, then even if the conduct complained of were "contrary to honest practices," the treaty apparently would not apply. For example, assume that breaking into computer security codes or tapping into telephone connections violates international norms of "honest practices." Assume also that, in the applicable forum, using the information thus acquired to create a related, but not directly competing program is not an act of "competition." In that case, the Paris Convention may not require awarding relief.

Similarly, even if the forum would classify the challenged act as "competition," if the act does not also violate international norms of "honest practices," then 10bis will not apply. Thus, if defendant "clones" a user interface, but does so using publicly available information, it is not clear that (in the absence of copyright protection) this act would violate international standards of fair play. As a result, one must question the ability of the Paris Convention to supply an alternative norm of intellectual property protection for computer programs.

## 5. THE CHOICE OF NATIONAL TREATMENT, RECIPROCITY OR MINIMUM RIGHTS

### (a) Territoriality and the Need for National Treatment

The "territorial" view of intellectual property, which maintained that an owner's rights ended at the border, necessarily gave rise to multinational efforts to establish international protection norms, culminating in the Berne and Paris Conventions in the latter part of the Nineteenth Century. Because of the accepted territorial nature of intellectual property rights, both Conventions relied largely upon a "national treatment" standard to assure uniform protection. Subsequent bilateral and multinational intellectual property treaties have similarly adopted a "national treatment" standard.

Where a "national treatment" standard is adopted, no agreement on the substantive rights granted an intellectual property owner is achieved; Each nation is required simply to provide identical protection under its domestic laws to both domestic and foreign rightsholders. Similarly, where "reciprocal treatment" is adopted, no agreement on an owner's substantive rights is achieved. Instead, each nation is required to provide identical protection under its domestic laws but only to the extent that the country of the foreign owner provides reciprocal rights.

Twentieth Century and twentyfirst century advances have called into question both the continuing viability of a territorial theory for intellectual property protection as well as the usefulness of a national treatment standard.

**(b) Territoriality and the Problem of Reciprocity**

There is now an attack on a widely accepted theory: the territoriality of intellectual property. There are more and more cases in which its difficult to localize the origin or the-infringement of intellectual property territorially. Research teams increasingly developing nation by collaborating in many countries at the same time within the framework of multinational corporations or consortiums. Authors increasingly collaborate within worldwide telecommunication networks, creating works that are in turn susceptible of instantaneous dissemination throughout such networks.[22] The difficulty is illustrated by the case in which the Nike company wanted to have its trademark attached to the clothing worn by Olympic athletes in Barcelona in 1992. A Spanish claimant had previously registered the name "Nike" ad a trademark in Spain and sued to prevent the Nike Company from using this name in Barcelona. National treatment results in subjecting Nike to prior registration in/ Spain, just as it would any Spinish national. But should this purely territorial priority preclude disseminating a trademark worldwide? That was, in any event, where Nike wanted its mark televised from the Olympics.[23]

The increasing difficulty of localizing such facts territory by territory has manifold consequences. Reciprocity, if it limits protection to the level established in a country of origin, requires localizing the fact of innovation, creation, or first use in that country. If that fact takes places across national borders, for example, because of coproduction in many countries, selecting any one country of origin will at least partially result in a legal fiction Further, to determine in what country to claim national treatment relative to rights of intellectual property, it is necessary to ascertain in what national territory to localize infringement of such property. Suppose, for example, that a pirate inputs a literary or artistic work into a world wide telecommunication network without consent; the copyright owner might not be sure in which country or countries to assert to assert infringement claims—at points of input or access in the network, or both. Finally, the judge might hesitate in deciding which country's or countries' laws to choose to determine rights enforceable at such points. All these Gordian knots may be cut by imposing much the same rights for any given property across many countries at once. This the Paris and Berne Conventions began to do in establishing minimum rights for intellectual properties.

Both material reciprocity and national treatment presuppose the old doctrine that intellectual property originates, and is enforced, territory by territory. Not only does the TRIPS agreement incorporate such territorial premises as the Paris-Berne regime brings with it, but it still bears traces of comparable premises in the GATT, which above all concerned trade in tangible goods that can always be located territorially, at given spots on this earth. The TRIPS Agreement effectively devotes many provisions to the old problem of controlling the traffic in infringing goods moving from one national territory to another. This perspective, however, is not necessarily always appropriate to more volatile forms of trade in intangibles, such as commerce in intellectual property or in services.

A purely territorial approach will not help us to confront the reality of the twenty-first century. Already today, the Internet is where prior art, relevant for determining the novelty of inventions, might be aired worldwide. Similarly, the Nike example illustrates how telecommunication allows trade and service marks to be used in transborder marketing campaigns.

### (c) The Continuing Viability of National Treatment[24]

The building blocks of international copyright seem to be territorial. In the past, these building blocks have always been nation-states, which concluded copyright treaties; these states have had to protect foreign works against acts of infringement localized within their territories.

The classic dynamics of international copyright started to gather momentum some five hundred years ago. Three types of classic processes followed each other in time; *first,* the impetus given by the print media to copyright lawmaking; *second,* the decentralization of copyright interests; and *third,* the emergence of international copyright.

*The first* classic process commenced in the fifteenth century. The printing press was introduced into Europe, and the church and kings sought to control the rising book trade. They gave publishers, in capitals such as Paris and London, state-protected monopolies to print and sell books the censors had approved. These monopolies; royal authorities—or, publishers, by powers delegated from the sovereign—policed these monopolies on national territories. Tensions arose, however, as print shop opened throughout the provinces, books were increasingly smuggled across borders, and the growing reading public also sought between access to printed works.

*The second* classic process, the decentralization of copyright interests, hit its stride in the eighteenth century. Control of the dissemination of works was shifted from centers of royal power, outward to individual authors and publishers. These parties were granted copyright as a private right, exploitable throughout the national marketplace and enforceable by any court on civil suit. Ultimately, neither the state nor copyright owners but the public buying books or the theater tickets in this marketplace decided which works were to gain the widest dissemination. Note also that the first copyright law, the Statute of Anne of 1709, was enacted at the very moment England and Scotland were being joined into a common market.

*The third classic process,* internationalization, began to take effect in the mid-nineteenth century. Books moved easily between the many countries of Europe sharing close borders. These countries began to cover Europe with a complicated web of bilateral treaties in order to protect the works of their respective nationals abroad. These treaties varied greatly, and authors, publishers and lawyers soon began to ask how to make more uniform law to govern the growing international market for works. Some proposed that all countries adopt the same copyright code at once, but a more modest proposal prevailed; simply conclude one copyright code at once, but a more modest proposal prevailed; simply conclude one copyright treaty, binding as many countries as possible, to compel the same choice of laws in cases of foreign works. This process culminated in 1886, when ten countries, seven of them European, established the Berne Convention.

The Berne Convention began what one commentator has called the "dissolution of the territoriality" of copyright.[25] Under the Berne principle of national treatment, the law of each Berne country applies when copyright in a Berne-protected work is infringed on its national territory. A court can easily localize the distribution of pirate copies or unauthorized theatrical performances in a given country. The court choosing law pursuant to the Berne Convention, however, need not sit within the territory of the country whose law it is to apply. For example, a court in the United States asserted jurisdiction to apply the Berne choice of low to infringement taking place in Latin America.[26]

In the twenty-first century, the media have been changing radically, setting new and continuing dynamics into motion.

*First,* the dominance of the print media gave way to a proliferation of other media. *Second,* as if in a kaleidoscope, copyright interests have been regrouping. New media have led copyright interests into turbulent regroupings. Performing artists acquired new importance with the advent of sound recording and motion pictures. Thus, Enrico Caruso became the first singer heard by fans, not merely in local concert halls, but in recordings sold worldwide. Enterprises specialized in different, competing media have lobbied for legal provisions serving their respective, conflicting interests.

*Third,* internationally, copyright has begun to splinter into uncoordinated rights [u]nder the pressure of new media and interests, copyright itself has begun to splinter into diverse rights. In response to these pressures, each Berne revision has introduced new minimum rights, such as the rights to control broadcasting and cable retransmission in Article 11bis and reproduction in Article 9 of the Paris Act. The Rome Convention has instituted neighboring artists, not only to satisfy performing artists reaching worldwide audiences, but also sound recording producers and broadcasting organizations.

This splintering of copyright threatens to undermine the Berne principle of national treatment for coordinating rights. For example, the Austrian copyright law imposed a levy on blank-tape cassettes to fund a royalty for the home recording of works. Austro-Mechana, an Austrian collecting society administering the levy, however, drew out over half of all such levies to finance programs that benefited only national authors, irrespective of foreign claims to share in all the levies. The German collecting society, GEMA, challenged that construction of the law, and the High Court of Austria reasoned that the "controlling principle of national treatment in the law of the international copyright conventions" precluded Austrian national law from allowing such a "one-sided discrimination against foreign citizens."[27] More subtle devices have been used to undercut national treatment elsewhere; for example, in France, the 1985 Act instituted so-called neighboring rights for audio-visual; producers, while specifying that holders of these rights are entitled to receive their distinct portion of blank-tape royalties. Of course, since no convention provides for national treatment relative to such so-called neighboring rights for audio-visual producers, this portion of the blank-tape royalties may be withheld from foreign claimants. More subtly yet, the local procedures of collecting societies sometimes have unintended consequences on the flow of copyright monies due to foreign claimants. Compounding these problems, there is great uncertainty concerning who owns splintering rights from country to country.[28]

At the threshold of the twenty-first century, more recent dynamics have been putting radically new stresses on the Berne system.

*The first* of these recent processes is political and legal. European nation-states, with their respective colonial empires, formed the Berne Union in 1886. European countries also played important roles in revising the Berne Convention repeatedly in this century. At present, however, these countries no longer need the Berne Union to stabilize legal conditions in the European media market. The reason is simple; the European Community has begun to function as a supra-national lawmaking authority in the field of copyright in Europe. Indeed, the Court of First Instance of the European Communities has recently declared that Berne provisions need not apply as between E.C. member countries if they conflict with E.C. law on point.

*The second* recent process represents a revolution in media trends. The media, once proliferating, are now being reconsolidated into telecommunication networks.

Works will continue to be available, albeit with decreasing frequency, both as hard copies obtained on the marketplace and as performances seen and heard in theater or concert halls. But there will be less and less need to clutter up our files and shelves with printed matter, tapes or discs, or to make photocopies or recordings from books or broadcasts. We will simply receive works on demand in digital form more or less centralized data bases, through more or less centralized telecommunication networks. The works will then be played back on highfidelity and high-definition multimedia monitors. There will accordingly be a decreasing need to buy, rent or make hard copies. We have to ask what the consequences will be for international copyright.

*The third recent* process involves a shift from private to public international law, as well as to supranational law. The Berne Convention is above all an instrument of private international law, assuring private parties of rights in literary and artistic works. To have effect, these rights must be vindicated in national courts, to which private parties may have recourse in copyright disputes with other private parties. The GATT, by contrast, is essentially an instrument of public international law; it governs disputes between public entities, notably nation states, and has procedures to adjudicate such disputes and to sanction states for violating its rules. European Community law is supranational: E.C. directives and judicial rulings may bind private parties or E.C. member states, eventually preempting national laws.

Think, for example, of Article 11bis of the Berne Convention. It is at the heart of the debate on the issue which has stretched the notion of territoriality to the breaking point; what country's law localizes acts of satellite broadcasting? One proposed resolution of this issue, I believe, illustrates how more powerful media drive us beyond the classically territorial framework of the private international law of copyright. The European Community is considering a proposed directive which defines acts of satellite communication to be subject to the law of the place where a work-carrying broadcast is unlinked to satellite. At the same time, it is argued, since the directive would harmonize the applicable laws throughout the Community, no significant choice-of-law issues would arise within any satellite footprint inside the Community. Thus the entire question of how to localize infringing acts territory by territory seems to be mooted by recourse to supranational law.

Consider this issue of territoriality more broadly. A book or a theatrical performance exists at a given point on this earth. By contrast, a work may arise and be virtually accessible at all points throughout a telecommunication network worldwide. Suppose an author collaborates by telephone, facsimile transmission or modem with a team of coauthors scattered over five continents in creating a work. Suppose, further, that our work is stored without our authorization in a data bank for release into a worldwide telecommunication network, accessible in all those continents at once. Suppose, finally, that the work is improperly indexed in the data bank and that authorship is not properly attributed to the members of the creative team. Would it make sense to localize this work in any one country of its origin or to localize its infringing storage or misattribution in any one protecting country? Indeed, in this case, creation and infringement quite simply take place throughout the network, across territorial boundaries.

As the Berne principle of national treatment is undercut, there is the clear risk of increasing the "Balkanization" of international copyright. That is, an increasing variety of copyright claims could be differently handled as between different pairs of countries.

In truth, international copyright now has to deal with more comprehensive telecommunication networks that transcend national territories. Only the European Community is now elaborating non-territorial copyright regimes for such networks.

The difficulty, however, is deeper. The Berne Union was Eurocentric from the start, in part because of European colonial dominance in the nineteenth century. Europe, with its many borders confined in a small space, also provided a microcosm of the world, in which to try out a territorial organized system of international copyright in uniting. Europe now provides a new laboratory in which to experiment with supranational copyright schemes. For a variety of reasons, however, its models may well diverge from those more appropriately adopted in other environments.

We believe and soon find ourselves faced with the following three options; *first,* adopt the new European models, if only for lack of anything better; *second,* adopt divergent schemes, thereby fracturing international copyright; or, *third,* develop a more comprehensive regime for copyright in the world at large. Such a regime could further bolster, or even in some cases supplant, national treatment with an even more comprehensive set of minimum rights. In any event, the media are making any territorial regime, with all its accompanying habits of thought, increasingly obsolete.

## 6. THE ESTABLISHMENT OF MINIMUM STANDARDS[29]

The absorption of classical intellectual property law into international economic law will gradually establish universal minimum a standards governing the relations between innovators and second comers in an integrated world market.

Among the many causes of the drive to overcome preexisting territorial limitations on intellectual property rights, two merit attention here. *First,* the growing capacity of manufacturers in developing countries to penetrate distant markets for traditional industrial products has forced the developed countries to rely more heavily on their comparative advantages in the production of intellectual goods than in the past. *Second,* the rise of knowledge-based industries radically altered the nature of competition and disrupted the equilibrium that had resulted from more traditional comparative advantages,. Not only is the cost of research and development often disproportionately higher than in the past, but the resulting innovation embodied in today's high-tech products has increasingly become more vulnerable to free-riding appropriators. Market access for developing countries like India and other countries in the South thus constituted a bargaining chip to be exchanged for greater protection of intellectual goods within a restructured global marketplace.

In response to these challenges, the TRIPS Agreement mandates mostly time-tested, basic norms of international intellectual property law as enshrined in the Paris Convention for the Protection of Industrial poperty and the Berne convention for the Protection of Literary and Artistic Works, or in certain domestic institutions, such as laws protecting confidential information, that all developed legal systems recognize in one form or another. It also leaves notable gaps and loopholes that will offset some of the gains accruing from the exercise, especially with respect to non-traditional objects of intellectual property protection. In this respect, both the strengths and weaknesses of the TRIPS Agreement stem from its essentially backward-looking character. To the extent that the TRIPS Agreement significantly elevates the level of protection beyond that found in existing conventions, as certainly occurs with respect to patents, for example, the developing countries are usually afforded safeguards that few would have predicted at the outset of the negotiations. Nevertheless; both developed and developing countries guarantee that detailed "enforcement procedures as specified in this [Agreement] are available under their national laws,"[30] and they all become liable to dispute-settlement machinery for claims of multification and impairof benefits that can lead to cross-sectoral trade sanctions.

**(a) Most Favoured Nation**

Perhaps the most important "basic principle" that applies virtually across the board is that of national treatment of (that is, non-discrimination against) foreign rights holders. This principle of equal treatment under the domestic laws is then carried over to relations between states in the most favored-nation (MFN) provisions of Article 4. The latter article ostensibly prevents one member country from offering a better intellectual property deal than is required by international law to nationals of a second member country and then denying similar advantages to the nationals of other member countries.

Taken together, the national treatment and MFN provisions attempt to rectify the damage that some states recently inflicted on the international intellectual property system by unilaterally asserting claims of material reciprocity with respect to hybrid legal regimes falling in the penumbra between the Paris and Berne Conventions. While the national treatment and MFN clauses both apply "with regard to the Protection of intellectual property," it turns out that, for purposes of the TRIPS Agreement, the term "intellectual property," refers only to seven of the eight subject matter categories (1) copyrights and related rights; (2) trademarks; (3) geographical indications; (4) industrial designs; (5) patents; (6) integrated circuit designs; and (7) trade secrets or confidential information. As regards neighboring rights covered by the International Convention for the Protection of Performers, Producers of Phonograms and Broadcasting Organizations (Rome Convention), national treatment and the MFN clause apply only to those rights that the TRIPS Agreement selectively provides, but not to rights generally flowing from that Convention.

**(b) The impact of National Treatment on Minimum Standards**[31]

Although computer software appears to be protectable under both the Berne Convention and the Universal Copyright Convention and the Universal Copyright Convention, the protection is not explicit. Because the protection is not explicit, computer software developers cannot be sure that computer programs will be protected. Even if it is conclusively determined that the copyright conventions protect computer software, their substantive terms are subject to criticism.

Both the Berne Convention and the Universal Convention provide for national treatment. National treatment means that member nations must treat non-nationals the same as they treat nationals. National treatment creates uncertainty as to the extent of protection granted to computer software by a given country. For computer software to be protected, two conditions must be satisfied. *First,* the country where the computer software was developed and the country where enforcement is being sought must be parties to one of the international copyright conventions. *Second,* the law of the country where enforcement is sought must protect computer software. The country where enforcement is sought, although a member of one or both international copyright conventions, may not protect computer software., A computer software developer would receive no protection in such a country. Alternatively, the extent of the protection granted buy the country where enforcement is sought may not be clear.

Even if both of the conditions are satisfied and the country where enforcement is sought clearly grants protection to computer software, national treatment is problematic because it results in inconsistent results. The rights of the computer software developer will depend on the country in which enforcement is sought.

The principle of national treatment is particularly problematic if a member nation grants authors moral rights in their works. Moral rights are incompatible with works that are predominantly utilitarian, such as computer software. They grant the author the power to control the use of the author's work, which limits the value of the work to owners of copies, particularly if the work is utilitarian. The right of an author to withdraw a work is particularly troubling because "allowing a programmer to withdraw his software could be devastating to those who have used, and become dependent on the program."

### (c) The Failings of National Treatment[32]

The argument that improving municipal laws will help secure intellectual property rights is founded on the related notions of "National Treatment" (NT), NT, as implemented in the Paris Convention for Protection of Industrial Property, requires signatory countries to treat individuals from a foreign country as they treat their own nationals. Thus, a host country is obligated to give foreign visitors, and their property the same protection that its municipal laws give to its own citizens.

However, shortcomings of applying, NT become obvious if the applicable municipal laws are themselves insufficient. For examiple, the Paris Convention grants each signatory country the right to determine what is patentable. This means that each country creates its own specific intellectual property regime. Thus, countries with the rescommunis ideology. India is having its own ideology that certain intellecutal properties, like *Yoga* and Ayurvedic (Medicine) are "the common Heritage of mankind"[33] have flexibility under the Paris Convention to enact very limited or even no laws recognizing patentability. Consequently, NT creates a disparate level of protection in different countries. It does not ensure substantive equivalence. Thus, according to NT Principles, a country with a high level of protection must grant this higher protection even to foreigners of countries with a lower level of protection. However, when citizens from the country with a higher level of protection visit the country with a lower level of protection, they must settle for the lower protection of that country. In many situations, NT only provides a foreigner with inadequate protection from the host country's municipal laws. Thus, municipal law coupled with NT does not offer an effective solution to the distortions of intellectual property trade.

**(d) Minimum Standards for What?**[34]

We now come to the theoretical heart of the problem: Paris, Berne, and related treaty provisions need not always mean the same thing in the abstract Cartesian universe of intellectual property as in the concrete Hobbesian world of trade wars and truces. In practice, domestic courts have interpreted the Paris-Berne regime, but only in cases between private parties, while TRIPS panels will apply Paris and Berne provisions in the TRIPS Agreement to disputes between public entities, that is, W.T.O. members. Domestic courts could construe Paris-Berne obligations differently than do TRIPS panels, resulting in jurisprudential schizophrenia between the private and public international laws of intellectual property.

Where is the source of such schizophrenia? It is not necessarily the distinction between private and public international laws. In principle, private and public international laws can reinforce each other, much like laminated sheets in plywood. A liberal system of private international law assures private parties of property rights in which they may freely trade across national borders. A liberal system of public international law, like the GATT, precludes nation-states from taking measures to restrain that freedom to trade in tangible goods at their own borders. The TRIPS Agreement coordinates these aims a bit differently, since it obligates W.T.O. members to undertake measures to protect property interests in intangibles both within and at their own borders. Nor does the danger of schizophrenia lie in the minimal rationale for protecting intellectual property at these points; technological innovations and media creations must at least be protected against misappropriation to assure some stable marketplace for them. The TRIPS Agreement imposes measures that, at a minimum, are intended to prevent pirates from raiding intellectual property anywhere in the global marketplace. Our danger rather arises out of the difficulty of fashioning rights of intellectual property at optimum levels to encourage investment without obstructing competition. Such rights should, to quote Professor Lehmann, serve as "restrictions in competition in order to promote competition.:"[35]

We would do well to ask just what the TRIPS consensus fixed; Is it confined to categories of rights which the TRIPS Agreement enumerate, or does it systematically embrace Paris-Berne Principles for adjusting levels of protection in the future? This question is critical for knowing how far TRIPS panels may go in resolving disputes between W.T.O. members, as well as the principles that might guide them on the way. Confined to standards that represent intellectual property at present levels, TRIPS panels may have to acquiesce in many gaps left in the present state of the law. The Paris and Berne Conventions share the same choice-of-law principles for adjusting protection in the future: national treatment bolstered by minimum rights. The GATT offered the comparable, if not stronger principle of most-favored-nation treatment, which was devised for trade cases. The Trips Agreement applies all these principles, but neither clearly nor coherently across the field of intellectual property.

Turing now to gaps endemic to the Paris-Berne regime which the TRIPS Agreement largely, if not altogether, incorporates, [t]he most obvious set of gaps arises because Paris and Berne provisions establishing minimum rights are subject to varying readings. Commentators have noted the open texture of such Paris and Berne rights: some are mandatory; some may be implemented with varying degrees of discretion; and some are altogether optional. However, to this point, only national courts have construed these rights, deciding which ones are mandatory and to what extent national legislators or courts themselves have discretion in formulating the other rights or fashioning remedies for them. For example, national courts have had to decide how to interpret the rather shadowy language which, in Article 10bis of the Paris Convention, assures relief against unfair competition in an open-ended range of cases. National courts may, of course, refer to the often-rich jurisprudence of their own constitutional and private international laws in applying international Paris and Berne provisions to diverse cases. The TRIPS Agreement in itself provides no such background against which TRIPS panels may understand the Paris and Berne minimum rights that it incorporates.[36]

**(e) Minimum Standards and Enforcement Procedures**

Even in those countries which make genuine efforts to comply with the strictures of TRIPs, copyright protection remains uncertain. Like the Berne Convention, protection under Trips is premised on national treatment. Thus, such critical issues ad the treatment of non-literal copying and the scope of protection to be afforded new rights not covered by the Berne Convention remain subject to the vagaries of national treatment. The only exception is the expressly stated inclusion under TRIPS of computer software as a covered "literary work"[37] under Berne under Article 10. Although one of the most significant development under TRIPs is the establishment of minimum procedural norms for the endorsement of copyright, such procedural norms are to be included within the structure of member's existing judicial system. Thus, procedures for protecting copyright will remain inconsistent even after TRIPS.[38]

**(f) The Retroactivity Principle**

When one state concludes a copyright agreement with another state, it is clear that the works created or published in either state after the effective date of the agreement will be protected in both states pursuant to the treaty. When, however, works created or published prior to the effective date of the agreement are afforded copyright protection in one state and not the other, problems may arise regarding the recapture of those pre-existing works out of the public domain of the other state.[39] This is particularly true when individuals in one state have invested time, money, and effort into exploiting the works of another state's authors in the absence of any legal duty not to do so, or when the term of copyright protection afforded to the works of one state's authors has expired in the other state. Although the exploiting individuals arguably are benefiting from the creative efforts of the authors and should not be entitled to have their interests protected, some scholars emphasize that these persons "have nonetheless acted in goods faith in reliance on the given state of affairs, namely that these works were in the public domain and could be used freely."[40]

The retroactivity doctrine seeks to achieve a balance between the newly acquired copyright protection accorded the authors of one state and the reliance interests of previous exploiters of those works in the other state. At a minimum, the doctrine creates a temporary time period during which prior exploiters may continue to use the work to recoup some or all of their investments, after which time the copyright owners are afforded full and exclusive protection under the terms of the Convention.

Today, Article 18 of the Berne Convention, which embodies the retroactivity principle, provides:

> (1) This Convention shall apply to all works which, at the moment of its coming into force, have not yet fallen into the public domain in the country of origin through the expiry of the term of protection.
> (2) If, however, through the expiry of the term of protection which was previously granted, a work has fallen into the public domain of the country where protection is claimed, that work shall not be protected anew.
> (3) The application of this principle shall be subject to any provisions contained in special conventions to that effect existing or to be concluded between countries of Union. In the absence of such provisions, the respective countries shall determine, each in so far as it is concerned, the conditions of application of this principle.
> (4) The preceding provisions shall also apply in the case of new accessions to the Union and to cases in which protection is extended by the application of article 7 or by abandonment of reservations.[41]

## 7. GATT *v.* WIPO

### (a) The Jurisdictional Dilemma[42]

From the initial preparatory work prior to the September 1986 Ministerial Declaration commencing the Uruguay Round, many developing countries, including Brazil and India, hotly contested the propriety of using GATT to establish international substantive norms in the area of intellectual property protection. The position of these countries, simply stated, was that if there was any need for the development of international norms, WIPO was the proper forum. Part of the reluctance to use GATT as a forum for addressing the desirability for new or additional international standards for intellectual property protection derived from the perception of many of these countries that GATT was primarily a forum for the "have" nations. Thus, many developing countries were concerned that their needs would not be given sufficient consideration in the GATT arena. Furthermore, to the extent that international norms for the protection of, for example, copyright might be required, these countries believed that the Berne Convention, with its emphasis on national treatment, had already resolved the issue and that any changes which might be required should be dealt with only through WIPO which had responsibility for overseeing the Convention. As the East German representative indicated in his support of a statement by Cuba on behalf of the "Group of 77"[43] challenging the use of GATT to address intellectual property protection issues:

> The strong international links between economy, science, technology and culture do not exclude other organizations or agreements in their activities to be concerned with the problems of implementing intellectual property rights. Moreover, for legal certainty and comprehensiveness, the competence of WIPO and its direct participation should be maintained since the solution of these problems belongs to the scope of its duties.[44]

By contrast, the developed nations, including the United States were strongly dissatisfied with efforts to resolve existing copyright issues under WIPO auspices. While developing nations saw WIPO as a generally hospitable forum for their concerns, many developed countries considered WIPO to be, at best, indifferent to their needs and, at worst, hostile, in view of renewed efforts by some developing countries to use WIPO to seek a lessening in the level of protection currently established under the Berne Convention.[45] The developed countries also perceived GATT as providing a forum where an international consensus could be reached regarding the scope of protection for works not covered by the Berne Convention—including software and computer databases—outside the potentially politicized open meetings required by WIPO.[46] Finally, developed nations sought to rectify a perceived lack of adequate enforcement mechanisms under the Berne Convention. Although Article 33 of the Berne Convention provided that disputes can be brought before the International Court of Justice, at the time of the Uruguay Round negotiations not one such dispute had been brought in over 45 years.[47] Since WIPO had no other enforcement procedures for assuring that a member's laws complied with Berne's agree-upon minimums, the developed countries sought to establish an endorsement mechanism under GATT which would force full compliance by all member countries, thereby assuring a minimum level of copyright protection in such countries.

**(b) The Enforcement Paradigm**

For rules to evolve into behaviour-influencing norms which ensure compliance with the rules by the players, particularly in the context of international law, the rules must be invested with a high degree of legitimacy by the players. Sanction or coercion is insufficient in itself to engender the legitimacy which ensures compliance with the law. The foundations, in international law, of the obligation to comply with a norm is difficult to explicate with reference to any one theory, however there is widespread agreement that the "acceptability" of a rule is critical to a nation's observance of a rule as law.

Acceptance of a rule is distinct from consent to enforcement of the rule. Acceptance, which endows the rule with norm-generative character usually precedes consent to the rule's enforcement; sometimes however, acceptance arises after consent to enforcement of a rule. In the event that acceptance precedes consent to the rule's enforcement, the shape of the rule begins to acquire a distinctly normative profile in its function—demarcating, with fair level of precision, the legal rights and obligations it creates.[48]

The roots of the *"GATT* v. *WIPO"* thesis with its pronounced emphasis on sanction based enforcement as the basis of a rule's binding character, derive from Austinian legal positivism. Austinian affinity for laws imperative nature locates the legally binding character of rules in their sanction based enforcement. Rules not supported by an effective sanction are defective for they cannot create any duty or obligation. Such laws are imperfect laws or deficient laws as they are without sanction. In consonance with its reasoning, international law, devoid as it is of any centralized sanction based enforcement system, cannot engender any binding obligation by itself. Thus it follows that in order to endow the rules created under international law with legitimacy it must be backed up by an enforcement mechanism.

The neo-analytic tradition, pioneered by H.L.A. Hart among others has lucidly elucidated the basic defect innate in the process of reasoning which predicates the validity of a rule on its enforceability. Such a process confuses "matters of fact with matters of right."[49] That X can by force compel Y to behave in a particular manner does not mean either that X has a right to compel Y to perform the act in question, nor can it imply that Y is under a duty or obligation to comply. Y may be "obliged" to obey but he is not under any "obligation" to do so. Enforcement alone, cannot imbue the rule with validity. The validity of enforcement in terms of its capacity to normatively ensure compliance with the rule will depend upon the legitimacy of the rule independently of the rule's enforceability. Enforcement presupposes the legitimacy of the rule being enforced. Legitimacy of the rule arises from its acceptance by the participant, who consents to its enforcement. "The law is not obligatory because it is enforced: it is enforced because it is obligatory; and enforcement would otherwise be illegal."[50]

If from the ineffective compliance with obligations created by a rule without sanctions we arrive at the conclusion that the validity or obligations of a rule originates in its capacity to be enforced, we are confusing the effectiveness of a rule with its legal validity. The legal validity of a rule is not contingent upon its effectiveness. Effectiveness of a rule may be an empirical condition however it cannot be the criterion of a rule's validity. Thus, if enforcement relates to the rule's effectiveness alone, then it cannot be the source of the rule's legitimacy. The normative legitimacy of a rule lies in its acceptance; a rule which is internalized by its acceptance may be effective in terms of compliance with its obligations, even in the absence of any enforcement mechanism.

Arguments which are either impervious or attribute secondary importance to the role of acceptance in the evolution of behaviour forming norms, particularly in the context of international law, are not well founded in theory and practice. Sanction–based enforcement may impart transient existence to rules in the short run, but it cannot be the basis for the normative legitimacy of the rules in the long run. In the absence of the former, rules cannot ascend to the status of behaviour forming obligations.

It is true that disenchantment with existing multilateral forums, enervated as they are both by the absence of minimum enforceable standards as well as by the non-existence of an effective enforcement mechanism, motivated strategic interest groups to successfully lobby for the inclusion of an intellectual property agenda in the Uruguay Round of multilateral trade negotiations. However the praxis which formed the backdrop for the debate attached, from its inception, importance to the need to promote complementarity between the work of GATT and that of WIPO and to avoid duplicating the work of WIPO. Indeed, beyond the rhetoric, the texts of the proceedings through the different stages of the negotiations, unequivocally resonate with the recognition by the dominant parties of the need for TRIP to complement WIPO's efforts.

The discourse on linking trade with intellectual property was animated by a limited agenda from its origin. The objective envisaged had four basic aspects: establish substantive standards for intellectual property protection; efficient enforcement measures; dispute settlement mechanism; and the application of certain GATT provisions to intellectual property. The spring board of the trade based approach was informed by the concept of trade sanction. To that extent its scope was circumscribed. With trade based sanctions forming the anchor, the primary objective was to concretize the intellectual property standards already obtained under the aegis of WIPO by weeding out ambiguities with respect to the form and content of these obligations. The objective was not to create an alternative regime under GATT as much as it was to build on WIPO's contributions.

## 8. MAJOR INTERNATIONAL INTELLECTUAL PROPERTY TREATIES

The major substantive international intellectual property rights treaties are the Paris Convention, the Universal Copyright Convention, and the Berne Convention. The Paris Convention protects patents and trademarks, while both the Universal Copyright Convention and the Berne Convention protect copyrights. In addition, the recently amended General Agreement on Tariffs and Trade ("GATT"), a trade treaty, includes provisions for protection of intellectual property entitled "Trade Related Aspects to Intellectual Property Rights" ("TRIPS"). Another important treaty, which in many ways served as a precursor to TRIPS is the North American Free Trade Agreement ("NAFTA"), a regional trade agreement between the United States, Canada and Mexico that included intellectual property protection provisions. All of these treaties provide integral international protection of intellectual property rights. Each, however, also contains its own defects that impedes its ability to provide comprehensive international protection.

### (a) The Bi-polar Structure

Governments adopt intellectual property laws in the belief that a privileged, monopolistic domain operating on the margins of the free-market economy promotes long-term cultural and technological progress better than a regime of unbridled competition. Ordinary tangible goods that acquire value by satisfying known human needs in more or less standardized ways cannot escape the price-setting function of the competitive market. In contrast, intellectual goods acquire value by deviating from standard solutions to known human needs in ways that yield more efficient outcomes or that capture the public's fancy. Because intellectual goods define relevant market segments in terms of the novelty or the originality they purvey, their creators invent their own markets by stimulating demand for goods that did not previously exist.[51]

The term "intellectual property" was not coined until the late nineteenth century. Only when Josef Kohler and Edmond Picard perceived that copyright, patent, and trademark laws and more in common with each other than with the older forms of property known to Roman law was it recognized that a new class of rights in intangible creations had arisen. Their use of the term "intellectual property" thus coincided with the drive for international regulation of both artistic and industrial property, a movement destined to produce a fully articulated and universally recognized legal discourse in little more than a century.

Taken together, the Paris and Berne Conventions purport to subdivide the international intellectual property system into two hermetically sealed compartments separated by a common line of demarcation. Literary and artistic property rights occupy one of these compartments; so called industrial property rights occupy the other.

The origins, of the bipolar structure can be traced to cornerstone provisions of the Great Conventions extant since their inception and to corresponding state practices recognized by most developed intellectual property systems. On the one hand, Article 1 of the Berne Convention established "a Union for the protection of the rights of authors in their literary and artistic works." Such works, categorized at length in Article 2(1), should receive automatic and mandatory protection in the domestic copyright laws of the member states. To avoid censorship and to liberate authors from overt and covert forms of patronage, these laws entitle almost all independently created works falling within the designated subject matter categories to a generous but relatively soft form of protection against copying only that lasts a long period of time.

On the other hand, Articles 1(1) and 1(2) of the Paris Convention established "a Union for the protection of industrial property" and identified certain legal institutions as the "object" of industrial property protection, namely, "patents, utility models, industrial designs, trademarks, service marks, trade names, indications of sources . . . and the repression of unfair competition." While some international minimum standards and the rule of national treatment apply to all these institutions, the Paris Convention entrusted the protection of industrial creations primarily to "the various kinds of industrial patents recognized by the laws of the countries of the Union." The patent paradigm and variants thereof classically confer a tougher form of protection on strict formal and substantive conditions for a relatively short period of time.

Governments seeking to maintain high levels of investment in technological innovations face an increasingly difficult task as the twentieth century closed and in the formative decades of the Twenty-first century. They must preserve or restore the bases for healthy competition at a time when information is increasingly becoming the medium from which the most socially valuable artifacts are likely to be constructed. This task will require the elaboration of a new intellectual property paradigm that looks "beyond art and inventions." Such a paradigm must deal directly with the pervasive threat of market failure facing investors in unpatentable, non-copyrightable innovation under present-day conditions, without multiplying ill-conceived, socially harmful regimes of exclusive property rights.

### (b) The Paris Convention

#### *(i) An Historical Overview*

The Paris Convention for the Protection of Industrial Property was first concluded in 1883. Since its inception, the Convention has been revised six times, the last revision occurring in 1967 at Stockholm. Concurrent with the latest revision was the establishment of WIPO, which assumed responsibility from the United International Bureau for the

Protection of Intellectual Property (BIRPI) for the performance of the administrative tasks of the Paris Union.

The national patent systems that existed prior to the Paris Convention often contained widely varying legal rules. The United States, for example, examined patent applications substantively, while many European countries did not. Most countries published the technical disclosure of patent applications upon grant, some held the disclosures in secret until after the patent expired, while still others published the disclosure immediately upon filing. Generally speaking, the variation between national provisions at the time appears to have been substantially larger than exists today.[52]

These variations in national patent practices created procedural obstacles to the international assertion of patent rights. In those countries that published patent disclosures immediately upon filing, for example, the mere act of applying for patent disclosed the invention publicly. At the same time; other countries conditioned patentability on absolute novelty worldwide. Applying for a patent in one country could thus create an absolute barrier to obtaining a valid patent in another.

These procedural obstacles to patenting generally appear to have arisen inadvertently. There also existed at this time, however, another category of obstacles that national governments had erected purposefully. The obstacles in this second category were essentially protectionist. By the late 1800s European and United States scholars had explored the economics of patenting extensively. As explained below, many granting sovereigns had begun to manipulate their national patent laws to enrich themselves in relation to their trading partners.

Patent systems are large-scale governmental intrusions into the free-market economy. They involve manipulating social costs and benefits to increase the national wealth. Perhaps the most significant cost of such systems is the higher prices imposed on consumers of the patented advance. If the patented technology has some economic value the patent owner is able to impose single source pricing on it a price that is higher than would exist in a truly competitive market.

Patent systems exist because this social cost of higher prices is presumed to result in an increased pace of invention. Higher prices transfer increased amounts of money from consumers of the patented technology to producers. Knowing this, inventors will strive to invent patentable technology more vigorously. Some will succeed who otherwise would have failed. The sophistication of the country's industrial base thus increases, and new technology becomes available to consumers. According to the presumption, the social benefits of this increased rate of invention are large enough to more than offset the costs of patenting.

In a purely domestics economy the national effects of these costs and benefits are linked together relatively tightly. Each unit of increased cost imposed on domestic consumers provides a unit of increased revenue to domestic industry. Evaluating such a patent system therefore involves, in large part, estimating the amount of increased invention that will actually result from a given increase in expected revenue. In addition, the increased resources diverted to a domestic patent owner are not wholly lost to the domestic economy. Rather, the domestic patent owner generally will reinvest all or a part of those resources, thereby mitigating the cost of patenting to some degree.

International patenting, on the other hand, de-couples the national effects of patenting. Assume that an inventor exploits the advance through patenting, not in his or her own country, but in a foreign country. In that situation industry domestic to the inventor's own country receives increased profits from patenting, but domestic consumers do not pay the associated higher prices. Instead, the higher prices are imposed on consumers in the foreign country. International patent transactions therefore reallocate wealth away from the granting country and into the country of the patent owner[53].

Prior to the Paris Convention many countries including India had acted on this basic economic truth. Their national laws included numerous, varied provisions that curtailed the domestic patent rights of foreign nationals. Some countries, for example, had adopted compulsory-licensing provisions. By their very nature, compulsory licenses lower the cost of the patented advance closer to multiple source pricing. In addition, if the compulsory license is given to a domestic entity a portion of the foreign trade is prevented outright. Both these mechanisms reduce the amount of wealth that flows out of the country into the hands of the foreign patent owner.

Another type of protectionist provision motivated by the same economic calculation was the widespread presence of national working requirements. Generally, these provisions required patent owners to supply domestic demand for the patented technology through domestic production. The failure to do so resulted in the patent becoming invalid or unenforceable. Facially neutral with regard to nationality, working requirements had an obviously greater, purposeful impact on patent owners who were foreign. In essence, foreign patentees were required to either abandon their patent rights or behave as if they were domestic entities.

In addition to increased prices, patents impose another social cost that is relevant to international patenting: they retard further research in the patented technology. Patents commonly dominate inventions that remain to be discovered and patented themselves. Once a patent issues, therefore, every person other than the patent owner has a reduced expectation of return from further research in the areas of technology that the patent dominates. Rationally, then, researchers will reduce their inventive efforts in technology that is dominated by another's patent. If competition spurs the speed of research, this reduction in competition will slow industrial development over time. The issue in a purely domestic economy is optimally balancing the initial incentive to the original patent owner with the detriment to future researchers.

With international patenting, however, the problem becomes more complex. The teachings of an issued patent can travel beyond the borders of the granting sovereign and into other countries. Corresponding patent rights in such other countries may, or may not, exist. In countries where they do not, the public learns of the advance and yet is free from the economic impediment of dominating patent rights. Technological development therefore continues unabated. In countries where dominant patent rights do exist, in contrast, only the holder of the dominant patent is fully motivated to continue researching. Over time, this risks reducing the industrial sophistication of the patenting country in comparison to that of the non-patenting country.

These economic considerations spurred a number of countries to act during the early period of international patenting. Primary among those actions were national provisions that caused domestic patents to expire as soon as any corresponding foreign patent expired. In operation, these provisions freed domestic industry from the constraining effects of patenting as soon as the industry in another country became free.

In total, these various protectionist provisions inflicted immense difficulties on patent owners. Often, one simply could not obtain patent rights in a foreign country. Even if a foreign patent could be obtained, many times its continued existence depended on the patent owner rapidly initiating manufacture in that foreign country. This could be disadvantageous for many different reasons.

Prior to the Paris Convention essentially no international agreements addressed the obstacles to international patenting set out in the preceding section. Instead, patent owners who wished to assert patent rights in foreign countries were forced to rely on their own resources. As a practical matter, they were forced to restrict the number of countries in which they sought patent protection.

In 1883, a decade-long process of negotiation culminated in a number of countries signing the Paris Convention. Although the creation of the convention was an act of international diplomacy, the participants in the negotiations included not only representatives of national governments, but representatives of industrial interests as well. It appears, in fact, that the negotiations began primarily at the insistence of industrial interests.

The Paris Convention addressed a portion of the obstacles to international patenting. At the same time, other obstacles remained unresolved. This partial failure raises an immediate questions: Why was agreement on those issues not reached? Many causes doubtlessly contributed. At the same time, however, the pattern of successes and failures suggests that the different economic interests of the various parties to the negotiations was a significant cause. In particular, agreement appears to have been possible only where the economic interests of national government and industry coincided.

It is axiomatic that the interests of national government will tend to be national in scope. With regard to patenting, these interests will include the full range of social costs and benefits of a patent system: the potential benefits of an increased rate of innovation, for example, as well as the costs of higher consumer prices, the costs of administering the patent system, and the costs borne by other endeavors from whom the increased resources spent on patenting have been diverted.

This focus on both the costs and the benefits of patenting should also hold true with regard to transactions of international patenting. A national government will be concerned with the increased incentive that patent rights in foreign countries bestow upon its domestic industry. Government will also be concerned with the domestic costs of awarding patents to foreigners: the loss of national wealth from importation of patented goods, and the potential stunting of domestic industry via international patenting that is uneven.

Industry's view of patenting, in contrast, is potentially quite different. Industry will be concerned with how patenting affects its own, private interests. Those interests will in all likelihood be very different from the interests of society as a whole. For example, patent systems rely entirely on the incentive of increased profits to spur innovative activity. Patenting therefore bestows large private benefits on industry. At the same time, the social costs of patenting are generally spread throughout society. They therefore impose private costs on industry to a much lesser degree.

This observation is very significant. Unless one views inventors as entitled to monopoly profits naturally, patent systems must be seen as societal mechanisms for providing an optimal amount of incentive to invent. To determine that amount of incentive, one must consider more than industry's narrow, private interests. The result of that broader calculation need not coincide with industry's preferences. Thus, society can prefer rules of patent law that industry would not choose. Stated conversely, industry can prefer rules of patent law that are adverse to society. The differences of position between the two groups should be systematic.

For the same reasons, industry and national governments should also have systematically different interests with regard to international patenting. If they behave rationally according to economic criteria, national governments will be interested in obtaining agreements that maximize the wealth of their individual countries. These will be agreements whose operation bestows on the particular national economy both larger benefits and small costs from international patenting. Industry, in contrast, will seek the private benefits of increased international patenting but will be relatively unconcerned with any associated social costs. In particular, industry will be largely unconcerned with whether a disproportionate share of such costs falls on any particular national economy, including that of its own country.

In essence, because the parties to an international sale of a patented item each belong to a different national economy, their private costs and gains become social costs and gains for the countries involved. For examples, where a national of the country under consideration holds a foreign patent, the sale of goods under that patent transfers wealth out of the foreign country into the hands of the patent-owning national. The national's private gain is thus a social gain for the national's own country. Conversely, where a country has granted one of its patents to a foreigner, the domestic sale of goods under the patent impoverishes domestic consumers and enriches the foreign patentee. The consumer's private cost is thus a social cost to the granting country. The outlook of national government differs from that of its patent-owning industry because the nation participates in both import and export transactions, while industry is largely preoccupied with exports.

The structure of the Paris Convention is consistent with the operation of these economic interests. Foreign patenting, for example, is crucial to the objectives of both industry and national government. Patents provide the market power that yield increased profits to industry. If such increased profits are to be had on foreign sales, industry must obtain foreign patents. Those same increased profits on foreign sales, moreover, appear to be the major mechanism by which countries enrich themselves through international patenting. National government is thus interested in seeing its citizens obtain as many foreign patents as possible. Additionally, foreign patents are needed to constrain the industrial development of competing countries while an advance is subject to domestic patent rights.[54]

For these reasons, one would expect easy agreement in the Paris Convention to increase the general availability of foreign patenting. The interest of national governments are more or less the same on this particular issue. In addition, the self interests of national governments and industry generally coincide.

The original text of the Paris Convention shows such easy agreement on this issue through the concept of foreign priority:

> Any one who shall have regularly deposited an application for a patent of invention . . . in one of the contracting States, shall enjoy for the purpose of making the deposit in the other States . . . a right of priority under the periods hereinafter determined.
>
> In consequence, the deposit subsequently made in one of the other States of the Union, before the expiration of [this] period cannot be invalidated by acts performed in the interval, especially by another deposit, by the publication of the invention or by its working by a third party . . .

As a result of this provision, an inventor could establish a date of filing in all member countries via an initial filing in a single country. The act of applying for patent rights on the same invention in several foreign countries was therefore made much easier.

As to protectionist provisions, the economic interests of

national government and patent owners appears to diverge. National government is critically interested in retaining the freedom to impose protectionist provisions. By definition, these provisions reduce the outflow of national wealth to foreign patentees. They are an important means of minimizing the domestic costs of international patenting.

Industry, in contract, will be generally opposed to protectionist provisions. Protectionist provisions reduce the market power of industry's foreign patents. Industry will therefore object to their presence in the patent systems of foreign countries and will seek their abolition. In addition, because others pay the private costs of increased patents on imports, industry as little reason to favour protectionist provisions in the domestic patent system of its own country.

Under an economic analysis, therefore, patent-owning industry will seek broad prohibitions against protectionist measures. In contrast, each national government will seek to preserve at least those protectionist provisions that operate to the country's own net benefit. Based upon these fundamentally different interests one would expect difficulty in achieving any agreement to eradicate protectionist provisions generally.

The historical course of negotiations over the Paris Convention is consistent with this analysis as well. The original text of the Paris Convention contained conspicuously little with regard to the two most widespread protectionist measures, working requirements and compulsory licenses:

> The introduction by the patentee into countries where the patent has been granted, of articles manufactured in any other of the States of the Union, shall not entail forfeiture.
>
> The patentee, however, shall be subject to the obligation of working his patent conformably to the laws of the country into which he has introduced the patented articles.

The text did require signatories to permit importation. At the same time, it specifically allowed the continued existence of national working requirements generally. It did not mention compulsory licenses at all.

In addition to the principle of foreign priority, the Paris Convention also adopted the principle of national treatment. "The subjects or citizens of each of the contracting States shall enjoy, in all other States of the Union, so far as concerns patents for inventions ... the advantages that the respective laws thereof at present accord, or shall thereafter accord to subjects or citizens." Stated simply, national treatment requires each government to apply the same provisions to both its own citizens and foreign nationals. It has been described, along with the principle of foreign priority, as a fundamental tenet of the Convention.

The Paris Union's agreement to provide for national treatment stands in apparent opposition to the economic analysis suggested in this article. At least in theory, national treatment prevents governments from employing the most effective tool for reducing the domestic cost of international patenting: expressly denying domestic patent rights to foreign inventors. In addition, the Paris Union consciously selected national treatment over the competing principle of reciprocity. Under reciprocity, each government need award to foreign inventors only those patent rights that the foreign inventor's own government awards to non-nationals. Reciprocity would thus seem a favorite of national governments: under it, the cost of awarding domestic patents to foreigners is tied directly to the benefits that domestic industry receives from patenting in foreign markets.

What, then, does the Paris Union's selection of national treatment imply? Does it invalidate the assertion that economic self-interest explains the Paris Convention's substantive provisions? More broadly, does it show the Paris Union to have adopted an internationalist, free-trade approach to foreign patenting?

When examined carefully, the adoption of national treatment probably does not support these suppositions. Reasons completely apart from a free-trade rationale can cause government to favour national treatment over reciprocity. A country applying reciprocity, for example, must be expert in the patent laws of every foreign country. Reciprocity thus risks large administrative costs.

In addition, a deeper examination shows that national treatment still permits government many forms of protectionist behaviour in patenting. Still possible, for example, are provisions that are facially neutral with regard to nationality, buy which impact foreigners disproportionately. Working requirements and compulsory licenses are examples of two such provisions; the restrictions in United States law against proof of invention by foreign activities are another.

Another, more subtle type of protectionist provision permitted under national treatment involves reducing the domestic costs of patenting generally. The loss of domestic wealth to foreign patentees can occur only when domestic patenting results in valuable rights. Thus, government can reduce the outflow of wealth to foreigners by simply reducing the economic value of the domestic patent rights that are available. Indeed, the loss can be reduced to zero by refusing to grant domestic patents altogether.

The Swiss patent system provides a historical example of a national government employing this latter technique. Switzerland progressed through the industrial revolution without a patent system. The economic rationale behind this decision was sound; without domestic patents Swiss consumers paid no increased prices for new technology, Switzerland thus minimized the outflow of its wealth to importers. Indeed, refusing to issue patents removed all the social costs of patenting from the domestic Swiss economy. At the same time, Switzerland continued to receive most of the benefits of patenting. True, Swiss industry could not expect patent profits from introducing new technology into the domestic Swiss economy. The absence of domestic patents, however, have Swiss industry free access to all the new technology that others developed. In addition, Swiss industry held patents in foreign countries, thus earning patent profits from exports and receiving an incentive to invent in that way. In fact, because the Swiss economy was small, the incentive that Swiss industry received from patented exports was arguably grater than the incentive that dominating the domestic Swiss economy via patenting might have supplied.

National treatment provided no obstacle to this strategy. The original Paris Convention did not commit its members to provide any minimum rights to patentees. Thus Switzerland could, and in fact did, adhere to the Paris Convention even though it had no patent system whatsoever. Its denial of patent rights equally to domestic nationals and foreigners satisfied the requirement of national treatment. Additionally, adhering to the Paris Convention guaranteed Swiss inventors national treatment from foreign governments, thereby ensuring Swiss industry access to patent profits on its exports. In fact, Switzerland did not find it in her interest to enact a national patent system until Germany threatened her with retaliatory tariff action.

Subsequent negotiations to revise the Paris Convention have continued to follow this pattern. It has been increasingly possible to harmonize the procedural requirements of patenting. At the same time, agreement to, limit the use of national patent provisions for protectionist purposes has not progressed very for. The Paris Union has repeatedly revisited the issues of working requirements and compulsory licensing since 1883. The resulting provisions place very few restrictions on national governments that wish to use these mechanisms. Compulsory licenses can be granted as soon as three years after the patent issues. The patent can be revoked for failure to work two years thereafter. Perhaps more significant, even today the Paris Convention Contains virtually no requirements that national governments grant any other minimum rights to patent holders. Indeed, the Convention still does not even require that national governments enact patent systems at all.

*(ii) Major Provisions*

The Paris Convention protects "industrial property," including "patents, utility models, industrial designs, trademarks, service marks, trade names, indications of source or appellations of origin, and the repression of unfair competition." In general, the Convention directs that each member country confer national treatment to other member nations. National treatment requires the member countries afford foreign intellectual property owners the same rights and protection as their own citizens. This includes affording national treatment to a foreign exporting company's manufacturing processes.

As a part of affording national treatment to foreign countries, the Convention requires all countries to honor prior applications of patents, and registration of utility models, industrial designs, or trademarks from a foreign country. In essence, this requires the foreign country to honor an applicant's original filing date in their own country, as long as the time between the original filing date and the filing in the foreign country is not longer than the "priority period." The period of priority begins at the date of filing the first application.[55]

Although the Convention affords a substantial amount of control to the intellectual property owners it is not absolute. Each member state has the right to grant compulsory licenses to prevent a patent holder from using an invention exclusively. In the extreme case, where granting compulsory licenses has not afforded the general population the benefit of the patented product, a Member may forfeit the patent holder's rights. However, industrial designs are never forfeitable.

What the Paris Convention lacks is an explicit mechanism for settling disputes between member countries. While Article 13 of the Convention does establish an assembly, it merely allows the assembly to take "appropriate action designed to further the objectives of the Union." Such a provision does not give any guidance as to the power of the assembly or the procedure one must follow to make a complaint about a member country's activity. In addition, Article 15 establishes an International Bureau that has the authority to "conduct studies" and "provide services, designed to facilitate the protection of industrial property." However, similar to the assembly, the scope of the Bureau's powers are not delineated, nor is there a set procedure for settling grievances.

The Paris Convention does not require a minimum patent term. [It] is silent regarding the disclosure and claims of a patent [and] does not specify patent protected subject matter. The Paris Convention defines criteria for patentability:

novelty, inventive step(non-obviousness) and industrial applicability. [It] does not specify the rights conferred by a patent.

*(iii) Exceptions to Protection*

The present text of Article 5A of the Paris Convention permits member countries to provide legislative remedies for patent abuses by the patentee, such as failure to work. In the event of failure to work or insufficient working of a patented invention, the issuing country may require the patentee to grant a compulsory license of his or her patent rights to a willing applicant. No one, however, may apply for a compulsory license until the expiration of either four years from the date the patentee applies for the patent or three years from the date the patentee receives the patent, whichever occurs last. Therefore, the patentee has from three to four years before any sanctions can be imposed. If the patentee has legitimate reasons that justify inactivity beyond the three to four year period, applicants for compulsory licenses will likewise be refused. In any event, compulsory licenses may only be nonexclusive. Thus, the license enables the licensee to work in addition to the patentee, rather than in place of the patentee.[56]

The present text of Article 5A prohibits revocation of patent rights for failure to work or insufficient working unless compulsory licenses were already granted and proved insufficient to prevent such abuses. In the event that compulsory licenses are granted and prove insufficient, forfeiture proceedings may not be instituted before the expiration of two years from the grant of the first compulsory license. Therefore, a patentee does not forfeit his or her patent rights unless the invention was not worked for the initial three to four year period, a compulsory license was then granted, and the invention was still not worked for another two years.

Under the present text of Article 5 quater of the Paris Convention, when a product is imported into a country where there is a patent for the process of manufacturing the product, the patentee has the same rights with regard to the imported product as he or she would have with regard to a product manufactured in the issuing country. Therefore, if the patentee of a manufacturing process is entitled to prevent anyone from making, using, or selling products manufactured according to the patented process within the issuing country, then he or she may also be permitted to prevent the use or sale of products manufactured outside but imported into the issuing country.

## Notes and References

1. Paris convention for the Protection of Industrial Property (As Revised at Stockholm, 1967).
2. Berne Convention for the Protection of Literary and Artistic works (As revised at Paris 1971), Universal Copyright Convention (Paris, 1971).
3. Agreement on Trade Related Aspects of Intellectual Property Rights (TRIPS).
4. North American Free Trade Agreement (NAFTA).
5. Protocol Relating to the Madrid Agreement concerning the International Registration of Marks, Patent Cooperation Treaty (Washington 1970).
6. Tara Kalagher Guinta, Lily H. Shang, "Ownership of Information in a Global Economy", 27 *George Washington Journal of International Law and Economics*, 327. Copyright 1994 George Washington University.
7. *The Hindu* "Delayed Action on Trademark Law" dated 25th September 2003. See for the recent legislation law passed by LokSabha The pattents Amendment Bill dated March 22, 2005.
8. 19 U.S.C. See. 2411(b); Indian patents Act of 1970;.
9. Robert A. Cinque, "Making Cyberspace Safe for Copyright: The Protection of Electronic Works in a protocol to the Berne Convention", 18 *Fordham International Law Journal*, 1258, copyright 1995 Fordham University School of Law.
10. *Supra* notes 1 to 7.
11. Monique L. Cordray, GATT *v.* WIPO, 76 J. Pat E. Trademark-off Society, 121.
12. Ian Johnstone, "Treaty Interpretation: The Authority of Interpretive Communities," 12 *Michigan Journal of International Law'* 371-72, 380-382, 385-91; 418-19 (1991).
13. Stanley Fish, *Doing What Comes Naturally* 141 (1989).
14. Nye, "Nuclear Learning and U.S-Soviet Security Regimes" 41 *International Organization* 371, 398 (1987).
15. Oscar Schoachter, "Self Defense and the Rule of Law" 83, *American Journal of International Law* 259, 264 (1989).

16. Louis Henkin, *How National Behave: Law and Foreign Policy* 52 (2nd ed. 1979).
17. Catherine Logan Piper, "Reservations to Multinational Treaties: The Goal of Universality" 71 *Iowa Law Review* 295, 298 (1985).
18. This Article is informally known as the "compatibility rule."
19. John king Gamble Jr, "Reservations to Multilateral Treaties: Macroscopic view of State Practice", 74 *American Journal of International Law* (1980).
20. Jane C. Ginsburg, "Four Reasons And a Paradox: The Manifest Superiority of Copyright Over Sui Generis Protection of Computer Software", 94, *Columbia Law Review.* 2559, (1994) Directors of *The Columbia Law Review Association.*
21. G.H.C. Bodenhausen, "Guide to the Application of the Paris Convention For the Protection of Industrial Property" 144 (1968). The Guide enjoys a high degree of authority, as it was written by the Director of the United International Bureau for the Protection of Intellectual Property (BIRIPI), the predecessor organization to World Intellectual Property Organization (WIPO), As an example of international trade norms the recent GATT/TRIPs accord incorporates Paris Convention Art, 10bis with respect to protection of trade secrets and defines "a manner contrary to honest commercial practices" as "at least practices such as breach of contract, breach of confidence and inducement to breach and includes the acquisition of undisclosed information by third parties who knew, or were grossly negligent in failing to know, that such practices were involved in the acquisition." TRIPS at Art. 39.1, 39.2 n. 10.
22. Paul Edward Geller, "Intellectual Property in the Global Marketplace: Impact of TRIPS Dispute Settlements?" *International Lawyer* 99, (1995).
23. Ultimately the case was decided on other grounds, notably the cancellation of the prior Spanish registration of a "Nike" mark Appeal 325/91, *America Nike* v. *Amigo,* Judgment of Dec. 10, 1993 Juzgado de Primera Instancia no. 9, section 1 (Court of first instance), Barcelona, Spain.
24. Paul Edward Gella "New Dynamics in International Copyright", 16 Columbia—*VLA Journal of Law and Arts.* 461 (1992).
25. Gyorgy Boytha, *Fragen Der Entstehung Des Internationalen Urheberrechts* in Wohrkommt Das Urheberrechts und Wohin Gehtes? 181, 182. (Robert Dittrich ed. (1988).
26. London Film Productions Ltd. *v.* Intercontinental communications, Inc., 580f. supp. 47 (S.D.N.Y. 1984)
27. Judgment of July 14, 1987 (Einbehaltungsuerpflichturg decision) Obersten Gerichtshof 1988 Gewerblicher Rechtsschutz und Urhebrrrecht Internationaler Teil (GRUR Int.) 365, 368.

28. Not all countries vest the same economic rights in the same parties worldwide, and many countries have developed their own rules concerning copyright transfers. No systematic international instrument guides the courts in tracing out chain of title from original owners to ultimate transferees of rights effective from country to country. Furthermore, while some countries have systems for putting copyright transfers on the public record, not all countries do, and no treaty instrument regulates the worldwide effect of such recordation.
29. J.H. Reichman, "Universal Minimum Standards of Intellectual Property Protection under the TRIPS Component the WTO Agreement", 29 *International Law* 345, (1995).
30. TRIPS Agreement at Articles 41-50.
31. Robert A. Arena, "A Proposal for the International Intellectual Property Protection of Computer Software" 14 *University Pensilvania Journal of International Business Law,* 213.
32. Jean M. Dettmann, "Gatt: An Opportunity for an Intellectual Property Rights Solution", 4 *Transnational Law* 347 (1991) University of the Pacific McGeorge School of Law.
33. Justice V.R. Krishna Iyer, "Piracy of Ayurvedic Heritage", *The Indian Express,* 13th October 2003.
34. Paul Edward Geller, "Intellectual Property in the Global Market Place: Impact of TRIPS Dispute Settlement", 29 *International Lawyer,* 99 (1995).
35. Michael Lehmann, "The Theory of Property Rights and Protection of Intellectual and Industrial Property" 16 *International Review of Industrial Property and Copyright Law,* 525 (1985).
36. Compare Articles 1(2) of TRIPS covers "categories of intellectual property that are the subject of Sections 1 to 7 of Part II 3(1) and 4(c) national and most-favored-nation treatment excluded for neighboring rights not "provided under this Agreement" with Articles 1(3), 2(1) of the Paris Convention (national treatment for industrial property "understood in the broadest sense" with respect to "advantage" that laws "now grant, or may hereafter grant" and Article 5(1) of the Berne Convention (such treatment for author's rights that laws" do now or may hereafter grant).
37. Doris Estelle Long, Copyright and the Uruguay Round Agreements: A New Era of Protection or an Illusory Promise? 22 AIPLA Q.J. 531. (1995).
38. See: For a further examination of the minimum procedural enforcement standards established under TRIPS.
39. Katherine S. Deters, "Retroactivity and Reliance Rights Under Article 18 of the Berne Copyright Convention", 24 VAND, *Journal of Transnational Law.* 971 (1991) Vanderbilt University School of Law.
40. Sam Ricketson, *The Berne Convention for the Protection of Literary and Artistic Works* 665 (1987).

41. Berne Convention for the Protection of Literary and Artistic Works of Article 18.

42. Doris Estelle Long Copyright and the Uruguay Round Agreement: A New Era of Protection or an Illusory Promised, 22 AIPLA *Quarterly Journal* 531 (1995).

43. The "Group of 77" was organised during the first United Nations Confernece on Trade and Development (UNCTAD) in Geneva in 1965 and is composed of less developed countries. The aim of the group was to organize developing countries so that they could speak with one voice, thereby gaining increased negotiating clout. Some commentators, however, viewed this development as representative of an ideological split between democracies who put their faith in economic growth and Third World countries who seek a redistribution of wealth to less technologically developed countries. This perceived ideological split led the US and other developed nations to distrust certain for a since developing countries often used discussions at the United Nations, and its specialized agencies such as WIPO, as vehicles for advancing political objectives, including mandatory transfer of technology from the "haves" to the "have nots."

44. GATT Negotiating Group sets Talk This Week on U.S. Proposal, WIPO Will Join Discussion, 4 INT'L TRADE REP. 1358, 1359 (1987).

45. "Some developing countries had already sought to reduce existing intellectual property protection under WIPO on the theory that such property is the "common heritage" of mankind and should be freely available to all. Such free availability, they believe, included the right of transfer to developing countries without payment of compensation.

46. WIPO meetings were almost always open meetings, thereby offering developing countries the opportunity for "political grandstanding at the expense of substantive discussion." By contrast, most GATT negotiations were generally conducted "outside the public spotlight, and the rhetoric used by the participants was ganteel by contrast."

47. Part of the reason for the lack of enforcement is the requirement under the UN Charter that a judgment by the International Court of Justice can only be enforced by voluntary cooperation or by referral to the Security Council. Since it is doubtful the Security Council would act to enforce an intellectual property judgment, absent consent, any such judgment would have no impact on the challenged conduct.

48. Bal Gopal Das, "Intellectual Property Dispute, GATT, WIPO: Of Playing By the Game Rules and Rules of the Game", 35 *IDEA Journal of Law and Technology*, L. & Tech. 149.

49. Terry Nardin, *"Law, Morality and Relations of States"*, (Princeton, 1983).

50. Gerald G. Fitzmaurice, General Principles at 45.

51. J.H. Raichman, "Charting the Collapse of the Patent—Copyright Dichotomy: Premises for a Restructured International Intellectual Property System" 13 *Cardozo Arts and Entertainment Law Journal* 475 (1993) Yeshiva University.
52. R. Carl Moy, "The History of the Patent Harmonization Treaty: Economic Self-Interest As An Influence", 26 *Journal Marshall Law Review* 457 (1993), The John Marshall Law School.
53. Biswajit Dhar, K.C. Niranjan Rao, "Third Amendment to Patents Act: Reflections on a TRIPS—Complaint Law", *Economic and Political Weekly*, April 9, 2005.
54. *Supra* Note 53.
55. Karen Waller, "NAFTA: The Latest Gun in the Fight to Protect Intellectual Property Rights", 13 *Dick Journal of International Law*, 347, (1994).
56. Adrienne Catanese, "Paris Convention Patent Protection and Technology Transfer", 3 *Boston University International Law Journal* 209 (1985).

CHAPTER

# 7

# Copyright under International Copyright Conventions

*The artist is a philosopher, perhaps without actually wanting to be. And even if he cannot, as the optimists do, declare this world to be the best of all possible worlds, and also does not wish to say that this world which surrounds us is too evil for us to take it as an example. Nevertheless he says: In this particular form it is not the only world there is! Thus be observes the things with which Nature presents him, already formed, with a penetrating eye.*
*He says: This world once looked different and this world will look different.*

—Paul Klee, 1879-1940

International copyright conventions have led to the harmonization of sometimes conflicting national copyright laws, thus achieving a more unified approach to the regulation of the trade of copyrighted goods and raising the general level of protection for copyright holders. For example, it was the Rome Convention that spurred the harmonization of the disparate legal traditions of the economically oriented Anglo-Saxon copyright system and the more artistically principled *droit d'auteur,* which is of French origin. In general, convention provisions are effective only when the conventions are either self-executing or when they have been adopted by domestic legislation. Even when the conventions have domestic effect, the extent of harmonization is limited by the principle of national treatment, which relies on the domestic law of the importing country to supply the appropriate legal norms.

## I. AN HISTORICAL OVERVIEW OF THE ORIGINS OF COPYRIGHT

As a result of the invention of the printing press by Gutenberg in 1436, the level of copying and publishing worldwide increased markedly. Prior to the printing press, book-sellers copied authors' manuscripts by hand, a lengthy procedure whose speed was only slightly increased through the use of slaves. After the invention of the printing press, however, booksellers could copy authors' manuscripts at a much faster rate. Profits from the sales of books helped the booksellers recover the costs of both the authors' manuscripts and the printing press.

The invention of the printing press also enabled "pirate" booksellers to copy books already published by "legitimate" booksellers. These pirate booksellers were able to sell these copied books at lower prices since they could avoid paying for the authors' manuscripts.[1] Neither the authors who had sold their manuscripts nor the legitimate booksellers had any legal recourse against these private booksellers, and it became increasingly clear that some protection was necessary.

The pressure for protection came not from authors but from booksellers, whose pecuniary interest was most threatened by the private booksellers. The booksellers successfully lobbied their respective sovereigns for protection in the form of an exclusive right, better known as a "privilege."[2] The privilege gave a legitimate bookseller the exclusive right to print and sell a specific author's manuscript for a limited time. In essence, government bestowed upon the printer a limited monopoly.[3]

The sovereigns also benefited from this arrangement, because they could decide which booksellers would receive a privilege—only those sellers holding views sympathetic to the government—and which manuscripts were suitable for printing. The sovereign censored manuscripts that it believed would threaten the public order.

The use of these privileges came to an end about two hundred years after they were introduced. The reasons for their demise are threefold. First, printers began to abuse their monopoly power, thereby angering their sovereigns in the process. Second, as governments became more mature, the need for censorship began to diminish. Finally, authors became more active in arguing for protection of their own rights.

The new system of protection that filled the vacuum left by the privilege system was a statutory form of protection, which focused, for the first time, on the rights of authors. Starting in Great Britain with the 1709 Statute of Anne, statutory copyright for the protection of authors spread throughout Europe and the United States.

When the focus of copyright switched from the bookseller to the author, a philosophical debate emerged as to the origin of the right. under the old privilege system, the right was justified on economic grounds; the booksellers needed an exclusive right for a limited duration in order to make adequate profit and cover the costs of a printing press and authors' manuscripts. Since the booksellers were not creators of a work, their only interest was pecuniary.

Authors, on the other hand, created the books; the ideas belonged to them and emanated from them. Thus, many philosophers argued that copyright should protect both the authors' economic and personal interests, and that those interests should be, as unlimited as possible. These philosophers pointed to natural law as the basis of authors' rights. Statutes existed only for the limited purpose of recognizing these naturally existing rights and to give them a more precise formulation.

The difference between the Anglo-American philosophy and the natural rights philosophy has caused much conflict at the international level during the various Berne revision conferences. Natural rights countries focus almost exclusively on the individual author while the Anglo-American countries focus more on the owner of the copyright, whether that be author, publisher, broadcaster, individual, or corporation. Moreover, authors' rights countries, referred to as *droit d'auteur* countries because of their focus on the authors, are less likely to find authors' rights out weighted by the public's interest in easy access to literary and artistic works. As a result of these different focal points, the copyright laws in *droit d'auteur* countries are more favorable to authors than the laws of Anglo-American countries.

### (a) Reciprocity Treaties and Bilateral Agreements[4]

The first international copyright treaties were based on a system of material reciprocity. Under material reciprocity, country A would grant country B's authors the same protection as country B would grant country A's authors. The reciprocity system, however, was complicated[5] and ineffective, and many countries maintained piracy as the central theme of their international copyright relations. They refused to enter into any treaties, and, if they did enter into such treaties, they failed to abide by the terms.

### (b) National Treatment under the French Decree of 1852

The Decree of 1852 was significant in many respects, not the least of which was its use of a national treatment system for the protection of foreign authors. Under national treatment, as opposed to material reciprocity, country A grants authors from country B the same protection that country A grants its own authors. A national treatment system is much easier to administer than a reciprocity system because courts need only interpret their own domestic copyright law. Moreover, any improvements in domestic authors' rights in country A automatically accrue to authors from country.

Following France's Decree, and during the latter half of the nineteenth century, a trend emerged in Europe for greater international protection of the rights of authors. The development of copyright exhibited a constant momentum toward, and focus on, authors. As the rights of authors received more and more attention in national legislation, authors emerged as an influential political group. In 1858, six years after France's landmark Decree, the first international Congress of Authors and Artists met in Brussels. The work of this group laid the groundwork for the drafting and signing of the Berne Convention.

## 2. THE UNIVERSAL COPYRIGHT CONVENTION

### (a) Major Provisions[6]

The Universal Copyright Convention (UCC) states that each member state will "provide for the adequate and effective protection of the rights of authors and other proprietors in literary, scientific, and artistic works, and including writings, musical, dramatic and cinematographic works, and paintings, engraving and sculptures." We can illustrate few from Indian National context. The architectual grandeur of the temples of Andal Rangamannar and Lord Vatapatrasayee, Srivilliputhur, Tamilnadu, rich in sculptural beauty fine workmanship of the Manimandapam in front of the Mahamandapam in stone and wood, and the Majestic Rajagopuram of Sri Nachiar (Andal) Temple, Srivilliputhur, the Town, incidentally, is the logo of the Government of Tamilnadu; The convention also requires each member to give national treatment to other nations. The term of protection for each copyrighted work is the author's life plus twenty-five years. One exception is the protection of photographic or "works of applied art", which are protected for only ten years.

The rights afforded the copyright holder include the author's exclusive right to authorize the reproduction of a public performance or broadcast in any manner. This includes both the original form and a form "recognizably derived from the original." The author also has the exclusive right to publish and authorize the making and publication of the translation of his works.

Like the Paris Convention, the UCC does allow member nations to limit copyright protection. The member states can restrict the right to translate writings. If the author has not translated the work after seven years from the date of first publication, any national in the country may translate the work. The UCC also allows a national to distribute a work without the author's consent if the translator uses the work for educational purposes or if the work has been distributed because of the public's need of the information.

As with the Paris Convention, the UCC does not delineate a dispute settlement procedure. While the UCC does establish an International Court of Justice that will decide any disputes arising under the Treaty, no details are provided about the scope of the Court's authority or about the proper procedure for settling a dispute.

The UCC has its foundations in the national treatment of foreign authors. Consequently, member states must afford foreign works the same protection afforded to domestic creations. Signatory nations must also modify domestic copyright laws to conform with [the] minimum standards [established under the Convention.] [E]ach member state must provide for the "adequate and effective protection of the rights of authors and other copyright proprietors in literary, scientific, and artistic works."

In addition, under the UCC, foreign works will satisfy all formalities (notice, registration, manufacture), if from the time of first publication all the copies of the work published with the authority of the author or other copyright proprietor bear the symbol (c) accompanied by the name of the copyright proprietor and the year of first publication placed in such manner and location as to give reasonable notice of claim of copyright.

The UCC contains a "Berne" conflict clause. This clause restricts Berne Convention Signatories from ignoring Berne Provisions and relying on the UCC in its copyright relations with another Berne Union member. The UCC is administered by the United Nations Educational, Scientific, and Cultural Organization (UNESCO).

### (b) Conflict with Berne[7]

The Universal Copyright Convention still governs relations between the United States and those countries that adhere to the Universal Copyright Convention but not to the Berne Convention, such as the Soviet Union. Relations between countries that belong to both treaties are generally governed by the Berne Convention. As between these countries, however, the Universal Copyright Convention may still determine whether existing works entered the public domain before they could be rescued by the retroactivity clause of the Berne Convention. The Precise Mesh between the Universal Copyright Convention and the Berne Convention as it will affect future United States copyright relations is controversial.

The preamble to the UCC expresses the hope that an international union for the protection of copyright would stimulate the creation and exchange of intellectual properties. It states: [A] system of copyright protection appropriate to all nations of the world and expressed in a universal convention . . . will ensure respect for the right of the individual and encourage the development of literature, the sciences and the arts . . . [and] will facilitate a wider dissemination of works of the human mind and increase international understanding."[8]

## 3. THE BERNE CONVENTION

### (a) An Historical Overview[9]

On September 27, 1858, the Congress of Authors and Artists held its first meeting in Brussels. The Congress was truly international in nature, with participants from many different countries[10] representing many different interests.[11] The participants passed five resolutions supporting greater international protection of authors' rights.[12] The Congress met twice more, in 1861 and 1877, and each time adopted resolutions asking governments to join together in passing legislation for the international protection of authors.

A new International Association, initially comprised only of authors and presided over by Victor Hugo, convened in 1878 and adopted five resolutions that eventually became the foundation for the original Berne Convention of 1886. In 1882, the International Association, later named L'Association Literature et Artistique International (ALAI), agreed that the only way to achieve its goal of increased international copyright protection would be to form a Union for the protection of literary property. Consequently, the International Association called a meeting in 1883 of all parties interested in creating such a Union. The meeting convened in Berne, Switzerland, where the participants drafted a treaty consisting of tenarticles, the most important of which provided for national treatment and the absence of formalities as a prerequisite for copyright protection. Following general approval of the draft treaty, the Swiss government invited various governments to meet in Berne on September 8, 1884, for the purpose of forming an international copyright Union.

Eleven nations responded affirmatively to the Swiss government's invitation to meet in Berne. The countries broke down into essentially three groups. The first group was comprised of those nations that favored a codified international law of copyright—a universal law. At the opposite end of the spectrum were those countries that wanted as little unification and as much national independence as possible. Moreover, they wanted the copyright treaty to be built lot on a reciprocity foundation. The final group of countries occupied a middle position. They favored a codified law of international copyright, but desired some domestic flexibility on issues such as the translation right and the term of protection Rather than adopting universal protection all at once, these countries wished to move slowly toward the goal of international copyright unification.

Of the three groups present at the 1884 Berne Conference, it was the middle group, representing those countries, which preferred some common legislation along with some provisions reserved for national law that emerged as the mainstream.

*The Berne Convention of 1886.*[13] The basic structure of the Berne Convention has remained relatively unchanged throughout each of the five revisions and two additional acts; the scope of authors' rights has, however, increased markedly. The original Convention provided an explicit, but not exclusive, list of works to be protected. The Convention also defined the conditions for protection, known as points of attachment, and specified rules governing the term of protection. Subsequent conferences have amended each of these provisions in order to increase the scope of authors' rights.

The Convention also established the concept of authors' exclusive rights, which functioned as minimum standards that all member countries were required to recognize. The translation right was the first exclusive right established by the 1886 Convention.

Although the Convention's primary focus was on the author, most contracting states agreed that in certain circumstances authors' rights had to be limited in order to assure public access to important information. The Convention, therefore, defined the situations in which a contracting state could permit certain works to be reproduced without the authors' express authorization. Many of these situations dealt with news of the day, newspaper articles or articles of political discussion. The Convention also allowed individual countries to create exceptions for the use of literary or artistic works in publications of a scientific or educational nature. These provisions have been both expanded and narrowed during Berne's subsequent revisions.

*The Substantive provisions of the Berne Convention of 1886.* Article I of the Berne Convention unequivocally stated that the Union was formed for the protection of the rights of authors. This focus was indicative of the continental European, *droit d'auteur* countries' influence in drafting the Convention.

The basic strategy of the Convention was to establish certain minimum standards, which all contracting countries were required to recognize and later to expand these minimum requirements to achieve the ultimate objective of a uniform international law of copyright. Individual countries could give foreign authors greater protection than required by the Convention, but in no case could they give less protection. The purpose and strategy of the Convention has not changed since of 1886 Convention.

The fundamental principle of the Berne Convention was, and continues to be national treatment. Under the national treatment concept, Berne signatories grant authors who are nationals of other Berne countries the same protection they accord to their own nationals. National treatment is significant because it ensures non-discriminatory treatment for authors in all contracting states.

Brussels Revision Conference of 1948. The Brussels revision created significant improvements in the substantive rights of authors.

After unsuccessful attempts at both the Berlin Conference of 1908 and the Rome Conference of 1928, the Brussels conferees succeeded in enacting a life-plus-fifty-year term of protection as a minimum Berne requirement. In all Union states, therefore, an author could expect a minimum term of protection of life plus fifty tears after death for almost all enumerated works. Union states could grant longer terms of protection within their domestic legislation. They could also limit the term of protection for foreign authors to the term granted in the foreign authors' country of origin if that term was shorter than in the Union country where protection was sought.

The life-plus-fifty-year term of protection did not apply to photographic works. - Works of applied art, and cinematographic works. The term of protection for these works was governed by the law of the country where protection was sought, but could not exceed the term granted in the country of origin of the work. The term of protection for pseudonymous works became fifty years after the date of publication of the work unless the pseudonym left no doubt as to the author's identity. If an author's identity became known, the author would receive the life-plus-fifty-year term of protection.

The Brussels conferees [also] strengthened the authors' moral right. Under the 1928 Rome revision, an author's moral right was guaranteed during his or her lifetime; contracting states were not bound to recognize the moral right after the author's death. Under the 1948 Brussels Convention, the contracting states were required to recognize the moral right for the whole term of copyright in most cases fifty years after death, if the legislation of the individual Union countries so permitted. The conferees did not require all Union countries to recognize the moral right after an author's death, because in some countries moral right was not protected under copyright law; rather, it was protected under alternative legislation or common law. Under the common law of torts in Great Britain for example, authors could only maintain a tort action during their lifetime. Great Britain, for example, authors could only maintain a troy action during their lifetime. Great Britain, therefore, could not agree to a Convention rule that would establish protection of the moral right beyond the author's death. Thus, it remained each individual contracting state's choice to extend the moral right past the author's life time, making the amendment rather insignificant in terms of effect. The amendment did, however, indicate the direction which Union members wanted the right to take at a subsequent revision conference.

Since the original Convention of 1886, authors had the exclusive right to authorize the public representation of dramatic or dramatic-musical works and the public performance of musical works only if the country in which protection was sought recognized those rights. In other words, the right of public representation and performance was not a minimum right under the Convention; an author would only benefit if the Union state in which protection was sought recognized the right.

Under the Brussels revision, the contracting states agreed to make the right of public performance and representation a minimum right. Consequently, authors of dramatic, dramatico-musical, or musical works enjoyed the exclusive right to authorize public presentations and performances of their works. The right of public performance was not subjected to a compulsory license. However, if the public performance were achieved through broadcast or through the playing of recording of a musical work, the compulsory licenses established under the broadcasting and recording rights would apply to the public performance. In these situations, an author's work could be publicly performed absent express authorization, but no contracting state could enact a compulsory license that would be prejudicial to the author's moral right or to the author's right to receive just remuneration.

The advances made in Brussels were significant and they secured a solid level of international protection for authors which endured until the Stockholm revision in 1967.

*Stockholm Revision Conference of 1967*

Almost twenty years after the Brussels Conference in 1948, the Berne Union members convened in Stockholm, once again with the intention of making substantive and structural improvements to the Convention. Although the contracting states made significant improvements in authors' rights and improved the Union's infrastructure, those results were almost destroyed by a conflict that the Union had never before confronted.

The problem emanated from the new composition of member states. Many of the Berne Union's fifty-nine members were a developing country that has achieved their independence in the post-World War II years. These developing countries needed literary and artistic resources from developed countries and, as a result, demanded special concessions from the developed countries such as compulsory licenses for translation and broadcasts and shorter terms of protection. In response to those demands, the contracting states drafted a protocol for the benefit of developing countries. The conferees also agreed to tie the substantive changes in Articles 1 through 20 of the Stockholm Convention to the protocol, this making it impossible to accept the substantive changes without the protocol. The developing country protocol was very controversial. Its compulsory license provisions and shortened terms of protection significantly weakened the rights of authors, rights that had been hard-won over Berne's five previous revisions.

Authors and publishers in the developed countries so opposed the protocol that they were willing to forego the substantive and structural improvements made in the Stockholm Convention in order to avoid enactment of the protocol's concessionary provisions. As a result, the Stockholm Convention did not receive the minimum number of ratifications necessary to enter into force.

Aside from Stockholm's developing country controversy, one other significant event occurred in Stockholm. The contracting states agreed to the formation of the World Intellectual Property Organization. WIPO's formation was achieved through a separate treaty; thus, the Union's inability to ratify the Stockholm revision did not affect WIPO's establishment.

The Stockholm revision significantly broadened the conditions for protection of non-Union authors by adopting a second point of attachment to accompany the previous requirement enacted in the 1886 Convention. Under previous Conventions, protection for non-Union authors was dependent on first or simultaneous publication in one of the Union countries. This was referred to as the "Geographical criterion." The Geographical criterion still exists, but it now accompanied by the "personal criterion," which provides that authors who are nationals or habitual residents of a Union country are protected in all Union countries no mater where first publication occurs. This protection also applies to unpublished works.

The Stockholm conferees [also] strengthened the Convention's moral right provisions. Under the original moral right provision, enacted at the Rome Revision Conference in 1928, contracting states were required to recognize the moral right until the author's death. At the Brussels Revision Conference, the contracting states strengthened the right somewhat by encouraging Union members to extend the moral right past the authors' death. Finally, at Stockholm, the conferees required Union members to recognize the authors' death. Finally, at Stockholm, the conferees required Union members to recognize the authors' moral right after death for at least as long as the author's economic right was protected.

The conferees enacted one exception to the new moral right: "those countries whose legislation, at the moment of their ratification of or accession to this Act, does not provide for the protection after death of the author of all the rights set out in the preceding paragraph ay provide that some of these rights may, after his death, cease to be maintained." This exception resulted from a compromise with Great Britain and other Anglo-American copyright countries that, like the United States, do not recognize the moral right under their copyright laws, but provide equivalent protection under other common laws. For example, in many countries the moral right is protected under the common law of defamation, which usually permits the maintenance of suit only during the author's lifetime.

**(b) Major Provisions**[14]

The Berne Convention protects "literary and artistic works," including:

> every production in literary, scientific and artistic domain . . . such as books, pamphlets and other writings; lectures, addresses, sermons and other works of the same nature; dramatic or dramatic-musical [sic] works; choreographic works and entertainments . . . musical compositions. . . . cinematographic works . . . works of drawing, painting, architecture, sculpture, engraving, and lithography; photographic works . . . works of applied art; illustrations, maps, plans, sketches and three-dimensional works relative to geography, topography, architecture or science.[15]

The Convention also covers "translations, adaptation, arrangements of music and other alterations of a literary or artistic works.

Like the Paris Convention and the UCC, the Berne Convention does not provide for enforcement measures, or for dispute resolution. Although the Berne Convention does provide for an assembly, which has the obligation to "take any . . . appropriate action designed to further the objectives of the Union," the Convention does not further provide for any enforcement measures. The convention also provides for an Executive Committee and an International Bureau. However, both of these groups are largely administrative.

**(c) Minimum Rights**[16]

The Berne Convention, unlike the U.C.C., sets forth specific minimum conditions to which each signatory must adhere. As a general matter these conditions may be broken into five categories; Primacy, Coverage, Activation of Coverage, Exclusive Rights, and Term of Protection.

*Primacy*

Each member nation is required to accord foreign authors the same level of copyright protection it provides to its own citizens. Signatory nations must grant protection at a level equal to or above the minimum standards espoused by the Convention. Unless otherwise provided in a given article, national discretion to rely on its own domestic law is not permitted. Convention provisions maintain primacy over national legislation.

*Coverage*

Coverage under the Convention extends to a broad variety of subject matters. Coverage extends to "every production in the literary, scientific, and artistic domain, whatever may be the mode or form of its expression. . . ." Expressly excluded, however, is "news of the day or to miscellaneous facts having the character of mere items of press information."[17] Coverage also extends to an author's unpublished works.

*Activation of Coverage*

The Berne Convention excludes all formalities that precondition the existence scope and duration of copyright protection. Once created, a work's entitlement to protection under the Convention is not premised on any administrative formality. Exercise of rights under the Convention is immediately available and independent of any exercise of protection in the work's country of origin.

*Exclusive Rights*

The Berne Convention protects an author's personal rights and the right created in his works. The Convention seeks to maintain minimum protective standards which signatories deem essential to the success of international copyright. Among these rights are the right of translation, reproduction, public performance, broadcasting, adaptation, and arrangement. Any reproduction of an author's work made in volition of any Convention exclusive right is subject to seizure.

*Term of Coverage*

The Berne Convention establishes a minimum term of copyright protection for life plus fifty years or an alternative term of fifty years from the date of first publication.

### (d) Minimum Rights[18] (Continued)

The Berne Convention requires members to protect all literary and artistic works. Berne defines a non-exhaustive list of protected works.

An author's exclusive rights under Berne, include; the right of reproduction of the work; the right of public performance of dramatic, dramatic-musical and musical works; the right of recitation of literary works; the right of recitation of literary works and the right of communication to the public of works performed or recited; the right of broadcasting of works or communication to the public by other means; right of translation of works; the right of adaptation arrangement or other alteration of works and the right of authorizing cinematographic adaptation of works and of authorizing the reproduction and distribution to the public of the works and the right of authorizing the public of the works thus adapted or reproduced and of the cinematographic works themselves.

Berne requires the protection of moral rights. The author has rights, independently of his economic rights, to claim authorship of his works and to object of any distortion, mutilation or other modification of, or other derogatory action in relation to, the work which would be prejudicial to his honour or reputation.

Berne also requires that members require no formalities or procedures for the recognition or maintenance of copyrights and oblige[s] parties to protect works for the life of the author plus 50 years, except a term of 25 years applies to photographic works and works of applied art.

### (e) Future Issues

> According to Holf Moroni, "a legacy for the future which benefits all mankind, because intellectual energy also creates material values without which man cannot survive and which will be of even more importance in a future in which the population of the world grows at a geometric rate. Consequently, it is of enormous importance, even today, to glimpse a vision of

> the future. This future has already begun for those who possess the mental capacity. It is, therefore apparent that every inventor already lives in the future, because he transcends his present environment through his inner vision to create as yet unimaginable treasures for the future.
>
> Spiritus est, qui vivificat. It is the spirit that moves the world. It is the spirit which alone shapes our world and thus our future.[19]

Historically, the Berne Union has protected authors from the divesting effect of new technologies such as television, radio, and cinematographs (by extending protection to these areas). An important element in solving the current copyright crisis is to continue that historical trend and develop copyright solutions to the problems posed buy audio and audio-visual reproduction, reprography, computer storage and retrieval, and satellite and cable television.

Aside from finding solutions to the threats caused by new reproduction technologies, the Berne Union and its member nations are attempting to determine how to protect new works such as computer programsl Many countries protect computer programs as literary and artistic works under their copyright law. Other nations favour sui genris non-copyright protection. The same pattern exists for semiconductor chips, although after the United States passed its Semiconductor Chip Protection Act in 1984, more ad more countries began considering sui generis legislation for chips as well.

The approach that a particular country purses is very important. Berne members that protect computer programs under their copyright law must accord national treatment to foreign authors of programs. A copyright approach avoids the need to establish a new treaty for the protection of software, because software is incorporated into the Convention under national treatment. If, on the other hand, a country protects software through domestic legislation, then protection is only accorded domestic authors, unless the country specifically provides otherwise through treaty oir bilateral agreement.

Thus, by incorporating new works into copyright, countries bring them into the international copyright conventions. The approach is favorable to authors of new books.[20]

On the other hand, what may be good for authors of new works may not be good for authors generally. For example, granting computer software or semiconductor chips full copyright status arguably weakens the overall status of copyright. This is so because software and chips have different characteristics that traditional literary and artistic works. Their economic lives, for example, are shorter than those of books and paintings. Thus, granting a life plus fifty-year term of protection to programs detracts, at least philosophically, from the status of books and other more traditional works. For this and other reasons, WIPO favours sui generis protection for programs. WIPO favours this approach even though sui generis legislation would require a new international agreement in order to protect authors of software.

The original contracting states to the Berne Union established the Convention to protect and promote the international rights of authors. That goal remains at the heart of the Convention. It has given the Berne Union the ability to increase the protection of author's rights, reach compromise solutions to overcome philosophical and economic differences, encourage growth in membership despite the difficulties in enacting Berne's high standards domestically, protect authors from the potential erosive effect of new technologies, and encourage greater author protection in non member countries.

At present, Berne must remain true to its original goal. It must continue to focus on the protection of authors. To lose sight of that goal would be to disarm the Berne Convention and leave authors hopelessly susceptible to the new wave of technologies.

## 4. TRIPS

### (a) An Historical Overview

#### *1. The Effort at Harmonization*[21]

Though varying in details, intellectual property laws throughout the world essentially seek to ensure that the creator is rewarded for his or her inventiveness and to motivate further creativity. These laws protect the creator from rival enterprises and competitors pirating the creator's process or idea. Since the creation of the GATT, however, intellectual property has undergone a fundamental conceptual change: the emphasis has moved away from sovereign matters—eg., one of protective norms restricted to the territory of the state—to restricted to the territory of the state—to issues of adequate protection of intellectual property rights abroad. As the economic importance of exports has increased, so have the needs for improved extra-territorial protection of intellectual property rights. This is particularly true for inventors and producers technological goods who, having spent great sums in research and development, demand that their national governments protect their investments from pirating and the subsequent undermining of their competitive positions. "As such, it was no longer the existence but rather the absence of, or deficiencies in, intellectual property protection which became the central issue in the international trade debate. . . ."[22] While strong intellectual property rights were once believed to create possible trade barriers, today the international exchange of goods is threatened by insufficient or nonexistent intellectual property rights.

The international dimension of intellectual property is not altogether new, however. The Berne Convention on Copyright protection has existed for over one hundred years and similar treaties have been adopted, including the Universal Copyright Convention and the Rome Phonograms Conventions. In addition, organizations such as WIPO predate the Uruguay Round. These treaties, conventions, and organizations largely provide permissive regulatory protection based upon the reciprocity of national treatment. What is new, however, is the awareness of the effect that intellectual property protection may have no international trade and an active desire to protect these rights abroad. It has been discovered that the absence of adequate protection of intellectual property or the existence of excessive protection can undermine the benefits derived from the elimination of high tariffs and the reduction of non-tariff barriers.

The growing interdependence of national economies in the increasing globalization and rationalization of markets has revealed insufficiencies in the present international regulatory framework. Many current market factors combine to demonstrate a growing need for effective transnational protection of intellectual property rights. As indicated above, intellectual creation and know-how increasingly comprise the value of products and services as well as represent a substantial cost in research and development. Given the relative ease that modern technology permits intellectual creation or know-how to be copied, inadequate international intellectual property safeguards hinder investment recoupment and inhibit further research and development. Furthermore, without intellectual property protection, the producer or supplier of services will find itself at a disadvantage in the highly competitive foreign market. This situation is exacerbated considering the trend toward research and development in one country and licensed development in another. One commentator noted that "[t]he present state of law in international intellectual property protection increasingly impairs or even nullifies acquired benefits accruing under the [GATT]."[23]

**(b) Intellectual Property Protection as a Trade Issue[24]**

Three propositions underlie the developed countries' drive for strengthened intellectual property rights within the framework of multilateral trade negotiations, known and the Uruguay Round, to revise the General Agreement on Tariffs and Trade:

(1) Strong intellectual property rights exert an unreservedly positive influence on developed free-market economies;
(2) Strong intellectual property rights benefit all countries regardless of the present stage of development:
(3) The acquisition of non-indigenous technologies by developing countries other than by imports or license usually constitutes an illicit economic loss to the technology exporting countries.

The first two propositions are counter-intuitive and neither historical experience nor the literature supports them. The social costs and relative efficiencies of intellectual property regimes remain the subject of continuing debate within the industrialized countries even today, and some conservative economists still maintain that a products market unfettered by intellectual property rights would attain greater efficiency that at present. On the whole, a consensus probably exists that industrialized societies are better off with established intellectual property regimes than without them. But there is not consensus concerning the levels of efficiency achieved by any particular regime, and considerable evidence suggests that all extant regimes yield serious inefficiencies under some circumstances. Opinions about the proper balance between the incentives of protection and the benefits of competition vary from country to country and from epoch to epoch within particular countries, and variations in attitude are especially prominent when shifts in the business cycle occur.

As regards the third proposition, that gains from unlicensed uses of foreign technologies in developing countries characteristically represent illicit losses to entrepreneurs in developed countries, this residual mercantilist attitude conflicts with the underlying competitive ethos from which intellectual property rights derogative and with the territorial nature of these derogations. Basic norms of free completion established in the nineteenth century often induced territorial legislators to provide relatively weak forms of intellectual property protection; the standards of protection currently prevailing in developing countries often resemble those applied in the developed world not too long age. Weak intellectual property laws ensure access to markets for second comers who provide cheaper and better products through imitation and incremental innovation. Innovators who fail to quality for protection under these laws can rely only on such factors as lead time, reputation for quality and continuing technical improvements to maintain their foothold in the market.

Undermining this classical nineteenth century outlook are two recent developments that lead directly to the inclusion of international intellectual property issues within the Uruguay Round of multilateral trade negations. First, the rise of information-based technologies altered the nature of completion and disrupted the equilibrium that had resulted from more traditional comparative advantages. Because such technologies are inherently vulnerable to rapid appropriation by free-riders who do not share in the costs of research and development, innovators demand both domestic and international measures to protect their investments. Second, the growing capacity of manufacturers in developing countries to penetrate distant markets for traditional industrial products has forced the developed countries to rely more heavily on their comparative advantages in the production of intellectual goods than in the past. Market access for developing countries thus became a bargaining chip to be exchanged for greater protection of intellectual goods within a restructured global marketplace.

These tensions largely account for the developed countries' demands for extraterritorial protection of intellectual property rights, which aim to curb free-riding practices seldom illegal under existing international law, and for unilateral trade sanctions that both the United States and the European Communities have exerted against countries that tolerate such practices. The paradox posed by these demands and the resistance they elicit has been characterized in the following terms:

> On the one hand, the industrialized countries that subscribe to free-market principles at home want to impose a highly regulated market for intellectual goods on the rest of the world, one in which authors and inventors my "reap where they have sown." On the other hand, the developing countries that restrict free competition at home envision a totally unregulated world market for intellectual goods, one in which "competition is the lifeblood of commerce."[25]

The resolution of this paradox lies in the gradual integration of international intellectual property law into the larger framework of international economic law. This project, however, requires a negotiated balancing of private and public interests valid for all states active in the international economic system.

Global economic integration requires that intangible creations, likely to become the most valuable form of property in the twenty-first century, should gradually be absorbed into the laws of state responsibility that otherwise protect alien property from confiscation and unlawful taking:

> To pretend that aliens have no legal claims arising from wholesale, unauthorized uses of their most valuable property while respecting laws that protect less valuable alien property only because it is tangible rather than intangible is to exalt from over substance. Sooner or later, both private and public international law must assimilate intellectual property rights to the general international minimum standards that preserve comity by dissuading states from authorizing uncompensated uses of alien property on their national territories.

As international minimum standards of intellectual property law become at least justifiable, if not enforceable, within the framework of the GATT's dispute-settlement procedures, the historical predilection for purely territorial intellectual property rights will give way to international economic law at some cost to national sovereignty.

Viewed in its most positive light, a transnational market for intellectual goods defended against free-riding imports by border control measures and by international machinery for the settlement of disputes could become a vehicle for implementing cultural and industrial policies on a grand scale. The larger rewards potentially accruing from successful innovation under these conditions could be factored into the aggregate investment calculus for research and development and for the dissemination of cultural products., To the extent that intellectual property laws overcome high risk-aversion by offering prospectors a kind of sweepstakes reward if they succeed, the stimulus afforded by minimum standards of legal protection operating across an enlarged and relatively undistorted market could greatly exceed that of similar laws operating in national markets that pursue different goals by different legal means. The ability of each legal subsystem to project more efficient uses of intellectual property throughout the worldwide domain governed by a TRIPS Agreement could thus magnify the capacity of the system as a whole to attain progressively higher levels of competition in the long run through appropriate short-term restrictions on free competition.

On the negative side, the norms of international economic law represent a delicate balance between the interests of states at different stages of development, and the adsorption of intellectual property will have to accommodate these norms and that balance. To the extent that a integrated world market becomes increasingly open and competitive, the desired equilibrium between legal protection of innovation and free competition must take account of the different economic policies of states at very different stages of development. Premature efforts to accelerate the process of harmonization without due regard to these differences and to the social costs of overcoming them could boomerang ageist those countries pressing for rapid change and could even widen the initial differences in the end.

The integration of intellectual property into international economic law will require entrepreneurs in both developed and developing countries to reevaluate the nature of competition in a more regulated global marketplace. While strengthened intellectual property norms benefit inventors and creators everywhere, there is no assurance that any particular countries will succeed in transforming short-term trade advantages accruing from a TRIPS agreement into solid and lasting commercial benefits. On the contrary, stronger intellectual property laws will ultimately benefit those states whose long-term development strategies best promote sustained technological innovation and the effective transfer of basic research from universities and laboratories to industry. The future prospects of the developed countries, including the united States, turn less on the level of intellectual property protection as such than on the level if investment in basic research and in high-risk commercial applications of the products it generates.

By the same token, the prospects for strengthened intellectual property regimes operating in open markets will require developing countries to formulate economic development strategies that are consistent with the new legal order. To maximize their opportunities, developing-country authorities mist foster and reward entrepreneurship in general, while entrepreneurs in developing countries must learn to think like small-and medium-sized firms in the industrialized countries. In time, affinities between small and medium-sized firms in both developed and developing countries will outweigh the affinities between small and large firms operating within any given national territory, and this transactional commonality of interests should strengthen the role of developing countries in future multilateral negotiations. Meanwhile, the developing countries will have to work harder to compete in general, and to acquire technological improvements in particular, under a post TRIPS regime. However, if the appropriate strategies are adopted in both the public and private sectors, any competitive efforts that yield a foothold in the world market, and any effective transfer of technology achieved in the process should yield greater potential returns than at present.

In all countries, efforts to implement higher intellectual property standards will put increasing strains on competition law, which is not directly covered by the TRIPS Agreement. Identifying the parameters of healthy competition valid for all players in an integrated world market will thus become pressing task for the international community in a post. TRIPS economic environment. Because innovators, users, and second coiners ask have different stakes in fashioning the rules of unfair competition law, their interests will increasingly very more with their economic roles than with the geopolitical affiliations of their respective national states. Developing countries that too aggressively promote the demands of large, multinational cop rations risk producing a competitive environment inimical to the needs of their own small-and medium-sized entrepreneurs. Developing countries that overly regulate large foreign firms operating in their territories urn the risk of suffocating their own small-and medium-sized firms.

Competition law must, accordingly, remain an integral part of ongoing international discussions of intellectual property rights. In this context, developed countries must eventually take steps to protect applied scientific know-how, which largely escapes the patent and copyright systems, and they will continue to press the developing countries to limit the pace at which second comers can appropriate the fruits of investment in unpatented; no copyrightable innovation. At the same time, the developing countries will require the cooperation of the industrialized countries in formulating guidelines for the licensing of both patented and unpatented technologies in order to effectuate transfers of technology without unduly discouraging direct foreign investment. If, in future negotiations, the developing countries proved willing to exchange greater short-term protection of products embodying unpatented know-how for a commitment by the industrialized countries to support an international Code of Conduct on the Transfer of Technology, it might open a new chapter in international unfair competition law.

Clearly, there is a great need for multilateral coordination and cooperation to ensure that all voices are heard in a collective endeavour to achieve a market-wide balance between incentives to create and reasonable opportunities to imitate and improve upon technological innovation. Future discussions seeking to reconcile the need for more effective transfers of technology with the drive for greater economic efficiency will require a high level of technical expertise and a no confrontational environment conductive to reasoned economic and social analysis. To the extent that cooperation between developed and developing countries succeeds, it will contribute a new perspective to the notion of fair competition that should strengthen the prospects of al participants in the global marketplace of the twenty-first century.

### (c) The Uruguay Round Negotiations[26]

Intellectual property piracy is rampant and affects a

wide range of industries. In particular, piracy hurts pharmaceutical industries, industries protected by trademark law, and producers and publishers who rely on copyright protection (i.e., developers of computer software, creators of literary and artistic works, and producers of audio and video recordings). Many nations deny patent protection to pharmaceutical products which by their nature require considerable time and expense to develop and bring to market. Consequently, some pharmaceutical companies face foreign competitors who misappropriate information with the active assistance and encouragement of their governments to produce inexpensive and potentially ineffective or dangerous imitations. New technology such a digital audio tapes, high quality digital broadcasts, optical character recognition scanners, and record able compact discs threaten to make piracy eraser and more difficult to detect. These technologies allow pirates to make high quality copies of copyrighted materials at minimal coast and effort. Inadequate trademark enforcement leads to the marketing of substandard counterfeit products that are sold in both origin markets as well as the trademark owner's home market. Trade distortions resulting from ineffective or non-existent intellectual property protection led the United States and other industrialized nations to discuss an international framework for the protection of intellectual property rights.

Proponents introduced the international protection of intellectual property rights to the GATT at the end of the Tokyo Round in the context of halting the counterfeiting of trademarked goods. Although the parties reached no agreement, the United States and the European Economic Community (EEC) succeeded in bringing the issue to the attention of the GATT's contracting parties and submitted a proposed agreement on measures to inhibit trade in counterfeit goods. Actions taken by developing nations at March 1980 Conference in the World Intellectual Property Organization (WIPO) further encouraged industrialized nations to pursue negotiations under the auspices of the GATT. At the conference, the Group of Developing Countries[27] attempted to weaken the already inadequate standards of protection provided by The Paris Convention for the Protection of Industrial Property. Although the industrialized nations blocked this initiative, this action demonstrated both the futility of seeking broad-based reform in this forum and the need to pursue other avenues to advance international intellectual property protection.

During various ministerial GATT meetings throughout the early 1980s, members continued discussing the possibility of including the subject of trade in counterfeit goods on the agenda of the next round of negotiations. Developing nations resisted the inclusion of intellectual property rights, asserting that such a topic exceeded the GATT's mandate.

The persistence of the United States and the other industrialized nations was rewarded by the inclusion of trade-related aspects of intellectual property rights in the Uruguay Round agenda by the Punta del Este Ministerial Declaration on the Uruguay Round.[28] Nations opposing strong international intellectual property protection continued to resist these negotiations by insisting that WIPO remained the appropriate forum for such a topic. This resistance creased when WIPO's Director-General was specifically mandated to participate in the GATT intellectual property negotiations. Further opposition to substantive TRIPS negotiations ended when India agreed to accept "the principle of policing trade related aspects of intellectual property rights within the framework of the Uruguay Round multilateral trade negotiations."[29] With this obstacle eliminated, substantive proposals could be considered.

### (d) Major Provisions

*Patents*

The proposed TRIPS Agreement provides minimum standards which closely match the initial proposal of the United States. The patent section provides a twenty-year term of protection from time of filing and defines patentable subject mater as any invention, whether product or process, that is new, involves in inventive step, and is capable of industrial application. Furthermore, the draft notes that "inventive step" and capable of industrial application" should be considered synonymous with the terms "non-obvious" and "useful" as commonly used in US patent law. The draft further strengthens the patent right by prohibiting patent discrimination based on the place of invention, the field of technology, or whether the product is imported or domestically produced. This language seeks to address problems common to the patent systems of many developing nations such as local working requirements and the exclusion of specific products, like pharmaceuticals and agrochemicals, from protection. This section represents a significant step towards establishing basic patent standards in international law.

Although the patent section provides a solid foundation for developing international patent protection, some problems exist. For example, the exclusions to paten table subject-matter contained in Article 27, Paragraphs 2 and 3 could be abused. Article 27 recognizes the following grounds for exclusion (1) protecting order public or morality; (2) protecting human, plant or animal life or health; and (3) avoiding serious prejudice to the environment. These exclusions are very broad and without a narrowing interpretation or interpretative statement, they could be understood to allow the continued exclusion of certain pharmaceutical products and processes from patentability. Nations may also exclude from patentability diagnostic, therapeutic, and surgical methods, as well as certain plants, animals, and biological processes for the production of plants or animals. In effect, much language substantially limits protection for the growing biotechnology industry.

The Proposed TRIPS Agreement effectively addresses the problem of compulsory licensing. Compulsory licensing is not specifically banned, but nations wishing to issue such licenses must satisfy important conditions. These conditions include the payment of adequate remuneration, non-exclusivity, non-assign ability, limited duration and scope, and the requirement that a compulsory license only be used after the prospective licensee has tried to obtain authorization from the right's holder on reasonable commercial terms and conditions Moreover, limitations on the use of compulsory licenses for the exploitation of dependent patents also exist. The language of Articles 27 and 31 states that local working requirements for compulsory licensing purposes remain satisfied through the importation of patented products sufficient to meet local needs. Such language in necessary to avoid requiring a patent holder to produce the product in every jurisdiction where it is patented or face a compulsory license. With certain exceptions, the substantive standards of the patent section and the compulsory licensing provisions provide a useful starting point for the further development and advancement of international patent protection.

*Copyrights*

Copyright protection is a particularly important aspect of the TRIPS Agreement due to advances in technology that have made copyright infringement significantly easier and less expensive. The copyright and related rights provisions of the proposed TRIPS Agreement generally codify traditional copyright standards by requiring a minimum fifty-year term as well as compliance with Articles 1 to 21 and the Appendix of The Berne Convention for the Protection of Literary and Artistic Works (971). This framework does not include provisions relating to moral rights. Copyright protection is extended to compilations of data and databases and to computer software, which is treated as a literary work. Sound recording also receives increased protection.

The primary area of conflict in the copyright and related rights provisions involves the role of national treatment. Many nations read their national treatment obligations narrowly thereby denying certain benefits to foreign nationals. These nations create what they consider to be new rights or subject-matters and then assert that their national treatment obligation under copyright and neighboring rights agreements does not extent to such new areas. The most controversial example of this practice is the European video levy system which collects and distributes funds to compensate copyright holders for private copying. While authors, performers, and video producers receive the levy funds, foreign video producers are denied their fair shares because video producers are not specifically covered by any agreement with a national treatment obligation. Advances in technology such as digital broadcasting make it likely that similar regimes will be developed with the potential to generate billions of dollars in revenue. Consequently American businesses with copyright and related rights interests stand to lose substantial revenue if national treatment concepts are not further extended in the ream of copyright and neighboring rights.

### *Transition Periods*

The issue of transition periods is an area of concern in both the patent and copyright provisions. It is asserted that developing nations need time to adjust their economies and legal systems to meet the requirements of the proposed TRIPS Agreement. It is unclear, however, that transition periods need be as long as provided in Articles 65 and 66. The proposed transition period allows one year with a four-year extension for developing countries and those nations shifting from a centrally planned economy to a market economy. Furthermore, an additional extension period of five years is granted for developing nations providing patent protection to areas not previously covered by their patent regimes, such ad pharmaceuticals and agro-chemicals.

Due to the fast pace of technological development, this extended transition period is extremely burdensome to high technology industries and other creative or research-oriented industries. It is also possible that the transition period may inhibit the use of Special 301 against signatory nations for the duration of the transition. Former General Counsel for the Office of the United States Trade Representative (USTR), Joshua Bolten, testified before Congress that the moral authority to use Special 301 might be constrained under an agreement that allows nations long transition periods. Excessive transition periods merely allow nations with thriving pirate industries to continue operating to the detriment of foreign and domestic innovators. Furthermore, long transition periods unnecessarily delay the development of such nations' economies and their further integration into the international marketplace. Therefore, shorter transition periods would be in the interests of the United States and the other industrialized nations.

*National Enforcement Measures*

Along with the establishment of substantive standards for patents, copyrights, trademarks, and other forms of intellectual property, the proposed TRIPS Agreement also requires the creation of effective national enforcement measures for rights holders. The proposal provides for both internal and border enforcement measures. Although it does not require a signatory state to create an entirely new or separate judicial system for intellectual property rights, the Agreement does mandate certain minimal obligations.

*Technological Advances*

In addition to providing for current forms of technology and intellectual property protection, the negotiators of the proposed TRIPS Agreement heeded the suggestion buy the United States of maintaining a flexible agreement capable of adjusting to the continuing dramatic advances in technological innovation. Accordingly copyright protection was extended to cover computer software and a sui generis system for the protection of semiconductor chips was created. The proposed agreement provides for a ten-year term of protection and requires the parties to declare unlawful; [I]mporting, selling, or otherwise distributing for commercial purposes a protected layout-design, an integrated circuit in which a protected layout-design in incorporated, or an article incorporating such an integrated circuit only insofar as it continues to contain an unlawfully reproduced layout design.

The use of these two different methods of protecting new innovations and the growing acceptance of this protection for these new technologies demonstrates the need for an ongoing mechanism for the adjustment of international intellectual property protection to meet new technological realities.

As a new form of [technology], the printing press once compelled governments to develop copyright rules as a means of protecting intellectual property. Technological innovations continue to exceed the conceptualizations of intellectual property law. In response to technological innovation, a more evolved body of intellectual property law will by necessity first originate in the domestic legal systems and later be incorporated into international law through negotiation. The development process of new intellectual property law, however, may affect its international acceptance, incorporation, and implementation. Two schools of though generally dominate the understanding of intellectual property right development. The first argues for the modification of existing forms of intellectual property rights such as patents and copyrights to cover new technologies; the other asserts that sui generis protection for such technology is more efficient.

These two methods of addressing ongoing technological advances will play a continuing role in the development of international intellectual property protection. As innovators create new technologies and problems for intellectual property law, domestic legal systems will have to respond with new forms of protection. With the increasing importance of the international marketplace, governments will need to extend this protection globally through one of the international intellectual property protection mechanisms.

### (e) Major Provisions (Another View)[30]

A formal consensus to regulate trademarks and unfair competition has always existed under the Paris Convention, for the reason that, as Ladas observed in 1949, "[i]nternational trade is inconceivable today without trademarks and their adequate protection."[31] In the past, however, lax enforcement prevailed and there was no recourse to dispute-resolution machinery. The Draft TRIPS provisions give pre-existing norms greater specificity by strengthening the protection of service marks, famous marks, and geographical indications of origin, including wines. Other provisions soften the use requirement and eliminate both compulsory licenses and local linkage requirements. Above all, the Draft Agreement subjects the international regime of trademarks and unfair competition to more stringent enforcement measures, including border controls against the import of "counterfeit trademark or pirated copyright goods."

The Primary effects of these provisions on the developing countries reside in the potential displacement of industries founded on counterfeiting and in the high cost of legal enforcement measures. To attenuate displacement costs, developing countries need to convert affected industries to the production of clearly marked, substitute goods that establish their own market niche by means of price competition with more costly foreign goods. Governments in the developing countries should generally encourage entrepreneurs to establish their own market identities through appropriate trademarks and to offer products that can be distinguished from those already in the market. Some developing countries may promote geographical appellations of their own, with a view to enhancing market identity in the future.

Strengthened trademark regimes should encourage both direct investment in developing countries and licensing by foreign producers who seek to monitor quality and to maintain brand names and goodwill in the international market generally. On the whole, more technology will be licensed to domestic firms when the licensor can both lower transaction costs by recourse to standard intellectual property norms and maintain quality controls through trademark license agreements. Local production under license then reduces the need for imports and helps to build an industrial infrastructure.

Governments in developing countries need to formulate policies and incentives that encourage foreign firms to allow licensees to adapt more of the licensed products for both domestic and export needs under local trademarks. The success of Japanese industry in importing foreign technology while developing indigenous marks constitutes an example for other countries to emulate. Countries at lesser stages of development may have less bargaining power when formulating appropriate regulations, however, and may remain more dependent on the introduction of foreign marks.

Although trademarks encourage the production of quality good, control over quality easily leads to control over price and other anticompetitive consequences. Accordingly, developing countries may respond to strengthened trade, mark regimes in a post TRIPS universe by replacing obsolete and restrictive trademark laws with up-to-date regulations dealing directly with the abusive licensing practices that flow from market power. While Article 21 of the Draft TRIPS Agreement expressly authorises parties to "determine conditions on the licensing and assignment of trademarks" the need of adeauate licensing regulations affects all subject matter areas covered by the TRIPS Agreement, including patents, now how and copyrights.

**(f) A step Forward[32]**

The TRIPS Agreement mandates mostly time-tested, basic norms of international intellectual property law as enshrined in the Paris Convention for the Protection of Industrial Property, and the Berne Convention for the Protection of Literary and Artistic Works.

The developed countries scored major achievements in elevating and harmonizing minimum standards of patent protection under TRIPS, especially with regard to basic criteria of eligibility and duration, which the Paris Convention had not addressed. The following provisions are noteworthy:

(1) Member states may not exclude any field of technology from patentability as a whole, and they may not discriminate as to the place of invention when rights are granted.

(2) The domestic patent laws (including that of the United States) must provide a uniform term of twenty years of protection from the filing date, such protection must depend on uniform conditions of eligibility, and specified exclusive rights must be granted.

(3) The patentees' bundle of exclusive rights must include the right to supply the market with imports of the patented products.

(4) Logically, the obligation to work patents locally under Article 5A of the Paris Convention appears overridden by the right to supply imports, at least in principle.

Single countries may deviate from these universal patent-law standards only to the extent that they benefit from longer or shorter periods of transitional relief, which very with the beneficiary's status as either a 'developing country' or a "least-developed country."

As regards information technologies, the TRIPS Agreement opts for copyright (and trade secret) protection of computer programs, not patent protection, the availability of which remains unsettled and controversial in most developed countries. Because the TRIPS provisions do prohibit field-specific exclusions of patentable subject-matter, one can nonetheless argue that the domestic patent laws must recognize some program-related inventions if they meet other criteria of eligibility, including the non-obviousness standard. There is, however, even less consensus concerning the proper application of patent-law doctrines to computer programs than exists with respect to biogenetic engineering. Hence, any developed or developing country that disfavours patent protection of computer software may allow its judicial or administrative authorities to emulate the many restrictive doctrines and practices recognized by developed legal systems, without running afoul of its TRIPS obligations.

Besides requiring all WTO member countries to comply with the relevant international minimum standards already set out in the Paris Convention, the TRIPS Agreement establishes a universally valid legal definition of a trademark. It then invests owners of registered marks with the exclusive right to prevent third parties from using similar marks for goods or services when such use would produce a "likelihood of confusion.." The trademark owner's exclusive right must last at least seven years after initial registration or after each renewal of registration, and the principle of indefinitely renewable registrations is established for trademarks, but not apparently for service marks.

While states may continue to condition registration-but not the filing of an application for registration—on actual use of a given trademark, cancellation requires "an uninterrupted period at least three years of non-use," and government actions that hinder such use will not constitute legally valid excuses. Member states can no longer require foreign trademark owners to couple their marks with the indigenous marks of local firms. Nor can they impose compulsory licenses or deny the principle of free assign ability of marks with, or without, the business to which they pertain.

Finally, the protection of well-known marks under Article 6bis of the Paris Convention has been strengthened in at least two ways. First, that article now applies expressly to services. Second, the same provision extends even to dissimilar goods or services when use of a resisted mark would likely indicate a harmful connection between those dissimilar goods or services and the owner of the registered mark. Whether US compliance with this provision will require the enactment of a federal dilution statute remains to be seen.

In bold move, the TRIPS Agreement recognizes some minimum standards of protection for phonogram producers, broadcast organizations, and performing artists, as derived from the Rome Convention, and it makes these rights universally applicable while, perhaps, discouraging further development of this Convention. For Example, producers of sound recordings must now obtain exclusive reproduction rights in their recordings, in keeping with Article 10 of the Rome Convention, and broadcasting organizations may prohibit unauthorized fixation, reproduction, retransmission, and communication to the public of their broadcasts. However, the TRIPS Agreement does not provide producers of sound recordings with an exclusive right to publicly perform or broadcast their recordings, nor does it man date even a right to equitable compensation for secondary uses of commercial recordings, which the Rome Convention tries to establish.

The neighboring rights provisions of the TRIPS Agreement are, to some extent, encumbered by the ability of member states to invoke the "conditions, limitations, exceptions and reservations" recognized by the Rome convention. Among other things, this opens the door to demands for reciprocity, rather than national treatment, with respect to payment of equitable compensation for public performances of sound recordings in countries that adopt such a system.

The TRIPS Agreement is the first international convention expressly to require member countries to protect undisclosed information. A systematic failure to provide either trade secret protection or equivalent laws governing confidential disclosures should thus become actionable as a distinct component of the international regime of unfair competition law that Article 10bis of the Paris Convention already covers. Violations of Article 10bis, in turn, become subject to the enforcement procedures and improved dispute-settlement machinery of the WTO Agreement as a whole.

The language that Article 39(2) of the TRIPS Agreement uses to mandate the protection of undisclosed information resembles that of the Uniform Trade Secrets Act, which is widely adopted at the local level in the United States. However, there is no express provision that guarantees third parties the right to reverse-engineer products made from secret processes by proper means. While the United States Supreme Court has invested this right with constitutional underpinnings, Article 39(2) merely invokes Article 10bis of the Paris Convention, which would require third parties not to acquire undisclosed information "in a manner contrary to honest commercial practices." A footnote to Article 39(2) precludes "at least practices such a breach of contract, breach of confidence and inducements to breach." But does not affirmatively endorse reverse-analysis as such.

Whether a duly appointed WTOP panel would regard a competitor's right to reverse-engineer by proper means as inherent in the "honest commercial practices" standard for purpose of dispute-settlement proceedings remains to be seen. A failure to do so should compromise both the economic functions of trade secret laws and a long-standing constitutional tradition concerning the rights and duties of competitors under US trade regulation law. It also remains to be seen whether a federal trade secret law is needed to comply with the United States' obligations under the TRIPS Agreement.

## 5. NAFTA

### (a) An Historical Overview[33]

The North American Free Trade Agreement negotiations are the most significant forum for the discussion of intellectual property protection in the Americas. In June 1991, the governments of the United States, Mexico and Canada formally began these trilateral negotiations to create a free trade agreement covering North America.

Once negotiated, the agreement will establish a free trade area covering substantially all trade between or among the parties involved. Generally, the parties agree to phase down and eliminate tariffs in order to encourage trade within the fr4ee trade area and implement other rules and measures to regulate trade in the region.

A successful NAFTA not only will create a free trade area with 355 million people and a combined gross national product of $5.5 trillion, but will also liberalize investment rules, open trade in services, and seek more effective intellectual property protection.

## CONCLUSIONS

IPR Treaties purports to define the nature and scope of the property rights that it confers by relying on the concept of originality. In fact, originality is an apparition; it does not, and cannot, provide a basis of deciding copyright cases. The vision of authorship on which it is based—portraying authorship as ineffable creation form nothing—is both flawed and misleading disserving the authors it seeks to extol. If we took that vision seriously we could not grant authors Scientists. Artists, Sculptures, Musicians and others copyrights without first dissecting their creative process to pare elements adapted from the works of others from the later authors recasting of them vision but nonetheless adhered unswervingly to the concept of originality, we would, most works of authorship Scientists. Artists, Sculptures, Musicians and others would find themselves enjoined by the owners of other copyrights.

The public domain rescues us from this dilemma. It permits us to continue to exalt originality without acknowledging that our claims to take originality seriously are mostly pretense. It furnishes a crucial device to an otherwise unworkable system by reserving the raw material of authorship to the commons, thus leaving that raw material available for other authors to use. The public domain thus permits the law of copyright to avoid a confrontation with the poverty of some of the assumptions on which it is based.

## Notes and References

1. The "pirate" booksellers also had the advantage of waiting to see which books were a commercial success. Thus, they would pirate only those books which had a high demand and thereby ensured themselves a profitable return.
2. The city of Venice apparently granted the first privilege to a publisher in approximately 1495. The exact date is not known, however, and some experts believe it could have been as early as 1469.
3. The privilege encompassed three essential aspects consistent with modern copyright law. the King would grant a printer an exclusive right to reproduce and distribute a certain work.
4. Peter Burger, "The Berne Convention: Its History and its Key Role in the Future," *Journal of Law and Technology,* Georgetown University Law Center.
5. A system of material reciprocity requires the courts of state A to interpret the laws of state B in order to determine whether country B gives adequate and reciprocal protection to an author from country.
6. Brad Swenson, "Intellectual Property Protection Through The Berne Convention: A Matter of Economic Survival for the Post-Soviet New Commonwealth of Independent States," 21 DENV. *Journal of International Law and Policy,* 77. (1992).
7. Universal Copyright Convention (Paris 1971) Article I.
8. Universal Copyright Convention, Preamble, Paris 1971.
9. Peter Burger, "The Berne Convention, It's History and its Key Role in the Future, 3, *Journal of Law and Technology* (1988).
10. The countries represented were Belgium, Canada, Denmark, France, Germany, Great Britain, Italy, the Netherlands, Portugal, Russia, Spain, Sweden, Norway, Switzerland, and the United States.
11. More than three hundred persons attended the meeting. Included in that number were 62 authors, 54 delegates of literary societies, 40 members of political assemblies, 29 lawyers, 29 librarians and printers, 24 artists, 21 economists and 16 journalists.
12. The resolutions were: (1) That the principle of international recognition of copyright in favour of authors must be made part of the legislation of all civilized countries. (2) This principle must be admitted regardless of reciprocity. (3) The assimilation of foreign to national authors (national treatment) must be absolute and complete. (4) Foreign authors should not be required to comply with any particular formalities for the recognition and protection of their

rights, provided they have complied with the formalities required in the country where publication first took place. (5) It is desirable that all countries adopt uniform legislation for the protection of literary and artistic works.

13. The Berne Convention.
14. Karen Kontje Waller, "NAFTA: The Latest Gun in the Fight to Protect International Intellectual Property Rights," 13, *Dickinson Journal of International Law*, 347 (1994).
15. Berne Convention for the Protection of Literary and Artistic Works (As Revised at Paris, 1971), Article 2.
16. Brad Swenson, Intellectual Property Protection Through the Berne Convention: A Matter of Economic Survival for the Post Soviet New Commonwealth of Independent States, 21 Denver *Journal of International Law and Policy* 77, (1992).
17. Berne Convention (Paris 1971), Article 2-8.
18. Monique L. Cordray, GATT *v.* WIPO, 76 J. PAT E. TRADEMARK OFF. SOC'Y, 121. (1994).
19. Dr. Holf Moroni, "The Individual's Contributions to Man's Progress", *Universities*, Vol. 17, No. 3, 1975, 229-234.
20. Peter Burger, Article: "The Berne Convention: Its History and its Key Role In the Future," 3 *Journal of Law and Technology*, (1998).
21. A David Derniray, "Intellectual Property and the External Power of the European Community: The New Extension, 16 *Michigan Journal of International Law*, 187 (1995).
22. INGA GOVAERE, "Intellectual Property Protection and Commercial Policy in the European Community's Commercial Policy After 1992: The Legal Dimension" 205-06 (Marc Maresceau ed. 1993).
23. Real trade liberalisation of technology based products could only be obtained through the abolishment of the reference to intellectual property protection in Article XX(d) GATT, or through the insertion of an explicit reference to the exhaustion of rights in case of parallel protection. The current TRIPS negotiations, which to a great extent focus on standards and norms of protection, will, however, lead to a partial trade liberalisation in the sense that new export markets will be created and secured against counterfeiting and piracy.
24. J.H. Reichman, "The Trips Component of the GATT's Uruguay Round: Competitive Prospects for Intellectual Property Owners in an Integrated World Market, 4 *Fordham Intellectual Property, Media and Entertainment Law Journal* (1993).
25. J.H. Reichman, "Intellectual Property in International Trade: Opportunities and Risks of a GATT Connection," 22 VAND. *Journal of Transnational Law*. 747, 795-96 (1989).
26. Michael L. Deane, "TRIPS and International Intellectual Property Protection In An Age of Advancing Technology", 9 American University *Journal of International Law & Policy*, 465. (1994).
27. The declaration Stated: "In order to reduce the distortions and impediments to international trade, and taking into account the need to promote the effective and adequate protection of intellectual

property rights, and to ensure that measures and procedures to enforce intellectual property rights do not themselves become barriers to legitimate trade, the negotiations shall aim to clarify GATT provisions and elaborate as appropriate new rules and disciplines.

Negotiations shall aim to develop a multilateral framework of principles, rules and disciplines dealing with international trade in counterfeit goods, taking into account work already undertaken in the GATT."

28. India Accepted Policing of Trade-Related Intellectual Property Rights in MTN Talks, 3 Int'l Trade Rep. (BNA) 244 (Sept. 20, 1989).
29. India Accepted Policing of Trade—Related Intellectual Property Rights in MTN Talks, 3 Int'l Trade Rep. (BNA) 244 (Sept. .20, 1989)
30. J.H. Reichman, "The Trips Component of the Gatt's Uruguay Round: Competitive Prospects for Intellectual Property Owners in an Integrated World Market", 4 *Fordham Intellectual Property Media and Entertainment Law Journal*, 171 (1993).
31. Stephen P. Ladas, *The Lanham Act and International Trade, 14 Law and Contemporary. Problems*. 269, (1949).
32. Paul Edward Geller, Intellectual Property in the Global Market Place: Impact of TRIPS Dispute Settlements? 29 *International Law* (1995).
33. M. Jean Anderson, Angela J. Paolini Ellard and Nima Shafran, "Intellectual Property Protection in the Americas: The Barriers are Being Removed," 4 *Journal Proprietary Rights* (1992) Prentice Hall Law and Business.

# Bibliography


**International Conventions Treaties Agreements and Acts**

Paris Convention for the Protection of Industrial Property (As revised at Stockholm, July 14, 1967).

Berne Convention for the Protection of Literary and Artistic Works (As Revised at Paris, July 24, 1971).

Treaty Establishing the European Community as Amended by Subsequent Treaties Rome 25th March, 1957.

International Convention for the Protection of Performers, Producers of Phonograms and Broadcasting Organizations (Rome 1961).

Universal Copyright Convention (UCC) (Paris 24th July, 1971).

Patent Cooperation Treaty (Washington, June 19, 1970).

European Communities Trademark Harmonization Directive (Brussels, December 21, 1988).

North American Free Trade Agreement (NAFTA).

Agreement on Trade Related Aspects of Intellectual Property Rights (TRIPS).

Protocol Relating to the Madrid Agreement Concerning the International Registration of Marks.

Trademark Registration Treaty.

The Patents (Amendment) Bill-15 Amendments by the Lok Sabha in 22nd March, 2005.

**Books and Research Articles Collected from various National and International Organisations**

*Classics*

Alberuni's, *Book of the Hind.*

Annie Besant's *India.*

Arnold J. Toynbee, *Experiences (OUP. 1969).*
Bana's *Harshacaritra.*
Bharathiyar's poems.
Basham, A.L., *The Wonder That was India,* OUP.
Buddha's *Dhammapada.*
Bhagavad Gida.
Mahabharata.
Kalhana's *Rajatarangini.*
Kalidasa's, *Meghasandesa, Kumarasambhava, Raghuvamsa.*
Kambar's *Ramayanam.*
Kautilya's *Arthasastra.*
*Manimegalai* and *Silappadigaram.*
Nanak's, *Granth Sahib.*
Narasimha's, *Kadambari*
Patanjali's *Yogasastra, Yogasutra.*
*Ettutogai.*
Pattuppattu.
*Padinenkelkanakku.*
Ralph Waldo Emerson, *Basic Writings of America's Sage* (Mentor Books, 1949).
Sekkizhar's *Periyapuranam.*
*Thevaram.*
*Thiruvasagam.*
Thiruvalluvar's *Thirukkural.*
Tholkappiyar's *Tholkappiyam.*
Tulsi Das, *Ramayana.*
Twelve Alvars, *Prabandhas.*
*Valmiki, Ramayana.*

A David Derniray, "Intellectual Property and the External Power of the European Community: The New Extension, 16 *Michigan Journal of International Law,* 187 (1995).
Adrienne Catanese, "Paris Convention Patent Protection and Technology Transfer", 3 *Boston University International Law Journal* 209 (1985).
Arthur B. Sackler, "The United States should not Adhere to the Berne Copyright Convention, 3 *Journal of Law and Technology* 207. (1978).
Article 32 of the French law of March 11, 1957.

Audio-visual Works and Phonogram, Preparatory Document for and Report of WIDO/UNESCO Committee of Governmental Experts, 22 Copyright 218, 2341 (1986).

Bal Gopal Das, "Intellectual Property Dispute, GATT, WIPO: of Playing by the Game Rules and Rules of the Game", 35 *IDEA Journal of Law and Technology*, 149.

Bartram S. Brown, "Developing Countries in the International Trade Order", 14 *Northern Illinios University Law Review* 347. (1994).

Biswajit Dhar, C. Niranjan Rao, "Third Amendment to Patent Act: Reflections on a TRIPS—Complaint Law" *Economic and Political Weekly*, April 9, 2005, OECD, Genetic Inventions, Intellectual Property Rights and Licensing Practices: Evidence and Policies 2005, 15.

Biswajit Dhar, K.C. Niranjan Rao, "Third Amendment to Patents Act: Reflections on a TRIPS—Complaint Law", *Economic and Political Weekly*, April 9, 2005.

Bodenhausen, G.H.C. "Guide to the Application of the Paris Convention for the Protection of Industrial Property" 144 (1968), *The Director of the United international Bureau for the Protection of Intellectual Property (BIRIPI).*

Bonnie Teller, "Toward Better Protection of Performance in the United States: A Comparative Look at Performer's Rights in the United States, Under the Rome Convention", 28 *Columbia Journal of Transnational Law* 775, (1990).

Brad Swenson, "Intellectual Property Protection Through the Berne Convention: A Matter of Economic Survival for the Post Soviet New Commonwealth of Independent States", 21 Denver *Journal of International Law and Policy* 77 (1992).

Brinson, "Copyrighted Software: Separating the Protected Expression from Unprotected Ideas: A Starting Point" 29 B.C.L. Review 803, 814 (1988).

Bundestagdtucksache 7.7.1989, nr. 11/4929.

Burreow-Giles Lithographi Co. 1.

California Art preservation Act. Cal. Civ. Code 987, 989.

Capital Records, Inc. V. Mercury Record Corp. 221. F. 2d 657 (2d (iv) 1955.

Carl H. Settlemyer III, "Between Thought and Possession:

Artists "Moral Right" and Public Access to Creative Works" 81 *Georgia Law Journal* 2291 (1993).

Carl Moy, R. "The History of the Patent Harmonization Treaty: Economic Self-Interest as an Influence", 26 *Journal Marshall Law Review* 457 (1993), The John Marshall Law School.

Carlos Alberto Primo Braga, "The Economics of Intellectual Property Rights and The GATT View from the South", 22 *Vanderbilt Journal of Transnational Law* 243 (1989).

Carlos Mouchet, Problems of the "Domaine Public Report", 8 *Columbia VLA Journal of Law and Arts* 137, 146 (1983).

Catherine Logan Piper, "Reservations to Multinational Treaties: The Goal of Universality" 71 *Iowa Law Review* 295, 298 (1985).

Cathryn A. Berryman, "Towards More Universal Protection of Intangible Cultural Property", 1 *Journal of Intellectual Property Law* 293. (1994 )

Charles Von Simson, "Feist or Famine American Database Copyright as an Economic Model for the European Union" 20 *Brooklyn Journal of International Law* 729. (1995).

Christopher Aide, "A more Comprehensive soul: Romantic Conceptions of Authorship and the copyright Doctrine of Moral Right." 48U, *Toranto Faculty Law Review* 211, (1990).

Cornish, *United Kingdom, id* at UK 62.

Cornish, W.R. *Intellectual Property* 275 (1989).

Dasilva, "Droit Moral and the A Moral Copyright: A Comparison of Artists' Rights in France and the U.S." 28 *Bull. Copyright Soc'y* 1, 12 (1980).

David Hurlbut, "Fixing The Biodiversity Convention: Toward A Special Protocol for related Intellectual Property", 34 *National Resources Journal* 379, (1994).

David M. Hang, "The International Transfer of Technology: Lessons that East Europe can Learn from the Failed Third World Experience", 5 *Harvard Journal of Law, Science and Technology* 209 (1992).

Dietz, Germany, Federal Republic in M. Nemer and P. Geller, *International Copyright Law and Practice at FRG* 122-130 1 (1989).

Doris Estella Long, *China, Russia an the United States: A Comparison of Cultural Choices* (1996).

Doris Estelle Long "Copyright and the Uruguay Round Agreement: A New Era of Protection or an Illusory Promised," 22 AIPLA *Quarterly Journal* 531 (1995).

Doris Estelle Long, "The Role of Intellectual Property in Developing Nations" (1995).

Dworkin "United Kingdom" in S.Stewart, *International Copyright and Neighbouring Rights,* 487 (1989).

Edward J. Damich, "The Right of Personality: A Common-law Basis for the Protection of the Moral Rights of Author 23 *Georgia Law Review* 1 (1988).

Ellies V. Hurst, 66 Misc. 235, 121 N.Y. Supp. 438 (Sup. Ct. 1910 (utilizing the right to privary); Clemens v. Press Publishing Co., 67 Misc. 183, 122 N.Y. Supp. 206 (Sup. Ct. 1910) Contract rights); Fischer *v.* Star Co., 231 N.Y. 414 132 N.E. 133 (1921) Unfair Competition.

Fox Film Co. *v.* Doyal, 286 U.S. 123, 127 (1932)

French Law of March 11, 1957.

GATT Negotiating Group sets Talk This Week on U.S. Proposal, WIPO Will Join Discussion, 4 *INT'L TRADE REP* 1358, 1359 (1987).

Gerald G. Fitzmaurice, *General Principles* at 45.

Ginsburg, "Sakotaging and Reconstructing History: A Comment on the Scope of Copyright Protection in Works of History after Hoehling V. Universal City Studios, 29 Bull. Copyright Society U.S.A. 647, 658 (1982).

Glassie, *Archaeology and Folklore: Common Anxieties, Common Hopes, in Historical, Archaeology and the Importance of Material Things* 23 (L. Ferguson ed. 1977).

Gopakumar K.M. and Tahir Amin, "Patents (Amendment) Bill 2005: A Critique", *Economic and Political Weekly,* April 9, 2005.

Gordon, "An Inquiry into the Merits of Copyright: The Challenges of Consistency Consent and Encouragement Theory", 41 *Stanford Law Review* 1378-79 (1989).

Gordon, "Fair Use as Market Failure: A Structural and Economic Analysis of the Betamax Case and Its Predecessors", 82 *Columbia Law Review,* 1600 (1982);

Gorman "Fact of Fancy? The Implication for Copyright", 29 Bull. Copyright Society U.S.A. 560, 560-561 (1982).

Gyorgy Boytha, *Fragen Der Entstehung Des Internationalen Urheberrechts* in Wohrkommt Das Urheberrechts und Wohin Gehtes? 181, 182. (Robert Dittrich ed (1988).

Halima Nice, "Legislative Models of Protection of Cultural Property" 27 *Hastings Law Journal*, 1098, (1976) Halina Nice.

Herman Cohen Jehoram, "The Nature of Neighboring Rights of Performing Artists, Phonogram Producers and Broadcasting Organisations: 15 *Columbia—VLA Journal of Law and the Arts* 75, (1990) Herman Cohen.

Herman Cohen Jehoram, *Netherlands, id.* at NETH 20-22.

Holf Moroni, Dr. "The Individual's Contributions to Man's Progress", *Universitas*, Vol. 17, No. 3, 1975, 229-234.

*Human Rights Tribune*, Vol. 7 No. 2&3, September 2000, 11-12.

Hyde, L. "The Gift: Imagination and the Erotic Life of Property" (vintage 1979).

Ian Johnstone, "Treaty Interpretation: The Authority of Interpretive Communities," 12 *Michigan Journal of International Law'* 371-72, 380-382, 385-91; 418-19 (1991).

INGA GOVAERE, "Intellectual Property Protection and Commercial Policy in the European Community's Commercial Policy After 1992: The Legal Dimension" 205-06 (Marc Maresceau ed. 1993).

International Convention for the Protection of Performance, Producer of Phonograms and Broadcasting Orgnisations (Rome 1961), Article 2(2).

Italian Copyright Law, at Arts. 38, 45, 88 (publishers of collective works), all obtain economic copyright interest); Spanish Copyright Law, at Arts 8.51 (Publishers of collective works acquire both economic and moral right copyright interest and employers acquire limited economic interest without contract).

Jack. A. Cline, "Moral Rights: The Long and Winding Road Towards Recognition", 14 *Nova Law Review* 435, (1990).

Jane C. Ginsburg, "A Tale of Two Copyrights: Literary Property in Revolutionary France and America" 64 *Tulane Law Review* 991, (1990).

Jane C. Ginsburg, "Four Reasons And a Paradox: The Manifest Superiority of Copyright Over *Sui Generis* Protection of Computer Software", 94, *Columbia Law Review,* 2559 (1994).

Jean Anderson, M., Angela J. Paolini Ellard and Nima Shafran, "Intellectual Property Protection in the Americas: The Barriers are Being Removed," 4 *Journal Proprietary Rights* (1992).

Jean M. Dettmann, "Gatt: An Opportunity for an Intellectual Property Rights Solution", 4 *Transnational Law* 347 (1991).

Jeff Berg, "Moral Rights; A legal Historical and Anthropological Reappraisal." 6I. P.J. 341. (1991).

Jeffrey M. Dine, "Authors" Moral Rights In Non-European Nations: International Agreements, Economics, Mannu Bhandari, and the Dead Sea Scrolls", 16 *Michigan Journal of International Law* (1995) 545.

John H. Merryman, "The Refrigerator of Bernard Buffet", 27 *Hastings law Journal,* 1023, 1028 (1976).

John H. Merryman, "Thinking about the Elgin Marbles", 83, *Michegan Law Review* 1881 (1985).

John Henry Merryman "The Rentention of Cultural Property" 21 *University of California Los Angels DAVIS LAW Review* 477 (1988).

John king Gamble Jr, "Reservations to Multilateral Treaties: Macroscopic View of State Practice", 74 *American Journal of International Law* (1980).

Johnthan Franklin, "Pay to Play: Emacting A Performing Right in Sound Recordings in the Age of Digital Audio Broadcasting" 10 University of Miami Entertainment & *Sports Law Review* 83, (1993) .

Judgement of Mar. 19, 1947. Courd' appel, Paris (1949) D.P. 20.

Judgement of May 28, 1991 (Huston V. La clinq) cass. civ. 1991 Bull;. civ. No. 89-19. 522 (Fr.).

Justice V.R. Krishna Iyer, "Piracy of Ayurvedic Heritage", *The Indian Express,* 13th October 2003.

Karen Kontje Waller, "NAFTA: The Latest Gun in the Fight to Protect International Intellectual Property Rights," 13, *Dickinson Journal of International Law,* 347 (1994).

Karen Waller, "NAFTA: The Latest Gun in the Fight to Protect Intellectual Property Rights", 13 *Dick Journal of International Law,* 347, (1994).

Katherine S. Deters, "Retroactivity and Reliance Rights Under Article 18 of the Berne Copyright Convention", 24 VAND, *Journal of Transnational Law.* 971 (1991).

Khullar G.D. "The National Museum" *Illustrated Weekly of India,* June 22, 1969.

Kirsten Peterson, "Recent Intellectual Property Trends in Developing Countries", 33 *Harvard International Law Journal,* 277 (1992).

Krishna Menon, A.G. "Rethinking Architecture", *The Hindu,* Folio, August, 1999.

Lawrence G.C. Kaplan, "The European Community's Television Without Frontiers Directive: Stimulating Europe to Regulate Culture," 8 *Emory International Law Review,* 255, (1994).

Library of Congress, *Copyright Enactments 1783-1900* (Copyright Office Bulletin No. 3) 10-11 (1900).

Lisa J. Borodkin "The Economics of Antiquities Looking and a Proposed Legal Alternative", 95 *Columbia Law Review* 377, (1995).

London Film Productions Ltd. *v.* Intercontinental communications, Inc., 580f. supp. 47 (S.D.N.Y. 1984)

Louis Henkin, *How National Behave: Law and Foreign Policy* 52 (2nd ed. 1979).

Lrie E. Simon, "Appellations of Origin: The Continuing Controversy", 5 *Journal of International Law Bus.* 132. (1983).

Mario Franzosi and Guistino de Sanctis, "Moral Rights and New Technology: Are Copyright and Patents Converging?" 2, EI.P.R. 63 (1995).

Mark C. Suchman, "Invention and Ritual: Notes on the Interrelation of Magic and Intellectual Property in Preliterate Societies," 89 *Columbia Law Review* 1264. (1989).

Markhan S.F. and H. Hargreaves, *The Museums of India* (London 1936); H. Sarkar, *Museums in Archeological Remains Monuments and Museums* (New Delhi, 1964) C. Sivaramamoorthy *Directory of Museums in India* (New Delhi 1959.)

Merryman J. & A. Elesen, *Law, Ethics and the Visual Arts* 147 (2d ed. 1987).

Michael L. Deane, "TRIPS and International Intellectual Property Protection in An Age of Advancing Technology", 9 *American University Journal of International Law & Policy* 465. (1994).

Michael Lehmann, "The Theory of Property Rights and Protection of Intellectual and Industrial Property" 16 *International Review of Industrial Property and Copyright Law,* 525 (1985).

Mira T. Sundara Rajan, "Bharati and His Copyright" *The Hindu,* 22.12.2004.

Monique L. Cordray, GATT *v.* WIPO, 76 J. Pat E. Trademark off Society, 121.

*New York Arts and Cultural Affairs Law,* 14. 51-14. 59 (1983).

Nimmer, "The Subject Matter of Copyright Under the Act of 1976" 24, *University of California Annual Law Review* 978, 1015-1016 (1977).

North American Free Trade Agreement (NAFTA).

Nye, "Nuclear Learning and U.S-Soviet Security Regimes" 41 *International Organization* 371, 398 (1987).

*One India One People*: "Lessons from History" June 2001.

Oscar Schoachter, "Self Defense and the Rule of Law" 83, *American Journal of International Law* 259, 264 (1989).

Pascal Kamina, "Authorship of Films and Implementation of the Term Directive: The Dramatic Tale of Two Copyrights", 8 *E.I.P.R.* 319. (1994).

Paul Edward Gella "New Dynamics in International copyright"16 Columbia- *VLA Journal of Law and Arts* 461 (1992).

Paul Edward Gellen, "Legal Transplants in International Copyright: Some Problems of Method", 13 *University of California Los Angels Pacific Basin Law Journal,* 199, (1994).

Paul Edward Geller, Intellectual Property in the Global Market Place: Impact of TRIPS Dispute Settlements? 29 *International Law* (1995).

Paul Goldstein (1991) *Copyright: Principles, Law and Practice,* 1.

Peter Burger, "The Berne Convention, It's History and its Key Role in the Future, 3, *Journal of Law and Technology* (1988)

Peter Jazsi, Toward a Theory of Copyright: The Metamorphoses of "Authorship," 1991 *Duke Law Journal.* 455, 497.

Pradip N. Thomas and Zaharom Nain (Editors) (2004) *Who owns? The Media?—Global Trends and Local Resistance* (Malaysia South Bound ?Sdn. Bhd. Suite 20 Fordham Northam House.

Pradip Thomas, "GATS and Trade in Audio-Visuals Culture, Politics and Empire", *Economic and Political Weekly,* August 16, 2003.

Raichman, J.H. "Charting the Collapse of the Patent—Copyright Dichotomy: Premises for a Restructured International Intellectual Property System" 13 *Cardozo Arts and Entertainment Law Journal* 475 (1993).

Rajeev Dhavan, "The Patent Controversy" *The Hindu* 10.12.2004, The Leader "Delayed Action on Trademark Law", *The Hindu,* 25.09.2003.

Ramamurthi, B. "Sixty-fourth Convocation Address", Annamalai University, 6th March 1997.

Raymond Sarraute, "Current Theory on the Moral Right of Authors and Artists under French Law", 16 *American Journal of Comparative Law* 465, 468 (1968).

Recht, P. le Droit D'Auteur, Une Nouelle Forme De Propriete 281.

Reichman, J. H. "Beyond the Historical Lines of Demarcation: Competition Law, Intellectual Property Rights, and International Trade After The Gatt's Uruguay Round", *20 Brooklyn Journal of International Law* 75 (1993).

Reichman, J.H. "Goldstein on Copyright Law: A Realist's Approach to a Technological Age" 43 *Stanford Law Review* 943 (1991).

Reichman, J.H. "Intellectual Property in International Trade: Opportunities and Risks of a GATT Connection," 22 VAND. *Journal of Transnational Law.* 747, 795-96 (1989).

Reichman, J.H. "The Trips Component of the Gatt's Uruguay Round: Competitive Prospects for Intellectual Property Owners in an Integrated World Market", 4 *Fordham Intellectual Property Media and Entertainment Law Journal,* 171 (1993).

Reichman, J.H. "Universal Minimum Standards of Intellectual Property Protection Under the TRIPS Component the WTO Agreement", 29 *International Law* 345, (1995).

Reymond Sarraute, "Current Theory in the Moral Rights of Authors and Artists under the French law" 16 *American Journal of Comparative Law* 465 (1968).

Robert A Cinque, "Making Cyberspace Safe for Copyright: The Protection of Electronic Works in a protocol to the Berne Convention" 18 *Fordham International Law Journal* 1258 (1995).

Robert A. Arena, "A Proposal for the International Intellectual Property Protection of Computer Software" 14 *University Pensilvania Journal of International Business Law*, 213.

Robert A. Gorman, "Federal Moral Rights Legislation: The Need for Caution", 14 *Nova Law Review*, 421, 423-24, (1990)

Robert A. Jacobs, "Work—for Hire and the Moral Right Dilemma in the European Community: A U.S. Perspective", 16 *B.C. International and Comparative Law Review* (1993).

Roger W. Mastalir, "A Proposal for Protecting the "Cultural" and "Property" Aspects of Cultural Property Under International Law," 16 *Fordham International Law Journal*. 1033, (1993).

Russell J. Da Silva, "Droit Moral and the Amoral Copyright" 28, Bull. copyright Society, 1, 17 (1980).

Russell J. Dasilva, "Droit Moral and the Amoral Copyright: A Comparison of Artists," *Rights in France and the United States*," 28 Bull. (1980).

Sam Ricketson, "Is Australia In Breach of Its International Obligations with Respect to the Protection of Moral Rights?" *17 Melbourne University Law Review* 462. (1990).

Sam Ricketson, *The Berne Convention for the Protection of Literary and Artistic Works* 665 (1987).

Sarkar, H. (1981), *Museums and Protection of Monuments and Antiquities in India*, (New Delhi Sundeep Prakashan) 14-17.

Seema Alavi "Lost Treasures", *Welath Folio The Hindu Supplement* 22 August 2000.

Seema Alavi "Lost Treasures", *Welath Folio The Hindu Supplement* 22 August 2000.

Sony Corporation of America, *v.* Universal City Studies, 464 U.S 417, 429 (1984).

Stacie I. Strong, "The Cultural Exclusion: Free Trade and Copyrighted Goods", 4 *Duke Journal of Comparative and International Law.*

Stanley Fish, *Doing What Comes Naturally* 141 (1989).

Stanley S. Madeja, "The Arts as a Cultural and Economic Factor in World Trade", 14 *Northern Illinois University Law Review,* 439 (1994).

Stefan Kirchanski, "Protection of US Patent Rights in Developing Countries: US Efforts to Enforce Pharmaceutical Patents in Thailand", 16 *Loyola of Los Angeles International and Comparative Law Journal,* 569 (1993).

Stephan A. Konighsberg, "Think Globally, Act Locally: North American Free Trade, Canadian Cultural Industry Exemption and the Liberalization of the Broadcast Ownership Laws" 12 *Cordozo Arts Entertainment Law Journal.*

Stephen P. Ladas, *The Lanham Act and International Trade, 14 Law and Contemporary. Problems.* 269, (1949).

Stephen Stewart International *Copyright and Neighboring Rights* 73, 7374 (2d ed. 1989). Jack. A. Cline, "Moral Rights: The Long and Winding Road Toward Recognition", 14 *Nova Law Review* 435, (1990).

Stromholum, 1 S. 1 *Droit Moral de L'Auteur* 159-53 (1996)

Suman Sahai, "Plant Variety Protection and Farmers' Rights Law" *Economic and Political Weekly,* September, 2001.

*Sunday Times* (London), May 22, 1983 at 15, Col. 2.

Tarakkalagher Giunta, Lily H. Shang, "Ownership of Information in a Global Economy", 27 *George Washington Journal of International Law and Economics* 327 (1994).

Ted L. McDorman, "U.S. Thailand Trade Disputes: Applying Section 301 to Cigarettes and Intellectual Property", 14 *Michigan Journal of International Law* 90. (1992).

Terry Nardin, *"Law, Morality and Relations of States"*, (Princeton, 1983).

"The Bellagio Declaration" March 11, 1993, *The International Journal of Cultural Property* (1995).

*The Hindu* "Delayed Action on Trademark Law" dated 25th September 2003. See for the recent legislation law passed by LokSabha The pattents Amendment Bill dated March 22, 2005.

The International Convention for the protection for performers, Producers of Phonograms and Broadcasting Organisations, 496, U.N.T.S. at Art. 12.

The New Palgrave: *A Dictionary of Economics,* Vol. 3 at 1014-1018 (J. Eatwell *et al.* eds, 1987).

The Patent (Amendment) Bill passed by Indian Parliament, March 22, 2005, "Two Cheers for Patents" (The Leader) *The Hindu,* March 24, 2005.

The UNESCO Convention on the means of Prohibiting and Preventing the Illicit Import, Expert and Transfer of Ownership of Cultural Property, Nov. 14, 1970, 823, U.N.T.S. 231 (1972).

Ultimately the case was decided on other grounds, notably the cancellation of the prior Spanish registration of a "Nike" mark Appeal 325/91, *America Nike v. Amigo,* Judgment of Dec. 10, 1993 Juzgado de Primera Instancia No. 9, section 1 (Court of first instance), Barcelona, Spain.

United Kingdom Copyright Designs and Patent Act 1988, Sec. 87(2).

United Nations Conference Environment and Development; Convention on Biological Diversity, 1992, 31 I.L.M. 818 (1992) at Art. 16.

Valerie L. Hummel, "The Search for A Solution to The US—Caribbean Copyright Enforcement Controversy" 16 *Fordham International Law Journal* 721 (1993).

Victora J. Vitrano "Protecting Cultural Object in an Internal Border—Free E.C: The EC Directive and Regulations for the Protection and Return of Cultural Objects", 17 *Fordham International Law Journal.* 1164 (1994).

Werner Rumphorst, "Neighbouring Rights Protection of Broadcasting Organizations", 18 EUPR 339, (1992).

Wheaton V. Peters, 33 U.S. (8.Pet.) 591 (1834).

William R. Cornish, "United Kingdom" in *International Copyright Law and Practice* (1991) at 31.

Working Group on Works in the Public Domain, *Copyright Bulletin*, Vol. 13, No.4 at 33, 34 (1979).

# Index

# C



# D



# E

## J



## K



## L



## M

# Q



# R



# S



# T

# U



# V



# W

## Y